The Anarchist Before the Law

ENCOUNTERS IN LAW AND PHILOSOPHY
SERIES EDITORS: Thanos Zartaloudis & Anton Schütz

This series interrogates, historically and theoretically, the encounters between philosophy and law. Each volume published takes a unique approach and challenges traditional systemic approaches to law and philosophy. The series is designed to expand the environment for law and thought.

Titles available in the series

STASIS: Civil War as a Political Paradigm
Giorgio Agamben

On the Idea of Potency: Juridical and Theological Roots of the Western Cultural Tradition
Emanuele Castrucci

Political Theology: Demystifying the Universal
Anton Schütz and Marinos Diamantides

The Birth of Nomos
Thanos Zartaloudis

Leibniz: A Contribution to the Archaeology of Power
Stephen Connelly

Legal Artifices: Ten Essays on Roman Law in the Present Tense
Yan Thomas

Form of Life: Agamben and the Destitution of Life
Gian-Giacomo Fusco

The Anarchist Before the Law: Law without Authority
Saul Newman and Massimo La Torre

edinburghuniversitypress.com/series/enlp

THE ANARCHIST BEFORE THE LAW

Law without Authority

Saul Newman and
Massimo La Torre

EDINBURGH
University Press

Edinburgh University Press is one of the leading university presses in the UK. We publish academic books and journals in our selected subject areas across the humanities and social sciences, combining cutting-edge scholarship with high editorial and production values to produce academic works of lasting importance. For more information visit our website: edinburghuniversitypress.com

Edinburgh University Press Ltd
13 Infirmary Street
Edinburgh, EH1 1LT

First published in hardback by Edinburgh University Press 2024

Typeset in 10.5/12 Palatino by
Cheshire Typesetting Ltd, Cuddington, Cheshire

A CIP record for this book is available from the British Library

ISBN 978 1 3995 1318 0 (hardback)
ISBN 978 1 3995 1319 7 (paperback)
ISBN 978 1 3995 1320 3 (webready PDF)
ISBN 978 1 3995 1321 0 (epub)

Contents

Preface

Does the law still function today? Does it continue to have any meaning or moral authority? Or is it, according to Giorgio Agamben's well-known formula, 'in force but without significance'? On the one hand, there are more laws than ever – law in late modern societies seems to govern virtually every single aspect of life, including the most intimate personal relations and social interactions. On the other hand, the very proliferation of laws in liberal democracies testifies to a certain crisis of legal legitimacy – what we might call a situation of *anomie* – defined not by the absence of the law as such, but by its hollowing out, its ontological emptiness, revealing the void at the heart of legal authority. From abuses of executive power and political lying to civil unrest and new forms of political dissent on both the left and the right; from 'post-truth' politics, 'fake news' and the spreading of wild conspiracy theories to the right-wing populist assault on the independence of the judiciary and the rule of law – such factors seem to point to a general loss of trust in traditional institutions and sources of authority, including the law itself.

This crisis of legitimacy afflicting liberal democracies was brought into sharp relief during the recent experience of the COVID-19 pandemic. The unprecedented restrictions imposed in a haphazard and chaotic fashion by governments everywhere, which seemed to blur the line between liberal democracies and authoritarian regimes, pointed at the same time to the incapacity of the sovereign state to effectively manage emergencies – an incapacity they also display particularly when it comes to dealing with much more profound crises like climate change. Moreover, the fact that measures taken to combat the pandemic were met with resistance – anti-lockdown protests, mis- and disinformation around vaccines and mask wearing, and so on – once again reflects this loss of legitimacy of governing institutions and discourses. The 'elites' are held in contempt, the political and legal 'establishment' (along with the media, the scientific establishment, and other traditional sources of authority) are openly despised, and the institutional procedures of liberal democracy have never seemed more fragile.

Could all this be symptomatic of what the Heideggerian philosopher Reiner Schürmann termed ontological anarchy? In his book, *Heidegger on Being and Acting: From Principles to Anarchy*, Schürmann argued that the late modern experience is characterised by an-archy – the absence of origin or foundation – a condition he relates to Heidegger's idea of the closure of metaphysics and the fading away of epochal principles. Unlike in metaphysical thinking, where action has always to be derived from and determined by a first principle – the *arché* – '"anarchy" … always designates the withering away of such a rule, the relaxing of its hold':

> The anarchy that will be at issue here is the name of a history affecting the ground or foundation of action, a history where the bedrock yields and where it becomes obvious that the principle of cohesion, be it authoritarian or 'rational', is no longer anything more than a blank space deprived of legislative, normative, power.[1]

This gesture of de-grounding, removing or questioning the *arché* – the original source or ground of authority – is also characteristic of theoretical moves such as deconstruction, which reveals the historicity and discursivity of our accepted structures of thought and experience, thus dislodging the centrality of the figure of Man and what Derrida terms the 'metaphysics of presence'. For Schürmann, the ontological ground has been pulled out from under our feet. Political and legal institutions can no longer derive their authority from a single ruling principle or point of origin, whether that be 'substance, God, cogito, discursive community', or the 'hierarchy of virtues, hierarchy of laws – divine, natural, and human – hierarchy of imperatives, and hierarchy of discursive interests'.[2] This obviously has implications for the consistency and bindingness of the law. Yet, for Schürmann, the experience of anarchy is one of a certain kind of freedom, where action is no longer determined by first principles or by a certain telos; action becomes contingent and anarchic.

In response to an anticipated objection to his anarchy principle (what he calls economic anarchy) – the risk that the disappearance of normative guidelines or 'practical standards' would lead to the 'anarchy of power', that is, to new forms of totalitarian power completely unhinged from the rule of law – Schürmann says that,

> Economic anarchy is not an anarchy of power. What I called the hypothesis of closure makes it impossible to conceive of public affairs according to the model of reference to the one, that is, according to the principial model that founds the delegation of functions and the investment of power in an ad hoc representative or titular. Economic anarchy is opposed to the anarchy of power as lawfulness is to lawlessness, as thinking is to the irrational, and as liberty is to oppression. The example of communal realizations ... should suffice to show that anarchy does not mean anomy. When, in the few instances of direct democracy in modern history, laws arose from a deliberation renewed, as it were, every day, positive legislation most closely followed the economic constellation shifting between eras. In those rare intervals, as perhaps again today with the 'turning,' laws lose their permanence ... It is one and the same deconstruction that breaks the prestige of referents and of constancy.[3]

So while the anarchy principle implies the de-grounding or deconstruction of all forms of authority, including law, this does not equate it with lawlessness (*anomie*). On the contrary, according to Schürmann, it implies a different understanding of *lawfulness*, in which law making becomes a contingent and entirely *human* activity, no longer predetermined by fixed principles or by an absolute sovereign authority. This is why he gives the example of laws being directly and democratically decided by a community, where 'laws arose from a deliberation renewed, as it were, everyday'. Such an approach to law and law-making could be described as anarchist.

While Schürmann is careful to distinguish his ontological anarchism from the political anarchism of Mikhail Bakunin, Pierre-Joseph Proudhon and Peter Kropotkin,[4] we contend – and indeed this is the premise of our book – that the 'withering away' of the *arché* can also be grasped politically.[5] While we are not quite so sanguine about the salutary effects of ontological anarchy – and indeed we are quite concerned about the dangers of the 'anarchy of power' filling the emptiness of the ontological void – we nevertheless believe that the condition that Schürmann describes invites a renewed consideration of the political philosophy of anarchism, and particularly of its rather complicated relationship with law. Indeed, the crisis of legitimacy of all political and legal institutions – institutions that *reign but do not govern*[6] – might be considered an opportune critical juncture for rethinking anarchism and for the development of an anarchist legal philosophy. This is precisely what this book aims to do.

The reader could be forgiven for being surprised at this endeavour. Anarchism is usually associated with an extreme antinomianism, that is, with a radical rejection of the law. In the popular imagination, anarchism is often seen as a wild, spontaneous rebellion against any form of authority, particularly the authority of the state and its laws. Certainly, the rejection of legal authority and the principle of political obligation – that is, the obligation to obey the law *because it is the law* – is absolutely central to anarchism, in both its philosophical and political forms. Indeed, amongst all the 'critical' approaches to law, anarchism offers the most radical and uncompromising critique of this institution. We explore the basis of the anarchist critique of legal authority in this book. However, we also reveal a certain ambivalence in anarchism on the question of the law: we show that what anarchists object to is not the concept of law itself – if understood as a series of norms of behaviour – but rather the sovereign dimension of legal authority, that is, the imposition of law from above in a hierarchical and coercive fashion. As we show, there is scope within anarchist theory for an alternative understanding of law: *law without coercion*. But what does this mean exactly? How can a legal system, which is meant to regulate human activity, operate without the threat of coercive sanctions? As we aim to show, anarchist law would derive its bindingness not from sovereign authority and the violence it threatens to inflict, but from a shared sense of moral obligation that arises from the kind of directly democratic activity that Schürmann has in mind. In other words, laws would be autonomously decided at a community level directly by its members; they would be shaped and reshaped through democratic deliberations, always remaining open to challenge and contestation. Lawmaking would become a creative, open and free process, based on cooperative agreements and horizontal processes of decision-making. Rather than seeing law as a series of regulations that limit and constrain human behaviour, law would be an ontologically anarchic, radically ungrounded, and flexible institution for promoting human autonomy and flourishing.

Therefore, what makes anarchism interesting as a philosophy and politics – and why we regard it as the essential 'test' of legal authority – is that it has both a *destituting* and *instituting* side, a destructive and creative impulse. As the great Russian anarchist of the nineteenth century, Mikhail Bakunin once said, 'the urge to destroy is also a creative urge'. Anarchism, as a revolutionary doctrine, has sought to destroy the state as an institution of sovereign authority, violence and domination, based on the firm belief that it has no legitimacy, that it masks class interests, and, furthermore, that it interferes with freely formed, natural relationships that would otherwise operate as the basis of social regulation. But this is also why anarchists regard anarchy, not as a situation of disorder – as in the Hobbesian scenario – but rather as a *different kind of order*, one based on autonomous human interactions, voluntary agreements between individuals, and spontaneous acts of cooperation and solidarity. Indeed, anarchism is unique as a political philosophy in openly affirming a more positive vision of 'anarchy'. The French anarchist Pierre-Joseph Proudhon, the first to openly call himself an anarchist, referred to anarchy as another kind of order. Anarchy, he said, was 'not the daughter but the mother of order'. And, certainly, many anarchists have proposed alternative visions of social organisation to replace the state, based on communal arrangements, federalist structures and mutualist principles. Moreover, anarchism, which is as much a *practice* as a philosophy, has long been associated with the attempt to build alternative communities, from the most mundane experiments in 'everyday anarchy' (cooperatives, squats, food exchanges, activist networks, mutual aid organisations, housing associations, free schools) right through to the anarchist republics established in Catalonia during the Spanish Civil War in the 1930s. Anarchism, as a practical form of social organisation, is particularly effective in emergency situations, in natural disasters, wars or even pandemics; during COVID-19 we saw a proliferation of mutual aid networks that sprang up more or less spontaneously to provide assistance to vulnerable people, in the wake of crumbling public infrastructure and state incapacity.[7] All these alternative forms of social organisation and community – even the most localised and horizontally arranged – are characterised by certain norms of conduct and behaviour, what we might call rules. But these are 'rules without rulers'[8] – that is, they are rules which are self-imposed by community members and participants, rather than by a sovereign legislator.

Proudhon defined anarchy as the 'absence of a master, of a sovereign'. Anarchy, as we know, comes from the Greek *anarkhia* (ἀναρχία) meaning without 'power' or 'authority.' This can be understood in both the ontological sense, as Schürmann proposes – that is, without a foundation, point of ultimate origin, or ruling principle – as well as in a political sense, indicating the desire to be free from, to live without, a ruler. The slogan of anarchism is 'No Gods, No Masters' – in other words, the rejection of authority and mastery in all its senses, theological, political, as well as economic, social and, above all, legal. Yet, as we show in this book, this is to be understood not only as a negative gesture, but also as a positive gesture: the desire to create new institutions and social arrangements, new forms of life, that are no longer based on sovereign mastery. This also means new kinds of legal institutions and arrangements designed to foster human freedom and autonomy rather than to limit it. Proudhon himself is particularly interesting in this regard, as he embodies this fundamental ambivalence when it comes to the question of the law. On the one hand – in his negative gesture – he rejects laws as the 'gossamer for the mighty and rich, fetters that no steel could smash for the little people and the poor, fishing nets in the hands of government'.[9] On the other hand – in a positive gesture – he proposes an alternative conception of law and legal justice, based not on the commands of the sovereign but on free contractual agreements between individuals.[10] In such alternative models, law operates as a way of instituting freedom, indeed as an *institution of freedom*. As the anarchist-inspired philosopher Miguel Abensour puts it, 'one quickly discovers how a certain conception of law can cohere with a libertarian idea of democracy and in this way belong to an anarchic constellation, particularly considering that the laws in favour of liberty are not laws like others'.[11]

So it is this institutionalising dimension of anarchism that we are interested in exploring. It is a mistake to think that anarchism is against institutions. Anarchism simply wants institutions of a different kind: institutions that are bottom-up rather than top-down; institutions that are contingent and adaptable, rather than fixed and pre-determined; institutions that are democratically deliberated on and always contestable rather than being imposed by a sovereign; institutions that promote, rather than restrict, human freedom. In other words, anarchist institution-building should be seen as a collective, open-ended, ontologically anarchic exercise intended to maximise autonomy and minimise coercion. Here we are particularly influenced by the Italian theorist Roberto Esposito and his recent work on *instituting thought*, which he distinguishes from constituting power, on the one hand, and destituting power, on the other. In his outline of these three political ontologies, destituting power is the negative gesture of withdrawal (associated with the thought of Heidegger and Agamben), and constituting power is the positive gesture of affirmation (associated with the Spinozist ontology of Deleuze), while the alternative paradigm of instituting thought derives from Claude Lefort and his neo-Machiavellian conflictual model of democracy. While we understand these paradigms somewhat differently to Esposito, seeing particularly, constituting power in the more familiar sense as the project of creating a new sovereign political and legal order based on the unmediated 'will of the people' (something we find in Carl Schmitt's legal theory and in today's authoritarian populisms), we nevertheless see something of value in Esposito's notion of instituting power[12] as a way of thinking through the paradoxes of anarchism's relation to law. In contrasting destituting and constituting thought with instituting thought, Esposito says:

> A radically different conception of the law separates them: the first two currents [destituting and constituting] rely on a paradigm that is enclosed in the language, also sovereign, of the primacy of the written law and of the will of the legislator; institutionalism on the other hand relies on a paradigm that is open to the pressures of society and to the exigencies of history, it has to respond to the urgencies of necessity and to the needs of life. In this sense the law is the object of a struggle that centers on its own meaning even before centering on the issue of specific rights. To say that the law, instead of responding to institutions that are fixed in time, never ceases to institute means attributing a performative force to it that unleashes all its performative power. Precisely insofar as it is 'unnatural' – entirely artificial – instituting law can intervene effectively in life: not in order to save it or re-create it anew, as the paradigms of political theology propose in a politically inactive manner, but in order to change it from within.[13]

In some ways, an anarchist approach to law embodies both the destituting gesture and the instituting gesture outlined here by Esposito. On the one hand, anarchism is a form of destituting thought, in the sense that it sees law in its politico-theological dimension as the sovereign will, and seeks to radically withdraw from it. We find this in much of the classical anarchist revolutionary tradition (Bakunin, Kropotkin) as well as in the alternative model of the insurrection proposed by the individualist anarchist, Max Stirner. We also find this destituting gesture in the anarchist-inspired thinking of Giorgio Agamben and Walter Benjamin, both of whom we engage with in this book. However, we also observe in anarchism an instituting form of thinking which frees law from the model of sovereign authority and political theology, seeing it as a flexible, open-ended, 'artificial', rather than fixed, institution, whose function is to change life 'from within' – which means, for us, to promote new forms of autonomous life. Anarchism, in this sense, makes law and legal institution a practice of freedom.

Methodology and approach

This book is an attempt to navigate a path for anarchism between these two poles of destituting and instituting thought. Rather than seeing the ambivalence of anarchism on the question of the law as an obstacle or a problem to be resolved decisively one way or the other, we see it as generating a productive tension that allows us to think both anarchism and legal theory in new ways. In staging this encounter between anarchism and law, we endeavour to find out what happens when law is forced to look at itself from an anarchist perspective, and when anarchism is forced to look at itself from a legal perspective. What sorts of questions arise here, what kinds of problems emerge, and how might these be reconciled, if indeed any reconciliation is possible?

Another productive set of tensions emerges from our different perspectives as authors. This book is a joint collaboration between a political theorist (Newman) and a legal scholar (La Torre), both of whom have a strong interest in and affinity with anarchism. Yet, our approach to anarchism is influenced by two different theoretical angles – continental and analytical. However, while some might regard this as an irreconcilable chasm, we believe that there is a fruitful dialogue to be had between these two styles of thinking. While they draw on different traditions and thinkers, there is considerable overlap between them, or at least important points of convergence which allow us to interrogate legal and political concepts in innovative ways. Analytical legal philosophy can benefit from the more historical or 'genealogical' approach taken by continental and critical social theory, while continental thought can be informed by the normative questions that analytical legal theory is typically engaged with. At the very least, when it comes to a consideration of jurisprudence and law, continental philosophy cannot shy away from normative questions about justice, rights, political obligation, and so on. In this book, Rawls, Dworkin, Raz, Hart, Finnis, Austin, and Kelsen are discussed alongside

Deleuze, Benjamin, Agamben, Foucault and Judith Butler. French and Italian legal institutionalists (Maurice Hauriou and Santi Romano) are made to tread the same ground as French poststructuralists and Italian biopolitical philosophers. The radical conservative Carl Schmitt is brought into critical dialogue with the anarchists Bakunin, Proudhon and Stirner. A genealogical arc is traced from the republican thought of Spinoza to the rationalist individualist anarchism of William Godwin. Unexpected parallels and rhizomatic connections crop up everywhere. We believe that this sort of heterogeneous, multiform approach is an appropriate way of exploring the possibility of an anarchist legal science.

However, developing an anarchist legal science is complicated by the fact that anarchism itself is an extremely diverse philosophy. Indeed, anarchism, compared with other ideologies like Marxism, has always been less homogeneous and, one could say, less doctrinal. While anarchism has a common set of inclinations – the rejection of authority and the desire for autonomy – it contains different and, at times conflicting, strands and perspectives. How can the anarchist communism of Kropotkin or the mutualism of Proudhon be made to cohere with the extreme individualism of Stirner? Does the rationalism of Godwin have any truck with the anarcho-mysticism of Gustav Landauer or the anarcho-messianism of Walter Benjamin? What would the violent revolution at times invoked by Bakunin have to do with the pacifist anarchism of Tolstoy, Thoreau or Gandhi? Then we have the difference between *philosophical anarchism* (Wolff, A. John Simmons, and to some extent Godwin) which adopts a sceptical position on the question of legal obligation but stops short of drawing any political conclusions from this, and *political anarchism* (Bakunin, Kropotkin, Malatesta) which calls for the revolutionary overthrow of the state and its laws and the creation of an alternative set of arrangements.

There are, moreover, many sub-strands within the anarchist tradition, including anarcha-feminism (Emma Goldman),[14] 'green' or eco-anarchism (Murray Bookchin),[15] and 'anti-civilizational' or 'primitivist' anarchism (John Zerzan).[16] This last sub-strand is particularly interesting from our point of view, in the sense that it is partly inspired by the work of the anarchist anthropologist Pierre Clastres, whose study of indigenous tribes in Amazonia as examples of stateless societies, or 'societies against the state', provides a kind of paradigm for thinking about how 'laws' can operate in a community without a command-and-control structure.[17] Moreover, this focus on indigenous and non-Western, even anti-modern communities and practices – and the important lessons they can teach anarchists and legal scholars alike – reflects the need to decolonise anarchism as a field of research.[18] Lastly, we should acknowledge the important contributions of anarchist criminology, which is obviously relevant to any discussion of the law. Anarchism has developed a powerful critique of systems of legal punishment and of the classification of the figure of the 'criminal' or 'deviant' as the one upon whom such oppressive and violent machinery is inflicted; they have sought to address the underlying social factors behind crime and have proposed prison abolition and alternative, more humane and less coercive, forms of social sanction.[19]

While our overall approach is influenced, in one way of another, by all these different perspectives, our aim is not to provide a comprehensive overview of anarchism as an ideology as such, but to explore anarchism's critical encounter with the law. Nevertheless, this sheer diversity of perspectives makes the rich tradition of anarchism somewhat difficult to pin down.

However, where we think a definitional distinction can and should be drawn is between anarchism and libertarianism (associated with the political philosopher Robert Nozick, who called his book *Anarchy, State and Utopia*) or so-called 'anarcho-capitalism' (associated with Murray Rothbard and others). While there are occasionally some important cross-overs in the history of these traditions, and while there are interesting debates in the libertarian/anarcho-capitalist milieu on legal theory,[20] these are quite different positions. Where does the difference lie? We have more to say about this later in the book – but basically, libertarianism/anarcho-capitalism confines its critique of authority and domination to the political or public sphere of the state, envisaging an organic society of free market transactions and unregulated private commercial relationships which the state – if it is to exist at all – does not interfere with. However, the problem with this scenario, for anarchists, is that it is utterly blind to the multiple forms of domination, coercion, hierarchy, inequality, and the restrictions on freedom (both negative and positive freedom) that inhere in the market, property relations, as well as within the family, patriarchy, and other spheres of private life. For anarchists, the state, or the political sphere, is only one sphere of domination and oppression in society; and while it might be central to upholding capitalist relations, it is naïve to imagine that if the state were to disappear domination would come to an end. It is therefore too simplistic, we argue, to see anarchism as being 'anti-state'; it is more precise to see it as 'anti-domination', as it is opposed to domination in all its forms and in all spheres of social life. In this matter, the individualist anarchism of Stirner would have more in common with the communist anarchism of Kropotkin or the collectivist anarchism of Bakunin, than with the 'libertarianism' of Nozick or Rothbard. Drawing this distinction becomes ever more important today when 'libertarianism' and 'anarcho-capitalism' have become associated – even if in a somewhat confused and incoherent way – with the ideology of far-right, which weaponises the idea of 'freedom' in order to justify gender and racial inequalities and entrenched privilege as part of a naturalised social order.[21]

Our impetus for writing this book was the absence of anarchism within the 'Critical Legal Studies'/'Critical Legal Theory'. Apart from a few notable exceptions,[22] anarchism as a distinct approach to legal thinking is generally overlooked in these fields of research. This may be largely due to the traditional dominance of Marxism, certainly with CLS.[23] However, although these fields have become considerably broadened and more diversified over time, under the influence of deconstruction (Derrida), poststructuralism (Foucault), psychoanalytic theory (Lacan), post-Heideggerian philosophy (Agamben, Nancy), queer studies (Butler),[24] feminism,[25] and postcolonial theory,[26] there is still a kind of silence when it comes to anarchism. This is slightly odd and vexing, given that anarchism offers the most radical critique of legal authority and therefore should be regarded as the ultimate ethical and political test of the limits of the law. Anarchism has always been a marginalised discourse in most academic disciplines (especially in political theory), and legal theory, even in its more 'critical' forms, is no exception to this. This may be due to the widely held belief – which we seek to dislodge – that anarchism is simply incompatible with the law and therefore has nothing of any importance to say on the matter. However, as we seek to show in this book, anarchism not only contains a valuable critical perspective on law, but also the opportunity to radically rethink it.

Outline of chapters

Chapter 1 outlines the anarchist critique of legal authority. Drawing mostly on the canon of nineteenth-century classical anarchism, it explores the radical positions of key anarchist thinkers like Bakunin, Kropotkin, Proudhon, Godwin and Stirner, as well as contemporary philosophical anarchists like Robert Paul Wolff and A. John Simmons, all of whom reject the principle of political obligation – the obligation to obey the law. They all seek to unmask what Montaigne called the 'mystical foundation of authority'. For these thinkers, the law has no legitimacy of its own, imposes unnecessary restrictions upon individual freedom and the right to private judgement, and that the various justifications of obligation usually provided, such as consent and the social contract, are simply unconvincing. Political anarchists, however, go a step beyond the merely sceptical position of the philosophical anarchists, proposing the destruction of state power and arguing that life can be lived and society organised in the absence of state law. Yet, we also show the way that, in making this critique, classical anarchism relies at the same time on some concept of natural law or a natural substratum, such as Kropotkin's theory of mutual aid, as a kind of moral and rational counterpoint to the artificial distortions of state law and as the bedrock for an anarchic principle of social organisation.

In Chapter 2 we explore, in much closer detail, the encounter between anarchism and legal jurisprudence, seeking to determine what theory of law – if any – might be compatible with anarchism. Positive law theory (Kelsen, Raz, Hart), in its 'exclusivist' and 'inclusivist' versions, is contrasted with natural law theory (Dworkin); yet, as we show, because both theories tend to regard coercion as essential, neither is really compatible with anarchism. Three different anarchist paradigms are then discussed – methodological, philosophical and political – all of which adopt a sceptical stance on legal obligation, and which would seem to widen the chasm between anarchism and the two dominant models of legal theory. However, a more promising approach is offered by legal institutionalism (Maurice Hariou, Santi Romano, as well as the neo-institutionalists like Ota Weinberger, Neil MacCormick). Here it is argued that while institutions can at times have a conservative function, institutionalism's *anti-prescriptivism* – whereby law is not a command as such but a contingent series of capacity-enabling rules that promote certain forms of life and action – opens up the possibility for thinking about *anarchist* legal institutions, a possibility we explore in the thought of David Graeber, Cornelius Castoriadis and Gilles Deleuze.

In Chapter 3 we lay the groundwork for a possible reconciliation between anarchism and law, by reconstructing a forgotten genealogy – what we call the long arc of anarchy – linking the materialist philosopher Spinoza with the anarchists Godwin and Proudhon. While Spinoza is not an anarchist in any obvious sense, we argue that his materialist ontology, in which free will is rejected and God is immanent within nature, leads to an alternative model of freedom understood not in the liberal negative sense of limiting others' interactions, but as the enhancement and intensification of human powers and capacities. This produces, we argue, new understandings of rights conceptualised as powers, not just as legal entitlements or protected areas of private liberty and enjoyment. Furthermore, in Spinoza's republicanism, the body politic is reshaped as a community of citizens who collectively deliberate about their destiny and a common way of life. Such ideas are taken up in the anarchist philosophy of Godwin and Proudhon, particularly in terms of their critique of capitalist relations and property rights. Furthermore, in this anti-authoritarian ontological paradigm we construct, institutions are not the embodiment of an external sovereign will but, rather, the expression of sociality and mutual deliberation. Here law operates as the constitutive act of a social space in which human capacities and powers can develop and expand. Law thus becomes a space of liberation rather than constraint and coercion, something that empowers individuals and fosters new forms of freedom.

Chapter 4 explores another even more unexpected encounter between the authoritarian conservative jurist and legal theorist Carl Schmitt and revolutionary anarchism. This is on the question of sovereignty and its relation to law. It is argued that Schmitt and the anarchists, coming from completely opposed sides of the question, expose the hidden politico-theological core of sovereignty – its exceptional position vis-à-vis law. For both sets of thinkers, political sovereignty is always an absolutist concept; something that Schmitt affirms as its highest good, and which anarchists condemn as its greatest evil. In tracing the dialogue that Schmitt sets up in his *Political Theology I*, between ultra-conservatives like Donoso Cortes and anarchists like Bakunin and Proudhon, as well as his critique of the anarchist conception of human nature in *The Concept of the Political*, we show that Schmitt's real target – his real ideological enemy – is not so much liberalism, as is commonly thought, but anarchism; and, moreover, that his conceptual apparatus of the sovereign state of exception, whereby the sovereign decides unilaterally to suspend the constitutional in moments of emergency, is a counter-revolutionary (or *katechontic*) weapon deployed to stave off the threat to political order posed by anarchism. Thus, the legal anarchy of the sovereign state of exception comes to resemble, in a paradoxical fashion, the real anarchy of the revolution.

In Chapter 5 we return to the enigma of the foundations of the law, and to the question of who or what can instantiate the legal order, given that this founding act is, by definition, *before* the law and therefore lacking in legal legitimacy. This problem is first explored through the idea of auto-immunity. Drawing on Esposito and Derrida, we discuss the ways in which the political-legal order is at times forced, in reaction to threats and emergencies, to violate its own principles and procedures as a way of bolstering its immune response. Secondly, we explore the question of revolution as a form of action that removes one politico-legal order and erects a new one in its place. Revolutions, in other words, are a form of constituting power (*pouvoir constituent*). Anarchism is an important means of interrogating this concept because, even though it is for the most part a revolutionary theory, it proposes a different way of understanding a revolution: not a revolution aimed at constituting a new form of state power (as in the liberal idea of a constitutional order, or the Marxian workers' state) but rather a revolution *against* power. One way of thinking about what this means, is the notion of destituting action – a form of action that withdraws from and deposes the politico-legal order, but which does not put anything in its place; a concept we develop through Stirner's idea of the insurrection and Agamben's notion of destituent power (which he derives from Benjamin's notion of divine violence). However, we propose here an alternative 'third way' – what we have referred to as anarchist *instituting* power, which we deploy, following Miguel Abensour, to think about how law and legal institutions might be redesigned to maximise freedom and autonomy.

Chapter 6 revisits the question of the state, which is obviously the central target of the anarchist critique of authority. Or is it? What we reveal in this chapter is a certain ambivalence on the part of anarchists on this question. Unlike libertarians/anarcho-capitalists, whose critique is solely focused on the state as a form of public authority and who are oblivious to the private sources of domination existing in the market and property relations, anarchists reject domination and exploitation in all its forms, private and public. Moreover, anarchists, once again unlike libertarians/anarcho-capitalists, will defend certain state functions such the public provision of welfare, social services, health care, environmental regulation and so on, even if they regard these as ultimately insufficient. This raises the question of whether it is possible to have a concept of the state – as a community and a set of public goods – that is compatible with anarchism. Therefore, in this chapter, we reflect the *dual nature* of the state: as a hierarchical, sovereign structure of command and obedience that retains a monopoly on violence; *and* as a public space that preserves the common good. After exploring different conceptions of the legal state (*Rechtsstaat*) in German legal thought (Hans Kelsen, Georg Jellinek, Gustav Radbruch, Hermann Kantorowicz), we turn to anarchism. We suggest that in thinkers like Proudhon, for instance, an alternative conception of the state can be found: no longer as an institution of violent domination, but rather as a public space of collective deliberation, in which legal institutions work to promote individual autonomy and human flourishing.

In Chapter 7 we turn to the question of violence and its relation to law. While law is supposed to put a stop to violence and to resolve conflict through peaceful, procedural means, anarchists, and other critical legal theorists (Robert Cover, Christophe Menke, Andreas Fischer-Lescano, Daniel Loick) recognise the law's intimate relationship to violence. We explore this relationship through an anarchist reading of Walter Benjamin's seminal essay *Zur Kritik der Gewalt* [1921] in which sovereign power – operating through the antinomies of lawmaking and law-preserving violence – is ultimately overcome through an altogether different form of violence, what Benjamin calls divine violence. This is a form of violence – indistinguishable from justice – which abolishes or deposes state authority and frees us from the law. Here we draw a close parallel between divine violence and Georges Sorel's anarcho-syndicalist notion of the proletarian general strike, understood as an autonomous action on the part of the working class to free themselves from capitalism and the state. Although the violence of the proletarian general strike involves a form of symbolic, mythical violence, and although Benjamin's divine violence should be understood in similar terms, as being 'lethal without spilling blood', this immediately raises the question of the place of violence in revolutionary emancipation, and indeed of anarchism's own ambivalent relationship with violence. Here we explore anarchist traditions of violence and non-violence, discussing thinkers like Peter Glenderloos, Judith Butler and Gustav Landauer.

Chapter 8 is devoted to a discussion of civil disobedience, of which anarchism is perhaps the most forthright expression. However, we register an important difference between liberal conceptions of civil disobedience – what Rawls calls 'principled law breaking' – which essentially seeks to uphold the constitutional order and which comes with so many conditions and restrictions as to make it entirely benign, and the much more radical anarchist idea of disobedience, which calls into the question the very idea of political obligation. However, we explore the question of disobedience from its opposite perspective, asking not why people disobey, but the more interesting question of why people obey in the first place, even when it is not in their interests to do so. Here we turn to the sixteenth-century French humanist writer Étiennne de La Boétie and his text *Discourse on Voluntary Servitude,* in which he explores the mystery of our voluntary obedience to tyrannical authority. We interpret this text in an emancipatory, and indeed anarchistic, sense, as a way of revealing the fragility of all systems of power and our ever-present capacity for freedom: to resist authority, all we must do is stop supporting it.

Chapter 9 addresses the question of human rights, and here is revealed a further point of ambivalence in anarchist philosophy. While anarchists invoke human rights against law, and have supported human rights struggles everywhere, they have also been conscious of the limitations of human rights discourse as conforming to a liberal legalistic framework and as reducing the individual to the status of a rights-bearing citizen of the nation state. Using Arendt's famous, although largely misunderstood, critique of the Rights of Man as the impetus for interrogating human rights discourse, we seek to develop a more radical, anarchist model of human rights: rights as genuinely cosmopolitan, rights as constructed through cross-border activism and solidarity, and rights as ontologically anarchic in the sense of providing a discourse and practice that opens up new terrains of struggle, different forms of experience and pleasure, and alternative modes of subjectivity.

Our concluding chapter briefly outlines some of the principles of an anarchist legal science. We restate our argument that anarchism is by no means incompatible with law, but seeks a different understanding of law: *law without coercion*. This requires legal institutions that are not constructed around the sovereign command and obedience principle. What might this look like? We show that laws in anarchist societies and communities might be understood as common rules and ethical norms of conduct, which provide a coordinating framework for collaborative social activity. These would be rules that members of the community voluntarily agree to, and yet which are open to democratic deliberation and ongoing interrogation. The role of law in anarchist societies and communities would not be to restrict human freedom but to promote it, and to enhance individuals' opportunities for autonomy and flourishing. We briefly explore some different ways of thinking about this: Gary Chartier's idea of the non-aggression maxim as the basis for law in a stateless society; Hermann Amborn's idea of 'law without hegemony', based on his ethnographic studies of traditional tribal communities in the Horn of Africa; and critical theorist Daniel Loick's engagement with Jewish thinkers like Walter Benjamin, Hermann Cohen and Franz Rosenzweig in order to propose an idea of legal obligation without the need for coercive sanctions. Above all, as Loick points out, one of the virtues of law, even in anarchist societies, would be not only to allow us to participate in collective deliberations when we so choose, but also to liberate us from the burden of always having to do so and to allow us to simply get on with our lives with as little interference as possible.

Notes

1. Reiner Schürmann, *Heidegger on Being and Acting: From Principles to Anarchy*, trans., C-M Gros. Bloomington: Indiana University Press, 1987, p. 6.
2. Ibid., p. 4.
3. Ibid., p. 290.
4. According to Schürmann, 'What these masters sought was to displace the origin, to substitute the "rational" power, principium, for the power of authority, princeps – as metaphysical an operation as has ever been. They sought to replace one focal point with another', p. 6.
5. On the connection between ontological anarchism and political anarchism, see Donatella di Cesare, *The Political Vocation of Philosophy*, trans., David Broder, Cambridge: Polity Press, 2021, pp. 131–137.
6. This is the famous maxim of the nineteenth-century French statesman, Louis Adolphe Thiers: *le roi regne, mais if ne gouverne pas*. Agamben adopts this to describe the way that power in modern liberal societies bears the 'anarchic' structure of administration or *oikonomia*, rather than sovereignty, which retains its rituals of authority, yet which conceals an empty throne. See Giorgio Agamben, *The Kingdom and the Glory: For a Theological Genealogy of Economy and* Government (Homo Sacer *II*, 2), trans. by L. Chiesa. Stanford, CA: Stanford University Press, 2011.

7. For a discussion of this, see Rhiannon Firth, *Disaster Anarchy: Mutual Aid and Radical Action*, London: Pluto Press, 2022.
8. See Matthew Wilson, *Rules without Rulers: The Possibilities and Limits of Anarchism*, Winchester UK: Zero Books, 2014.
9. Pierre-Joseph Proudhon, 'The Authority Principle', in Daniel Guérin, ed., *No Gods, No Masters: An Anthology of Anarchism*, trans., Paul Sharkey, Oakland, CA: AK Press, 2006, 81–98, p. 90.
10. See Pierre-Joseph Proudhon, *Du principe fédératif et oeuvres diverses sur les problems politiques européens*, ed. by C. Bouglé and H. Moysset, Marcel Rivière, Paris 1959.
11. Miguel Abensour, *Democracy against the State. Marx and the Machiavellian Moment*, trans. M. Blechman and M. Breaugh, Cambridge: Polity, p. 122.
12. Here we would regard Deleuze also as a thinker of institutions – as we show in Chapter 2.
13. Roberto Esposito, *Instituting Thought: Three Paradigms of Political Ontology*, trans., Mark William Epstein, Cambridge: Polity Press, p. 13.
14. For a recent discussion on anarcha-feminism, see Chiara Bottici, *Anarchafeminism*, London: Bloomsbury, 2021.
15. Bookchin, *The Ecology of Freedom*, Oakland CA: AK Press, 1982, p. 31.
16. John Zerzan, *Future Primitive*, New York: Autonomedia, 1991.
17. See Hermann Amborn, *Law as Refuge of Anarchy: Societies without Hegemony or State*, trans., Adrian Nathan West, Cambridge, MA: MIT Press, 2019.
18. See for instance the work of Maia Ramnath, *Decolonizing Anarchism: An Anti-authoritarian History of India's Liberation Struggle*, Oakland CA: AK Press, 2011.
19. See for instance, the work of: Jeff Ferrell, 'Against the Law: Anarchist Criminology', *Recent Developments in Criminology: Towards Disciplinary Diversity and Theoretical Integration*, ed., Stuart Henry, London: Routledge, 2016; Geoffroy de Lagasnerie, *Judge and Punish: The Penal State on Trial*, trans., L. Vergnaud, Stanford, CA: Stanford University Press, 2018; Larry L. Tifft and Dennis Sullivan, *The Struggle to be Human: Crime, Criminology and Anarchism*, Cienfuegos Press, 1980; and Jacques Lesage de La Haye, *The Abolition of Prison*, trans., Scott Branson, Oakland CA: AK Press.
20. See Edward Stringham, ed., *Anarchy and the Law: The Political Economy of Choice*, Oakland CA: The Independent Institute, 2006.

21. This convergence is discussed by Melinda Cooper. See 'The Alt-Right: Neoliberalism, Libertarianism and the Fascist Temptation', *Theory, Culture & Society* (Special Issue: *Post-Neoliberalism*), 38: 6 (2021), 28–50.
22. See Elena Loizidou's *Anarchism: An Art of Living without Law*, Abingdon, Oxon: Routledge, 2023; Christos Marneros, '"It is a Nomos Very Different from the Law": On Anarchy and the Law', *Acta Universitatis Lodziensis: Folia Juridica* 92 (2021): 125–139.
23. See Roberto Mangabeira Unger, *The Critical Legal Studies Movement*, Cambridge, MA: Harvard University Press, 1986.
24. See for instance, Matthew Stone, Illan Rua Wall and Costas Douzinas, eds., *New Critical Legal Thinking: Law and the Political*, Abingdon, Oxon: Routledge, 2012.
25. See Carrie Menkel-Meadow, 'Feminist Legal Theory, Critical Legal Studies, and Legal Education, or "The Fem-Crits Go to Law School"', *Journal of Legal Education*, 38: 1/2 (March–June 1988), 61–85; Matthew Kramer, *Critical Legal Theory and the Challenge of Feminism, Lanham*, MA: Rowman & Littlefield, 1995.
26. Denise Ferreira da Silva and Mark Harris eds., *Postcolonialism and the Law*, London: Routledge, 2017.

One
Classical Anarchism and Legal Authority

'In a word, we reject all legislation – privileged, licensed, official, and legal – and all authority, and influence, even though they may emanate from universal suffrage, for we are convinced that it can turn only to the advantage of a dominant minority of exploiters against the interests of the vast majority in subjection to them. It is in this sense that we are really Anarchists.'

(Mikhail Bakunin).[1]

It is interesting to read the court transcripts from famous trials of anarchists. Pierre-Joseph Proudhon, the first to call himself an anarchist, and who, in 1842, found himself facing legal proceedings because of his radical views on property, defended his economic theories to the jury, who apparently found them so obscure and difficult to follow that they could not condemn them. At the trial of the Haymarket anarchists in 1886 – convicted of conspiring to detonate a bomb targeted at police officers amidst labour unrest in Chicago – one of the accused, German immigrant Louis Lingg, declared: 'I die gladly upon the gallows in the sure hope that hundreds and thousands of people to whom I have spoken will now recognize and make use of dynamite. In this hope I despise you and despise your laws. Hang me for it'.[2] Emma Goldmann, publisher of the anarchist journal *Mother Earth*, who found herself, along with Alexander Berkmann, in front of a court in New York in 1917 charged with disseminating anti-war propaganda and seeking to dissuade people from enlisting, called into question the legality of the judicial proceedings against her. Felix Feneon, editor of the journal *La Revue Anarchiste*, prosecuted as part of a widespread government crackdown on the anarchist movement in France in 1894, used humour to derail the proceedings. When confronted by the prosecutor with the allegation – 'It has been established that you surrounded yourself with Cohen and Ortoz' – Feneon replied 'One can hardly be surrounded by two persons; you need at least three', which was greeted with laughter from the courtroom. The prosecutor continued – 'You were seen conferring with them behind a lamppost' – to which Feneon replied 'A lamppost is round. Can Your Honour tell me where behind a lamppost is?' More laughter erupted.

Whether with irreverent humour[3] or revolutionary defiance, with legal arguments or complicated doctrines, anarchists have used different strategies in confronting the repressive machinery of a judicial system. They stage a conflict with the law that is at once political, philosophical, even theatrical. If, in the words of Geoffroy de Lagasnerie, '*Living under the rule of law means living in a context in which the state has the right to dispose of us*',[4] anarchists seek to reveal the violent domination behind the principle of legal authority.

Of all the radical and revolutionary political philosophies, none is more implacably opposed to the institution of the law than anarchism. Central to anarchism is the rejection of the law's claim to authority.[5] This is a claim anarchists regard as morally questionable, irrational and altogether unjustified. In holding this view, the anarchist takes aim at the very foundation of the law, revealing the ignominy of the demand that the law be obeyed *simply* because it is the law, not because of any separate rational or moral criteria. The anarchist critique thus goes to the very heart of what Michel de Montaigne called 'the mystical foundation of authority'.[6] In a radically demystifying gesture, the anarchist questions the rather perverse tautological reasoning that lies at the base of all arguments about legal obligation. And at least some anarchists go further. They contend that the law is an unnecessary imposition, and that life can be lived and society organised without legal authority. Whereas law bases its claim to our obedience on its supposed ability to put a stop to the violent anarchy of the state of nature, anarchists refuse this artifice of social contract theory, affirming instead a completely different and more positive vision of anarchy: a rational social order based on voluntary cooperation rather than on centralised authority.

In the Preface we introduced the notion of *ontological anarchy* – the indeterminacy and emptiness of meaning (*anomie*) that is increasingly the condition of social life. *An-archy* is the absence of origin and authority, in other words the absence of a ruling principle that founds and determines political and legal institutions. Such institutions continue to exist but more as empty shells without life or legitimacy, relying on coercive force rather than moral authority. Anarchy is therefore a fundamentally ambivalent condition. While the crisis of authority facing all governing institutions today produces dangerous and violent paroxysms, and while the temptation is always to fill in the empty place of authority with new and more despotic forms of power, the condition of anarchy also invites ethical reflection on the limits of legal obligation and presents the opportunity for transforming institutions in radically different directions. This is why we consider the political and ethical project of anarchism as being so important at this critical juncture. Anarchism is the transformation of anarchy into a positive vision of social relations, one based on autonomy, self-determination, and voluntary cooperation rather than on legal coercion. Anarchism shifts the meaning of anarchy from one of disorder to a *different kind of order*, one where the principle of the sovereign *arché* is transcended.

This chapter will explore the anarchist critique of law. Anarchism, as we have argued, is the most radical form of antinomianism. Certainly, other radical political philosophies, like Marxism, are critical of law, or at least a certain form of law, which they see as the instrument of class domination.[7] Yet, anarchism takes issue with the very principle of legal obligation itself. It asks the fundamental question: why should we obey *any* law? And, taking essentially a sceptical position on this question, it regards the law's moral claim to our obedience as fundamentally spurious. This rejection centres on two interrelated claims: firstly, that law and legal obligation violate individual freedom and the right to private judgement; and secondly, that the law has no legitimate authority – that it is founded on force, violence and deception, and that it merely enshrines economic inequality and political domination.

For anarchists, the principle of legal and political obligation necessarily conflicts with the principle of individual autonomy and acting according to the dictates of one's own conscience. The starting point for philosophical anarchism[8] is the assertion of the moral autonomy of the individual, a position which *might*, as Robert Paul Wolff argues, lead him or her to at certain times comply with particular commands for prudential reasons, for instance, or if they concern a technical matter in which the individual has no expertise and is prepared to defer judgement to someone who does, but which at the same time *never* means that the individual obeys a command *simply* because it is a command.[9] Obeying commands[10] – whether political commands or even legal decisions – is a recognition of another's authority over oneself, and therefore an abrogation of one's own autonomy. The principle of authority as embodied in the state and the principle of individual autonomy are irreconcilable. As Wolff puts it, 'The defining mark of the state is authority, the right to rule. The primary obligation of man is autonomy, the refusal to be ruled'.[11] In a similar vein, A. John Simmons distinguishes between legal and moral duties: within any legal system there is an in-built expectation to obey, defined by a system of sanctions for disobedience. However, the question of *moral* obedience suggests an autonomous realm of judgement outside the system of legal norms. From this perspective, the anarchist – while perhaps agreeing to obey particular laws on pragmatic grounds or because they align with his or her sense of morality in specific cases – never considers it his moral duty to obey law in general. The law's absolute claim on our moral obedience is never justified, and the anarchist reserves the right to judge laws according to her own conscience. As Simmons puts it: 'A moral duty to obey the law would be a duty to do as the law requires *because* it is the law, a duty to obey the valid law as such … not to do as it requires just insofar as it happens to overlap with independent moral duties'.[12] To accept such a duty would be, according to Simmons, to surrender one's own autonomous moral judgement. Moreover, the fact that there are different legal systems in the world, with vastly different standards of justice and morality, emphasises that the duty to obey cannot be absolute, unless we are willing to accept the idea that we should comply with commands that are patently unjust.[13]

Anarchists therefore regard independent moral judgement as pre-eminent over legal obligation. For the eighteenth-nineteenth century anarchist philosopher William Godwin, we could not hope to arrive at a more virtuous existence unless we can freely make our own decisions on the basis of our own moral and rational judgement. Yet, the obedience demanded by law undermines the independent development of one's rational capacities: if people are used to simply obeying rules for their own sake, then their rational faculties would not be exercised and their minds would remain in a slumber. Our independent judgement – and not any external compulsion – should therefore be the only thing that determines our actions and which can legitimately impose obligations upon the individual. Any interference with this right is something that diminishes the sanctity of the human being. That is why Godwin believed that the right of private judgement should translate into civil affairs as well as matters of individual conscience; indeed, the two domains are inseparable. However, this right to freely form one's own opinions and to shape the conditions in which one lives always runs up against the determining violence of the law and political authority: 'I have deeply reflected, suppose, upon the nature of virtue, and am convinced that a certain proceeding is incumbent upon me. But the hangman, supported by an act of parliament, assures me I am mistaken'.[14]

Furthermore, the law involves the application of abstract universal rules to singular situations, thus often doing a real injustice to them. According to Godwin, jurisprudence was a sort of Procrustes' bed of general rules, no less spurious than creeds and catechisms, which reduced individual differences to arbitrary determinations. Laws were based upon antiquated traditions and obscure precedents made long ago, whose reasons were forgotten; and yet their authority over the individual remains absolute. Justice, on the contrary, can only be observed if the particularities of each individual case are taken into account. Therefore, the strict application of the law is an unjust tyranny wielded over the individual. For Godwin, then, 'we can scarcely hesitate to conclude universally that law is an institution of the most pernicious tendency'.[15] The problem with the law is that it totalises and determines all spheres of life according to a rigid formula, a fixed set of norms and rules, leading to the abdication of individual decision-making. We are so used to law deciding every dispute and solving every problem that we have lost all power of independent judgement and autonomous action. We have been made dependent on the law, and it has bred within us a slavish and servile mentality. We regard the law as sacred, and unthinkingly submit to its authority. As Kropotkin put it:

> We are so perverted by an education which from infancy seeks to kill in us the spirit of revolt, and to develop that of submission to authority; we are so perverted by this existence under the ferule of a law, which regulates every event in life – our birth, our education, our development, our love, our friendship – that, if this state of things continues, we shall lose all initiative, all habit of thinking for ourselves. Our society seems no longer able to understand that it is possible to exist otherwise than under the reign of Law, elaborated by a representative government and administered by a handful of rulers; and even when it has gone so far as to emancipate itself from the thraldom, its first care had been to reconstitute it immediately.[16]

Indeed, law, in its blind and absolutist application, was no different from the exercise of political force. According to Godwin, the punishments and coercions of the law are simply the violent and arbitrary infliction of one will upon another – the 'right' of the stronger to enforce his will upon the weaker:

> The case of punishment, in the view in which we now consider it, is the case of you and me differing in opinion, and your telling me that you must be right, since you have a more brawny arm, or have applied your mind more to the acquiring skill in your weapons than I have.[17]

This idea is also echoed by the individualist anarchist Max Stirner, who regarded the rule of law as an intolerable imposition of an alien will upon that of the individual: 'People are at pains to distinguish *law* from arbitrary *orders* [*Befehl*], from an ordinance: the former comes from a duly entitled authority. But a law over human action (ethical law, state law, etc.) is always a *declaration of will*, and so an order.'[18] If, therefore, law cannot be distinguished from arbitrary rule, from orders imposed from above – if it is no different, in other words, from power and force – then there is little to actually justify the authority of the politico-legal order.

Most of the discourses that have, at one time or another, served to legitimise the violence and domination of the state are, anarchists argue, theoretically fraudulent, mere ideological mystifications which mask the real workings of power. Consent and social contract justifications for legal obligation are no more convincing than the old doctrine of divine right. For Mikhail Bakunin, social contract theory was an 'unworthy hoax' and an 'absurd fiction' – a cheap trick foisted on people to make them think the state legitimate and based on their consent. The contradiction of social contract theories was that while they imagined a condition of either primitive savagery or egotistical competition, they at the same time claimed that people suddenly had the foresight to come together to form a rational collective agreement.[19] The origins of our supposed consent to government are highly dubious and paradoxical. Rather than having freely sacrificed our natural freedom, anarchists claim that government and legal systems had been violently imposed upon us through conquest. Law and state power are imposed not in the general interests of society, but in the interest of economic and political elites. Laws were, as Pierre-Joseph Proudhon put it, 'gossamer for the mighty and rich, fetters that no steel could smash for the little people and the poor, fishing nets in the hands of government'.[20] Moreover, legal systems emerged, as Bakunin recognised, not through a collective agreement between individuals but rather through a struggle between powerful groups, where one group vanquishes all the rest and establishes its domination.[21] Similarly, Kropotkin describes the way that in European societies during the sixteenth century, independent entities such as guilds, free associations, village communities and medieval cities began to be taken over and displaced by an increasingly centralised and absolutist state apparatus – a process that was accomplished through violence rather than consent, and led to the annihilation of these autonomous social entities.[22] It was this process of state capture which, moreover, fostered more hierarchical and unequal forms of society, and led to domination by political, religious and economic elites. So, the dangerous conditions of liberty and equality that Hobbes believed constituted the state of nature, and which he saw as so destructive of human coexistence, are precisely the conditions which anarchists see as the basis of ethical community – conditions which have been obscured beneath the looming shadow of Leviathan. Rather, the violent state of nature, based on egotistical competition, exists *now* and has been fostered by the state and capitalism.

The idea of democratic legitimacy fares little better than the social contract in providing a convincing justification for obedience to the law. The fact that laws are made today in a democratic system, by elected representatives, does not furnish them with any greater legitimacy. It is not that a democratic state would not be in itself preferable to say an authoritarian state or absolutist monarchy, but that mechanisms of universal suffrage and elected representation do not in fact guarantee equality and liberty, and indeed often work to deny them. According to anarchists, the idea of democratic accountability, and government representing the will and interests of the people, is simply an illusion that conceals the absolute gulf between the people and power.[23] Voting in elections cannot be taken as a sign of consent. Leaving aside the question of unfair and disproportionate voting systems, voting simply authorises a new set of masters who make decisions for the people and exercise authority over them. Moreover, to endorse one particular government over another does not mean one has consented directly to everything it does or to all the laws it makes. Furthermore, the idea of democratic representation assumes that people cannot speak for themselves or articulate their own wishes. As Proudhon complained:

> what are all these elections to me? What need have I of proxies, or indeed of representatives? And since I must set out my wishes, can I not articulate them without help from anyone? Will the cost to me be any greater, and will I not be all the surer of myself than of my advocate?[24]

Democracy is therefore simply the guise for the rule of elites and the transfer of political power from absolutist monarchs to a new set of masters. While representative democracy was meant to enshrine political equality – the equality of all citizens – it simply alienated the will of the people and institutionalised a new form of inequality between the people and the governing class. As Bakunin put it,

> But the instinctive aims of those who govern – of those who frame the laws of the country as well as those who exercise the executive power, are, because of their exceptional position diametrically opposed to the instinctive popular aspirations. Whatever their democratic sentiments and intentions may be, viewing society from the high position in which they find themselves, they cannot consider this society in any other way in which a schoolmaster views his pupils.[25]

For anarchists, it is the *structure* of political power – the principle of sovereignty in other words – that is more important than the *form* political power takes. This is why they do not place much value on the distinction between democratic regimes and other types of regimes, why Proudhon sees no essential difference between the principle of democratic government and the principle of divine right,[26] and why, for Stirner, the transition from monarchical regimes to modern republics did not so much guarantee liberty but introduced a new form of servitude: '"Political liberty", what are we to understand by that? Perhaps the individual's independence of the state and its laws? No; on the contrary, the individual's subjection in the state and to the state's laws.'[27]

For philosophical anarchists like Wolff, the *idea* of democracy – wherein people freely determine the laws and rules by which they were governed – offered some sort of solution to the problem of legal obligation. Yet this would only apply in a situation of *direct* democracy based on unanimous consensus, rather than in representative and majoritarian democracies in which the will of the individual was only indirectly expressed or drowned out by that of the majority.[28] Anarchists have long been interested in more direct and consensus-based forms of democratic decision-making – as we have seen, for instance, in activist movements like Occupy Wall Street.[29] Indeed, from a certain perspective, the anarchist project can be seen as a *democratisation of democracy* – an ongoing, open-ended form of democratic experimentation and innovation. However, while there is an important convergence – both historically and politically – between anarchism and the radical democratic tradition, the insufficiencies of actually existing forms of democracy render them incapable of accounting for legal obligation. The symptoms of the current dysfunction of democratic regimes – seen in everything from voter apathy, disinterest, cynicism and distrust of elected politicians, the resurgence of far-right populism, to the mobilisation of new social movements and forms of dissent – all point to the limits of the idea of democratic consent as a foundation for legal authority.

A further claim for the sanctity of the rule of law in a democratic society is the idea that law protects us from the excesses of sovereignty, that it checks and limits executive power. As the liberal argument goes, the rule of law must be respected because it protects us not only from one another, but also from the government, which must itself abide by the law. However, from an anarchist perspective, this contention must be also questioned. While it is true that in some cases the law protects individual rights and can be used to appeal against particular government decisions, the liberal's faith in law's capacity to limit power is naïve and misplaced. Legal protections are afforded to some and denied to others – asylum seekers and minorities, for instance; rights can be, indeed often are, curtailed and suspended by constitutional states for all sorts of reasons, particular on security grounds. Nothing exposes this better than the logic of the state of exception which, for the theorist of sovereignty, Carl Schmitt, was absolutely central to state power. For Schmitt, sovereignty ultimately lay in the prerogative to suspend the constitutional order and the rule of law, and to act in an extra-legal capacity. This sovereign right to decide on the exception[30] was essential not only in defending the constitutional order from an existential threat, but also in acting as the law's ultimate point of application. In other words, the legal system is grounded in a force that exceeds it; it derives its authority from an existential domain that is beyond its limits. This was something that, according to Schmitt, positive law theorists and liberal constitutionalists simply could not grasp. We shall discuss Schmitt in greater detail in a later chapter, especially in relation to his subterranean dialogue with anarchism. Yet, we can observe here that Schmitt and the anarchists unmask the limits of the liberal theory of the law from opposite sides of the argument. Both see the spectre of the sovereign exception behind the visage of the law – but Schmitt invokes this as a way of bolstering the law's authority and legitimacy, whereas anarchists want to strip away the ideological veils of the law to reveal the naked power and domination concealed behind. Furthermore, as Giorgio Agamben has pointed out, while the exception exceeds the law, some sort of provision is nevertheless made within most legal systems for their own suspension in times of emergency.[31] The law thus embodies its own lack, its own suspension; there is a paradoxical relationship between law and lawlessness, between the rule of law and its abrogation. The state of exception is neither outside nor inside the law, but rather inside and outside at the same time. It is a sort of black hole or abyss into which law falls, or rather which law opens up for itself, where the distinctions between law, power and violence collapse. Have we not seen an increasing extension, indeed one could say *normalisation*, of the state of exception in liberal democracies over recent decades with emergency legislation and security measures in order to combat all manner of threats and crises, such as terrorism, political dissent or pandemics?[32]

Finally – and this is perhaps their most radical claim – anarchists have contended that the law is *unnecessary*; that the legal-political structure enshrined in the state is an unwarranted, disruptive and parasitical imposition upon society. In the words of Godwin, governments 'lay their hand on the spring there is in society, and put a stop to its motion'.[33] Society is seen as an organism driven by natural mechanisms and forces. It has the capacity for self-regulation and self-organisation, based on voluntary agreements and cooperation at a community level, without the need for legal coercion. Central to anarchism, then, is the counter-image of the state. Rather than the Hobbesian Leviathan which towers over society, enforcing the law with coercive force ('covenants without the sword are but words, with no strength to secure a man at all'),[34] anarchists envisage an alternative image of anarchy as self-organised society composed of autonomous individuals who agree freely amongst themselves on the rules of their community. Later in the book, we will reflect on what this alternative, non-coercive system of rules might actually mean, and whether it can still be considered a form of law – even if of a radically different kind. However, anarchists have always pointed to the possibility of alternative communities and social relationships no longer governed by the principle of legal authority. Whether this is understood as the kind of social order that would emerge once the artificial and coercive institutions of state power had been overthrown, or whether as a series of relations already immanent within current social arrangements – embodied for instance in everyday practices of mutual aid, cooperation and solidarity – anarchists have imagined and fought for the possibility of life outside the constraints of the law.

The possibility of this kind of free life is based, for classical anarchists, on a sort of natural substratum, an order of natural law which conflicts with the laws of the state. Indeed, Bakunin drew a distinction between natural law and man-made law. Whereas man-made laws – the laws imposed by the state and enforced through violence – were irrational, corrupt and an artificial and unnecessary constraint upon society, natural laws were part of the human makeup and therefore provided an alternative moral and rational basis for human action. Indeed, for Bakunin, it was to this alternative order of natural law that we owed our obedience:

> But it is necessary to distinguish natural laws from authoritarian, arbitrary, political, religions, and civil laws ... laws which under the pretext of a fictitious morality, have always been the source of the deepest immorality. Thus we have the involuntary and inevitable obedience to all laws which constitute, independently of all human will, the very fate of Nature and society; but on the other hand, there should be independence (as nearly unconditional as it is possible to attain) on the part of everyone with respect to all claims to dictate to other people, with respect to all human wills (collective as well as individual) tending to impose not their natural influence but their law, their despotism.[35]

Bakunin thus constructs a sort of Manichean opposition between two ontological orders of law: one natural, rational, moral, the well-spring of human freedom and sociability, and whose authority we obey absolutely; the other, artificial, corrupt, irrational, immoral, destructive of human freedom and sociability, and whose despotic authority we have a right to defy.[36]

The idea of a natural order therefore provides the foundation for the classical anarchist critique of legal authority and for its contention that an alternative stateless society is possible. The potential for human freedom and autonomy is contained within natural and material forces, even biological instincts and evolutionary drives, that are immanent to social processes yet buried beneath the artificial order of the state and its laws. Murray Bookchin's Hegelian-inspired philosophy of 'dialectical naturalism' sees the possibilities of a rationally ordered society embedded within a sort of social totality immanent within nature, and whose dialectical unfolding would produce a flowering of human freedom.[37] Kropotkin believed that the principle of human sociability could be derived from a permanent biological instinct towards mutual aid inherited from animal species.[38] In opposition to Herbert Spencer's reduction of Darwin's theory of evolution to the 'survival of the fittest', Kropotkin – who based his conclusions on countless geographical, historical and zoological studies – believed that the key factor in the survival of species, both animal and human, was not competition but cooperation. Yet it was this natural instinct for cooperation that was gradually obscured by the growth of the centralised state, leading not only to the loss of freedom but also to a narrow-minded individualism and egoistic competition. The 'war of everyman against everyman' depicted by Hobbes as our natural condition, was actually the *outcome* of the imposition of sovereign authority rather than what preceded it. For Kropotkin, then, solidarity, rather than individualistic competition, formed the true basis of human societies. Many of our daily interactions involved spontaneous forms of mutual assistance and cooperation, without the need for state coordination and legal regulation, and the extension of this principle of solidarity could function as the moral and organisational framework for an anarchist society. Recent commentators have pointed, for instance, to spontaneous mutual aid networks emerging in the context of the COVID-19 pandemic and other crises, in the shadow of an increasingly dysfunctional and ineffectual state, as evidence of the liberatory potential of social solidarity.[39]

It seems to us that there is an urgent need to rethink the idea of mutual aid and to consider what it might mean today in the context of crumbling state institutions, whose inability to manage manifold crises and emergencies is plain for all to see. The question we shall address over the following chapters is how mutual aid and social solidarity might transform the idea of law, allowing law to operate in a less coercive and less regulatory way, allowing more spaces of social life to operate on the basis of autonomous interactions, voluntary agreement and self-management. However, our argument will be that while there are plenty of examples of mutual aid and solidarity in everyday life, the possibility of an anarchist community is *contingent* rather than pre-determined (either by natural laws or biological instincts), and its future therefore lies in ongoing experimentation in redesigning legal institutions and in the invention of new practices of freedom.

Notes

1. Mikhail Bakunin, *The Political Philosophy of Bakunin*, ed., G. P. Maximoff, London: The Free Press of Glencoe, 1953, p. 241.
2. Timothy Messer-Kruse, *The Trial of the Haymarket Anarchists*, Palgrave Macmillan, 2011, p. 136.
3. See the discussion of humour as an anarchist strategy in Loizidou's *Anarchism*.
4. See de Lagasnerie, *Judge and Punish*, p. 40.
5. See Paul McLaughlin, *Anarchism and Authority: A Philosophical Introduction to Classical Anarchism*, Aldershot, Hampshire: Ashgate, 2007.
6. For Montaigne, 'laws keep up their good standing not because they are just, but because they are the laws; that is the mystical foundation of their authority, they have no other ... Anyone who obeys them because they are just is not obeying them the way he ought to.' *Essais*, book 3, Ch. 13. www.gutenberg.org/files/3600/3600-h/3600-h.htm.
7. Indeed, Marxist theory has had a major influence on the Critical Legal Studies movement. See Mark Tushnet, 'Marxism as Metaphor' (1983) 68 *Cornell Law Review* 281. 37; Duncan Kennedy, 'The Role of Law in Economic

Thought: Essays on the Fetishism of Commodities', *American University Law Review* 34, 939 (1985).

8. Philosophical anarchism reflects a general position of scepticism with regard to the question of political obligation. See, for instance, Robert Paul Wolff, R. P. Wolff, *In Defense of Anarchism*, University of California Press: Los Angeles, 1970; Leslie Green, *The Authority of the State*, Oxford: Clarendon Press, 1988; A. John Simmons, *Moral Principles and Political Obligations*, Princeton: Princeton University Press, 1979; A. John Simmons, 'The Anarchist Position: A Reply to Klosko and Senor' Philosophy and Public Affairs, Vol. 16 (1979); Chaim Gans, *Philosophical Anarchism and Political Disobedience*, Cambridge: Cambridge University Press, 2012.
9. Wolff, *In Defense of Anarchism*, p. 16.
10. Seeing law in terms of commands, disobedience towards which is punishable, is the basic premise of John Austin's theory of jurisprudence. See *The Province of Jurisprudence Determined*, Cambridge: Cambridge University Press, 1995.
11. Wolff, *In Defense of Anarchism*, p. 18.
12. Christopher Heath Wellman and A. John Simmons, *Is there a Duty to Obey the Law?* Cambridge: Cambridge University Press, 2005, p. 95.
13. Simmons nevertheless recognises a distinction between philosophical anarchism, which simply retains a sceptical position on legal obligation, upholding that we do not have a moral duty to obey the law, and *political* anarchism, which argues that we have a moral duty to disobey, certainly when it comes to unjust laws – a position that leads to resistance and revolution (Ibid., pp. 191–192). See also on this distinction, Magda Egoumenides, *Philosophical Anarchism and Political Obligation*, London: Bloomsbury, 2014, p. 2.
14. William Godwin, *Enquiry Concerning Justice* (1793), Ontario: Batoche Books, 2001, p. 111.
15. Ibid., p. 514.
16. Peter Kropotkin, 'Law and Authority: an Anarchist Essay' http://dwardmac.pitzer.edu/Anarchist_Archives/kropotkin/lawauthority.html.
17. Godwin, *Enquiry*, p. 112.
18. Max Stirner, *The Ego and Its Own*, trans., Steven Byington, ed., David Leopold, Cambridge: Cambridge University Press, 1995, p. 174.
19. Bakunin, *Political Philosophy*, p. 165. Simmons argues that consent-based theories – whether actual or tacit – suffer

from a similar lack of realism. (Wellman and Simmons, *Is there a Duty to Obey the Law?*, pp. 117–118).

20. Proudhon, 'The Authority Principle', p. 90.
21. Bakunin, *Political Philosophy*, p. 354.
22. See Peter Kropotkin, *The State: Its Historic Role*, London: Freedom Press, 1943.
23. Bakunin, *Political Philosophy*, pp. 217–218.
24. Proudhon, 'The Authority Principle', p. 93.
25. Bakunin, *Political Philosophy*, p. 218.
26. Proudhon says: 'Government is government by divine right or it is not'. 'The Authority Principle', p. 91.
27. Stirner, *The Ego and Its Own*, p. 137.
28. Wolff, *In Defense of Anarchism*, p. 21.
29. See David Graeber's *The Democracy Project: A History, a Crisis, a Movement*, London: Penguin, 2014.
30. For Schmitt, the sovereign is 'he who decides on the state of exception'. Carl Schmitt, *Political Theology: Four Chapters on the Concept of Sovereignty*, trans., George Schwab, Chicago: University of Chicago Press, 2005, p. 5.
31. Giorgio Agamben, *State of Exception*, trans. Kevin Attell, Chicago and London: University of Chicago Press, 2005, p. 1.
32. See Agamben's recent series of interventions from the start of the pandemic in 2019: *Where are we Now? The Epidemic as Politics*, London: Eris, 2021.
33. Godwin, *Enquiry*, p. 151.
34. Thomas Hobbes, *Leviathan* [1651] Chapter XVII www.gutenberg.org/files/3207/3207-h/3207-h.htm.
35. Bakunin, *Political Philosophy*, 1953, p. 168.
36. We must nevertheless distinguish this from the more familiar understanding of natural law found in jurisprudence or in the classical liberal tradition. Here, while natural law is seen to supersede and normatively circumscribe positive law and the authority of government (see J. Finnis, *Natural Law and Natural Rights*, Oxford: Clarendon, 1980, pp. 23–24), at the same time it is the ontological ground upon which law and government emerge. For instance, in Lockeian social contract theory, natural law and natural rights can only be realised insofar as they are instituted within a sovereign political community; their function is to provide the foundation for a legitimate form of government, even as they impose – in theory at least – normative limits on government power. By contrast, the idea of natural law proposed by Bakunin embodies not the constitution of a 'just' state

order, but rather the dissolution of all state orders. Natural law, for anarchists, is not a basis upon which to reform, moderate or ameliorate political-legal authority (to make it adhere to the 'rule of law' or to natural principles of justice) but to destroy it. The notion of natural law proposed here by Bakunin is perhaps closer to Ernst Bloch's idea of natural law as embodying a utopian dimension of human emancipation, dignity and justice which is always pitted against the domination and injustice of the state: 'The pride of the upright carriage, natural law ... is the element that resists, the insurgent element in all revolution.' (Ernst Bloch, *The Principle of Hope*, Cambridge MA.: MIT Press, 1986 p. 275; see also Costas Douzinas, *The End of Human Rights*, Oxford: Hart Publishing, 2000).

37. See Bookchin, *The Ecology of Freedom*, p. 31.
38. See Peter Kropotkin, *Mutual Aid: A Factor in Evolution*, McCure, Phillips & Co. 1902.
39. For an extended discussion of this, see Dan Swain, Petr Urban, Catherine Malabou, Petr Kouba eds., *Unchaining Solidarity: Mutual Aid and Anarchism with Catherine Malabou*, Landham, Maryland: Rowman and Littlefield, 2022. See also Firth, *Disaster Anarchy*.

Two

Anarchism and Law: A Jurisprudential Conundrum

A thorny relationship

This chapter's aim is to determine which concept of law best fits anarchism. This question will be pursued from the perspective of the rich tradition of legal theory and philosophy of law, and thus also from the angle of the self-understanding of what legal practice is and means.

As law is central to the question of the coordination of conducts, and for a general scheme of a social order, anarchism is immediately confronted with the question of what law is, what purposes it should serve and how it should be deployed. Anarchism's attitude towards law is displayed according to the five different views it assumes in its 'classical' theory, aspects of which were explored in the preceding chapter: (a) Godwin's objectivist rationalism; (b) Stirner's existential individualism; (c) Proudhon's social pluralism; (d) Bakunin's dialectical communitarianism; and (e) Kropotkin's evolutionary naturalism. Yet, while the approach of classical anarchism to the law is generally a critical one, we need to consider the degree to which a certain form of anarchism might be reconcilable with a concept of law, as well as the extent to which jurisprudence and legal theory could possibly integrate an anarchist political option. Our claim, in other words, is that, notwithstanding the traditional critical stance of anarchism with regard to the law, there might be some way of rethinking law in order to make it more compatible with anarchist principles.

When being confronted with the concept of law we have of course to face the classical opposition between legal positivism and natural law. Natural law refers law to justice, or morality, through a necessary conceptual connection. From this perspective, law is considered malleable. Law is plastic and it is mostly a matter of what people believe it is by acting according to the law. Through law, people determine the shape and content of their life and entitlements and the powers and procedures instrumental to giving sense to social life and to the satisfaction of their basic needs. The issue of what law is can thus overlap with the question of what kind of society and coordination of human relations one has to choose and realise. This is, of course, a controversial issue, depending on the distinct interests and values people have, and, consequently, it is intrinsically open to discussion and contestation. We might thus conclude that law is an essentially contested concept,[1] one that is permanently open to debate and disagreement.

Legal positivism, by contrast, denies any necessary connection between law and morality. While from a natural law perspective, law is a question of justification, for legal positivism, law is simply a matter of ascertaining certain facts. For the legal positivist, the entirety of law is contained in 'sources' that are there to be discovered and highlighted. In his seminal essay on the critique of violence, *Zur Kritik der Gewalt*,[2] Walter Benjamin re-elaborates the distinction between these two grand doctrines of law by outlining that, while natural law subjects the legality of legal instruments to the material justice of their aim, legal positivism, on the contrary, considers the legality of the aims pursued by legal provisions from the perspective of the adequacy of such rules to the aims taken as fundamental. In this sense, one might also argue that natural law is a *material* doctrine, based on a substantive notion of justice, while legal positivism is a *formal* or *procedural* doctrine, being focused on the adoption of formalities dictated by the legal provisions that are to be enforced. For natural law theory, the law's rationality is to found in its aims and the values they embody, and only in these, while for legal positivism law's rationality is simply instrumental, a question of the means it adopts to reach ends that could be freely, arbitrarily, fixed.

Thus, legal positivism makes law's content a matter of decision and autonomy, which is, however, open to factual description. One might therefore think this to be more in line with an anarchist approach to social and political relations, according to which agreement and reflexivity are central to normative legitimacy. Moreover, in tracing law back to the empirical world, without any rhetorical reference to principles of morality, or of an ideal dimension, legal positivism could be, in a paradoxical way, compatible with a radical critique of law, in which its pretences to morality are unmasked as an ideological guise for violence, domination and arbitrary power.

At the same time, legal positivism depends on a notion of authority where individual reasons are largely replaced by exclusionary directives in a way that cannot be reconciled with a robust requirement of self-government and a strong sense of individual autonomy. Positivism is especially hostile to any attempt to refer law to morality, to moral principles and justice, in such a way that makes law impermeable to questions of legitimacy and contestations of injustice. This would possibly render it incongruent or incompatible with a strong moral critique of power and authority, such as is presupposed in an anarchist approach to politics.

Legal positivism all too quickly leads to imperativism, and operationalises a strong, hierarchical concept of sovereignty. For it is authority, not truth, nor justice, that makes law. Furthermore, for political anarchism to be legitimate requires a radical universal move, that of general acceptability, and the reference to a model of a good life in which autonomy is much more than simply a procedural value. In this sense, some version of natural law, giving autonomy an objective and sometimes even an ontological value, would seem more appropriate to anarchism. However, natural law may have quietist implications, such as those that are derivable from a view of law as already given in the structure of being and its internal ontological hierarchy as reflected by society. Natural law might imply that the rules of the good life are independent from people's deliberation.

Natural law is too easily prone to presupposing goods that do not need a reflective endorsement by those said to be the beneficiaries or the holders of the given 'goods'. The same would be the case, if in the positivist reconstruction of legal rules as secondary order reasons, those primary order reasons that allegedly are better satisfied through their preemption by legal rules could be identified without an exercise of self-reflection by the people to whom they apply. This is the gist of 'exclusive' legal positivism as it has been presented in the work of Joseph Raz. Paradoxically, something of a similar tenor happens within natural law, especially in its equally 'exclusivist' approach.[3] However, 'exclusive' natural law and 'exclusive' legal positivism defend quite different theses. The former 'excludes' deliberation from the realm of the most important basic goods, which are given and are operative without a specific intermediation of discourse and decision. Legal positivism is 'exclusive' in a different sense; it 'excludes' morality from the precinct of law, at least from the domain of the definition of law. Law can be without any reference to morality or justice. An intolerably unjust law would thus still be law. In 'exclusive' natural law 'essences' or 'correctness' are detached from a practice of public deliberation. The absence of autonomy and reflexivity in this approach is hardly congruent with an intense theory of political freedom such as is defended by anarchists. Nor could anarchism be satisfied with a theory, especially in its more radical, 'exclusivist', version, that never confronts the question of the justification and legitimacy of legal rules. Thus, anarchism would appear to be incompatible with both legal positivism or natural law theory, and points towards a 'third theory' of law.

Versions of legal positivism

Legal positivism doctrines are split into two opposing 'camps' – 'exclusive' and 'inclusive'. 'Exclusivists' claim that law and morality are forever disconnected, in the sense that for the law to be legally valid it does not need to refer to moral criteria or principles. 'Inclusivists' raise a partially opposing claim: law may *sometimes* need to include moral principles in order to be what it is. Accordingly, it would only depend on the content of the basic rule which is the foundation of the legal system and its norm of recognition. If this basic rule – for instance Herbert Hart's 'rule of recognition'[4] – contains some reference to morality, then morality is incorporated into positive law.

This point, however, is not perspicuous in the debate between the two camps. 'Exclusivists' believe that law's essence must be factual and thus authoritative in order to be enforceable. Being enforceable here means that there has been a first act of enforcement, and this justifies the following events of enforcement. Enforceability in this perspective does not refer to a special normative claim. It is not an opening towards some sense of 'ought'. The argument here runs more or less as follows: since law claims to be authoritative, then it should be factually able to be authoritative. This is a strange logic. It will be also used to defend law as essentially coercive. Since law is something that claims to be enforced, the capacity of enforcement – identified here tout court with coercion and violence – should be a property of the nature of law. For the 'inclusivist', on the contrary, law's 'nature', although it once again rests on factuality, might need some reference to an 'ought'. For the 'inclusivist', law's essence is again factuality and enforceability, but the latter could sometimes require a normative support. The 'is' may be complemented by an 'ought' to be what really is.

However, this ontological difference is not further elaborated or conceptualised. The 'inclusivist', *malgré lui* perhaps, remains loyal to a factual view of the law that is the one rigidly defended by the 'exclusivist'. There is no clear distance between their respective views of what a fact of law is. In short, their basic ontology of law is the same, and this is given by a notion of social fact in terms of decision and authoritative coordination. There is no room here for an anarchist re-elaboration of law in terms of a practice liberated from coercion and hierarchy, and responsive to strong criteria of justice.

Between 'exclusivists' and 'inclusivists' there might be a significant distinction, in so far as the 'exclusivists' tend to see law as the outcome of an individual making, a kind of artifact, while 'inclusivists' might tend towards a view that underlines law as a collective social fact. For both, however, law – to use Hannah Arendt's terminology – remains a *making*.[5] This view of law as a 'making' rather than a 'doing' becomes explicit, once the nature of law is severed off from the practice of law, as is the case in Raz's jurisprudence.[6] Here, we are told, legal reasoning – lawyers' and citizens' way of using legal rules and concepts – is not relevant for the definition of what law is. The participants' internal point of view is no longer assumed to be needed. To have access to the 'nature' of law, to the essence of what law is, the correct position to take is the observer's one, a pure external, conceptual (not practical), philosophical enterprise, intended as a domain that is fully independent from legal practice. While, according to Hart, the concept of law is still in the hands of those who practice it, this is no longer accepted by Raz. Hence, law is viewed simply as a 'making', a kind of production, a special 'tool' or 'artifact'. This epistemologically 'essentialist' approach – one that programmatically abandons Hart's hermeneutical perspective – is indeed possible only if we consider the rule and its use as entities and situations unrelated to the core of law's existence, that is, its practice. 'Essence' is the pure, privileged outcome of an external observer's expertise, not of the community of citizens who actually practice law and modify its rules. This kind of essentialism is at odds with an anarchist, pragmatist approach to law, since it turns law into a rarified, abstract, fixed system of rules and norms removed from the everyday practice of citizens. People are thus expelled from law's 'essence'. 'Exclusive' positivism in this sense is hardly compatible with an anarchist commitment to law as self-definition and self-determination by ordinary people. Law's autonomy is pitted here against people's autonomy. The autonomy of law is obtained by denying citizens autonomy in the determination of what law is and should be. In short, law's autonomy is an achievement of legal positivism, which is obtained in so far as it implies its closure against citizens' queries for justification and possible readjustment. Autopoietic or systemic theories of law, such as those proposed by Niklas Luhmann and his disciples, radicalise this view, and interpret citizens' possible contestation of law as an illegitimate disturbance of the autonomous, autopoietic system of law.[7]

But there are two other recent declinations of positivism that should be mentioned here. One is that we need positivism – that is a law that is authoritative in the sense of being ultimately ascertainable only by descriptions – if we want to have certainty and democracy. Were we to accept that law is ever referable to considerations of morality and justice, we would be opening up greater scope for controversy, conflict, and eventually judicial assessment and discretion.

Citizens' self-determination implies that citizens are able to determine the definitive rules of their being together and their form of life. Moral controversy should be once and for all decided and ultimately solved by citizens' legal determinations. The law that is their product cannot be reopened again to moral controversy; otherwise citizens' decisions would be eventually derogated, overrun by judges and other actors. Consequently, we need legal positivism – undisputable legal determinations open only to description, not to valuation – in order to guarantee democracy. For moral reasons we have to assume a ground rule that would prescribe that subjects obey legal rules, irrespective of their content. This is echoed by Kelsen in his *Reine Rechtslehre*, his 'pure legal theory', where it is claimed that legal rules can have whatever content.[8]

That we need law in order to solve moral controversies among citizens and to avoid moral pluralism corrosive to social stability and the common good, seems *prima facie* a sound argument. But this 'ethical' version of positivism[9] – 'normative' or 'ethical positivism' – depends heavily on the validity of *methodological positivism*. This claims that we can epistemologically assess what a law is from just a source of law, a fact of its determination, without any additional argument than a purely descriptive interpretation. In a sense, we should presuppose here that conducts can only be determined through definitive rules, and that principles (general norms without conditions of applications) do not play any role in the application of rules and their interpretation. However, whether this methodological assumption is sound can be legitimately doubted. Even if the law as a source, as a statute, or as a precedent, decides about and solves moral conflict, this could and would be reopened in the dimension of interpretation. Interpretation is not just a description of the rule, but involves an adjustment and thus some revision of its semantic purpose, of its sense, and especially of its capacity to give an answer to concrete cases. Of course, the issued rule to be interpreted and applied narrows down the scope of the possible interpretation and application, otherwise there would be no point in having a rule. However, it cannot apply by itself ('rules cannot provide for their own application' – says Hart,[10] repeating a prior consideration of Wittgenstein);[11] in particular, the rule cannot fully preempt the question of justice and morality. This is exactly the weak point of Raz's 'exclusive' positivism that, on the contrary, centres on the efficacy of the said preemption, that is, the exclusion of normative reasons beyond those dictated by authority through command.

Now, an anarchist legal theory is premised on an awareness of this permanent gap between facticity and normativity, or, taken from a different angle, between individual primary reasons for action, and secondary reasons that are called to replace the primary reasons. A comparison and reflective judgement between these two kinds of reasons is inevitable in the phenomenology of practical reasoning. That gap necessarily leaves room open for further discussion and deliberation. And it is good indeed that there is such a gap, since cases are ever a result of changing reality, and law, as outlined by William Godwin, cannot be a bed of Procrustes, a rule that does not take into account the diversity of cases and the multiple qualities and values that exist in the world of human actions; for the law to be applied in this way would be an exertion of violence on the world of facts.

A further version of legal positivism is actually the revival of a very traditional view. This is the one that sees the core of law as coercion and violence. Its exertion of force and violence over reality and the world is its basic nature. Now, we might accept that law sometimes, indeed more often not, involves coercion and violence. Law, for instance, can enforce the death penalty or sanction the use of torture. In recent decades, for instance, the US has attempted to re-legalise torture.[12] Law is not resistant to violence. Just the opposite – something that we explore in a later chapter. However, one could argue whether violence is the central experience and property of law. Recently, an American jurisprudent, Kenneth E. Himma, has advanced a radical thesis according to which law and coercion would be *conceptually* connected: 'It is a conceptual truth that anything that counts as a system of law backs some mandatory legal norms governing non-official behaviour with the threat of a coercive sanction'.[13] This statement is somewhat baroque in tenor, and full of strong theoretical assumptions, implying for instance the idea of a 'conceptual truth', sort of *a priori* notion, applied to a practice of social life as law. Here we are clearly confronted with a resurrection of an old 'essentialism' according to which states of affairs in the world are to be referred back to their presupposed 'nature' or 'essence', independently of their 'existence'. A law without coercion would be like the shadow seen by the people chained together in the Platonic cavern. Once exposed to the light, law would appear with its most terrible face, a thesis that Kelsen could have shared, for he believes that if one had ever a chance of looking law in the face, one would be petrified by the sight of power's image, a sort of Gorgon, revealing the naked force and the terror underlying the fact of law.[14]

The essentialist approach to law and coercion might be considered a sort of revival of a legal or political theology, whereby 'ideas' without mediation direct and produce the facts in the world and especially human and social facts. This is a thesis that anarchism could hardly accept, at least as far as the social world is concerned, since it simply affirms the status quo and denies the possibility of reshaping the world according to an alternative vision of social relations. A reason that is not mediated through imagination, deliberation and action would not allow individuals to interrogate and even resist it, if it is so dictated by subjective needs. Such irresistible rationality, detached from subjective perceptions, feelings, and imagination, could hardly be conducive to individual autonomy and human flourishing. It would put a stop to change and the emergence of novelty in the world.[15] From this perspective, the world is merely the outcome of 'concepts' or 'essences' or 'natures' that can be assessed *a priori*. In any case, Hart would reject the strong view of law and coercion. According to him, sanctions, as distinct from sheer acts of violence or from suffering or loss of benefits and goods, need to be referred to some previous rule that provides a general standard of conduct for citizens. Sanctions would make sense, and are understood and applied as such, only once those substantive rules of conduct are infringed.[16]

A strong connection between law and coercion, one could argue, might be found in Ronald Dworkin's doctrine of law. Dworkin is a critic of Hart's legal positivism, objecting to its genealogical derivation of the rule for the case at hand from a putative sum of sources that are purely factual, and which can be assessed in a merely descriptive mood.

Dworkin argues that law is not just a system of rules, but also and essentially includes principles, and these are distinct from rules as normative standards in so far as they do not have a definitive condition of application. Principles, moreover, cannot be interpreted literally or genealogically. They instead require a hermeneutical approach and a form of moral reasoning. The interpretation of a legal provision is not just a semantic exercise. Legal controversies are not conflicts about the semantic meaning of prescriptions, where a case could be subsumed under a discrete linguistic rule. There is much more involved here. Conventionalism, he says, should leave room for interpretivism and the operative criterion of integrity as the general ground rule of law. Integrity means both a requirement of universalisation and the attention to all circumstances relevant to the case at hand.[17]

Dworkin thus argues against the two systems approach, according to which law and morality are distinct normative orders. Instead, he defends a one-system approach, where law and morality are part of the same system of normative criteria for human action.[18] However, Dworkin lays down a formulation of what the role of law is that seems to include coercion as one of its necessary tenets: 'Law provides a justification in principle for official coercion'.[19] Here coercion is not so much a *property of* law, but it is nevertheless *presupposed by* it. Law offers legitimacy to the pre-existing requirement of coercion. From this perspective, law is a justificatory device, rather than an ontological entity. It is something that gives normative justification to coercion. But this is a view that is hardly acceptable to anarchism, which rejects the use of legally sanctioned violence against individuals as a violation of their autonomy and human dignity.

In spite of its *prima facie* plausibility, the strong view of law and coercion has to face elements of the phenomenology of law that cannot be easily reconciled with it. A law whose first aim would be punishing people without considering their conducts would be not only irrational, but also fully ineffective, because people could then be punished irrespective of their behaviour and mutual expectations. Kant, when discussing immoral forms of convivence, defines such a model as the one of *Zuchthaus*,[20] a penitentiary, where people are permanently sanctioned without reason. Punishment, being ontologically necessary, does not need a justificatory support, an additional normative legitimacy. No *nulla poena sine lege previa* principle, no punishment without a previous legal standard, is conceptually applicable here. Let us suppose a judge sentences someone to life imprisonment, and then justifies this decision only on the basis that she is using a law whose conceptual core is sanction, or coercion, irrespective of other, more relevant considerations and features of what the law is and ought to be. Such a decision would be entirely inappropriate, unjust, and indefensible, even for the legal system within which it is taken. A 'conceptual truth' about law should either be able to be operative first and foremost from the internal point of view of people practising law, or, if not, it should be dismissed as useless and finally considered as only a 'conceptual game' without relevance for the practice of law. It might still be true for 'philosophers', but it could not claim to elucidate and guide, even implicitly, the work of citizens and lawyers.

A concept of law that irremediably relates law to violence would be incompatible with anarchism, whose first existential justification is the revolt against hierarchy and authority and the use of violence against persons. If law is conceived in such terms, it should be *in toto* rejected as a way of organising social life, unless there is the possibility of some sort of social coordination that could be based on rules without sanction and coercion.

Three forms of anarchism

We can identify three basic anarchist approaches to the question of legal authority: a *methodological*, a *philosophical* and, finally, a *political* anarchism, each, respectively, suspicious or hostile to authority and law in the domains of knowledge, morality, and in the public space of politics. The latter form, political anarchism, we might also label 'paradigmatic' anarchism, since it is the form that directly challenges social hierarchies and alienation, and their corresponding basic form of a modern political and legal order – the *state*.

The first form of anarchism – methodological anarchism – founds itself on Cartesian doubt and therefore on a fundamental questioning of established sources of authority.

The authority deriving from tradition is radically questioned and subverted. There is a preliminary refusal of the established body of cognitive assumptions. Knowledge is only considered legitimate if it is first based on self-examination and supported by individual acknowledgement. No other source could claim epistemological authority. In this perspective, ontology, the examination of what 'is', is practically displaced by epistemology, the examination of what I myself can know.

In this sense, contemporary methodological negations of scientific legality are not so distant from the originary source of modern rationalism. While Cartesianism only accepts what is rooted in an existential feeling of individual certainty, Paul Feyerabend's methodological anarchism deconstructs scientific legality and redefines this as a pragmatic 'everything goes' approach. Descartes' perspective bets on the merits of an overarching reason which would open up a path to truth. Methodological anarchism, in Feyerabend's vein, does not believe in the possibility or even the merits of such an absolute truth. Rather, reason is viewed with some suspicion as an authoritarian faculty that tends to belittle the plurality of human attitudes to knowledge and good life. Methodological anarchism refuses scientific legality, and preaches a kind of 'science par provision', a provisional contextual science, a fully contingent body of knowledge, which is unavoidably rooted in a parochial context. This is radicalised in Feyerabend's account: now methodological anarchism extends the rule of contingency to the whole area of the human predicament, both in the field of practice and knowledge, including science. However, in this perspective, the step from law-scepticism in the domain of science to the denial of law in the political domain is not clear or straightforward, or even explicit.[21] Nonetheless, a free society from this perspective is only possible if there is a conflict of claimed truths that might then be arranged in a conciliatory way, through a *modus vivendi*. There is no need for one prevailing truth to be operative or effective in coping with reality. The same would hold for politics where good decisions and rules cannot be fixed once and for all, without taking into account the ever-changing multiplicity of different interests, preferences and life plans, and, accordingly, of findings and knowledge. Otherwise, a free society would succumb to domination. It is therefore the abstractness and distance from concrete single situations that produces authority and power. The principle of methodological anarchism consequently cannot but be a mere 'anything goes', as it *affirms* a plurality of positions, perspectives, and life plans. Another conclusion of such approach, once it is reconnected with metaphysical existentialism, especially with Heidegger's later philosophy, is the conclusion that no theory, nor any ethical or political engagement, could be given a foundational bedrock. This is the principle of 'anarchy', proposed by Reiner Schürmann and reformulated in Miguel Abensour's thesis of 'savage democracy',[22] a political and social regime constantly open to contestation. Here anarchy is no longer the type of society anarchists aim for, but is, rather, equated with the lack of *arché*, of any original determining principle. This ontologically anarchic approach explicitly takes a certain distance from traditional political anarchism, rejecting its foundationalism and affirming instead a plurality and contingency of outcomes.

A similar route leads to *philosophical* anarchism. Here, radical doubt is applied to the moral justification of obedience in intersubjective relations, that is, of political authority or of positive law. While liberalism would single out politics as the privileged arena of power and domination, to be then checked and balanced through a system of rights and a separation of powers, anarchism believes that power and domination arise in all areas of social life, included those concerning private relationships, for instance, in the family, the market and contractual relations. This move universalises the need for autonomy, and does not confine it to the sphere of institutional politics or along a vertical relationship between the state and the subject, as is the case with liberalism. For law to be justified, it requires a universalisation of individual recognition and deliberation. There is no reason, it is claimed, beyond a subjectively dependent one, beyond individual autonomy, or conscience, that could endorse the binding force of law.

There are various ways of justifying legal obedience. The claim of fairness is most commonly used. Law – so runs here the argument broadly stated – grants me a series of benefits, and therefore it is only fair that in return I obey the law. But a question is raised immediately about my originally asking for those benefits. I *am* granted them – but often without actually *asking* for them in the first place. They are essentially imposed upon me. The fairness principle demanding that I reciprocate would only apply if I could have a say in the granting of benefits, if I could decide which benefits to accept and which to refuse. Fairness always involves a two-sided relationship, and presupposes a freedom to accept or refuse the benefits offered to me. However, in the form of life embodied in the state, this element of freedom is excluded, since I find the law already given and I am asked only to comply.

A similar objection could also be directed to a second reason for compliance: community. I am told that I am a member of community, that I am what I am by virtue of my membership of this community; therefore, I cannot but abide by its rules. Revolt or disobedience would be an impossible act of self-denial and ingratitude. Socrates' argument in Plato's *Crito* goes in this direction – although he also makes obedience conditional on the right to interact with the law and to persuade citizens to amend unjust laws. However, the problem with the argument from community is that I am not given the chance of making my community accountable for what it had done to me, and for what it is requiring from me. The reflexivity that I receive from my community, will induce me to put in question the merits of the community itself. My community might have wanted me to interrogate its justification. If am disobedient, this could be interpreted as a feature or an attitude simply imposed upon me by my communal environment and education, and therefore without justification.

Then here is the well-worn Hobbesian argument according to which order, legality, is preferable to anarchy. Law provides certainty, stability, and security. But sometimes it might be better for the well-being and survival of people that there should not be such absolute 'security'. An excess of 'security' can become repressive and produce its own experience of insecurity, as victims of authoritarian and totalitarian regimes experienced when confronted with what Arendt, Neumann and others termed the 'anarchy of power'.

The conclusion of all these failed attempts to support authority and legality would then be that there is not a rational justification for a general obligation to obey the legal rule.[23] Democracy believes itself to be able to circumvent philosophical anarchism in so far as the obligation to law can be assimilated to a freely assumed promise to engage in certain conduct (to obey) and such a promise is unanimously taken. Nonetheless, as A. John Simmons says, once we move from individual autonomy as a basic moral and political principle, and one that is inalienable because Archimedean, 'the problem remains, that those who submit to laws against which they have voted are no longer autonomous, even though they may have submitted voluntarily'.[24]

However, philosophical anarchism does not project a form of sociality that might be implied by its own normative stance. Philosophical anarchists do not talk about an anarchist society, and seem almost indifferent to political goals and projects. This is not its business, or so it seems. We curiously find doctrines that, on the one hand, defend the lack of bindingness of legal rules, but that, on the other hand, more or less prudentially propose a concept of law as a sum of commands, or else of exclusionary reasons, that is, reasons that preempt the individual reasons for action.[25] There is thus no necessary connection, or so it would seem, between philosophical anarchism – the view according which there is no obligation to obey law, as a theory that denies the moral legitimacy of law – and a view of a sociality, or of a form of life, that could do without law as an independent and exclusionary reason for action. It is only political anarchism – the anarchism that not only radically rejects legal and political authority but proposes alternatives to it – that acknowledges this gap and tries to fill it.[26]

An anarchist test for jurisprudence

It is telling that the anarchist is a figure who haunts traditional jurisprudence and legal theory. This is the case not only with Kelsen, but also with the Danish jurisprudent Alf Ross, and Herbert Hart. The issue here curiously is whether an anarchist could be a professor of law. Could an anarchist teach positive law without being condemned to incoherence? That is, could we have a standpoint about law that is both external (in the sense that it does not share or endorse the legitimacy claimed by the law in question) and internal (in the sense that it can impartially or neutrally interpret the law)? Put in a different way, could we have propositions *about law* that are not at the same time propositions *of law*?

Kelsen believes that even an anarchist could teach law, since legal theory can assume a strictly 'pure', neutral, form. True, he tells us that to say what the law is one should presuppose a 'ground rule' as a sort of transcendental category. Such a 'ground rule' as a matter of fact is not 'posed', but is only 'presupposed'. It is not a positive law. Moreover, this *Grundnorm* has solely an epistemological function, that of allowing us to claim the validity of our descriptions of the law. But it does not have any function to justify the legitimacy of the law in question. It does not imply that that law so identified and described should also be obeyed.

From this perspective, then, we might argue, the definition of the law would depend on the observer's, the jurist's, point of view. We could thus perhaps have a plurality of views, that is a plurality of 'ground rules'. But, once we accept that there is room for plural doctrinal views about the law, and that at least some of them are open to a notion of law that is not referred to sanction, punishment or coercion, Kelsen's account of the legal rules as being focused entirely on coercion or sanction would no longer be plausible. Forced to choose between alternative accounts of law, an anarchist would probably prefer the one that is more coherent with an anti-authoritarian narrative. On the other hand, this alternative would be open only at the higher abstract level of legal theory or philosophy of law. We could thus have an anarchist legal theorist or philosopher of law.

Yet, how could we account, from an anarchist point of view, for laws that involve punishment and coercion? We could only follow one route, one that is typical of anarchism: the complete denial of legal obligation as such. But could we still interpret law without the implication that it has to be obeyed? For Kelsen, it would seem that this is possible, since there is a semantic irreducible difference between legal propositions and political or moral statements. And Herbert Hart would probably say the same, since he sharply distinguishes between *propositions of* law (those issued by a judge, for instance) and *propositions about* the law (those stated by a professor that just describe what the law of a country is). However, there is a complication here, since Hart also tells us that to be able to issue a proposition about the law, we should simulate the position of someone issuing propositions *of* law (the internal point of view).

An anarchist law teacher should then hypothetically assume the standpoint of a judge to first understand and then to explain what the law is. But is this possible without some form of moral commitment? John Finnis' natural law doctrine would deny this. To understand the law we should somehow presuppose a good form of law that nonetheless, in its concrete instances, might prove defective.[27] And according to him this good and paradigmatic essence of law implies coercion, authority, and does not need consent. A similar conclusion could be drawn from a stance taken from Ronald Dworkin's 'integrity' theory. If, as he claims, there is no real difference between a proposition *of law* and a proposition *about the law* – and in any case law is understood through interpreting it in the best possible light – we should interrogate coercion and its moral legitimacy within our view of the law.

Joseph Raz's proposal could perhaps help and indeed rescue the anarchist perspective. He severs legal reasoning, and thus the internal standpoint of officials and people endorsing legal legitimacy, from the theory about the nature of law. An anarchist from this perspective, could then teach law without too many pangs of conscience, since she is not required to assent to the legitimacy of the law in question. She is not asked to endorse or justify the law; her attitude can be fully detached. But can this be so? We may doubt it, at least if we still share Raz's views about the nature of law, which is strongly related to authority, to its capacity to impose its directives, and to a concept of legal rules that are seen here as exclusionary reasons, that is, as independent reasons. Law, as a bundle of exclusionary reasons, would necessarily render individual autonomy inert. An anarchist could not accept such a thesis.

An interesting test to prove the universality (the overcoming of parochial strictness) of jurisprudence might be whether a concept of law is compatible with an anarchist view of social relationships. Anarchist sociality is basically given through discourse, and mutual recognition and agreement. No violence or coercion is admitted here. Now, do we find in traditional legal theory a concept of law that could be integrated into this form of sociality? Most legal philosophies are hostile to anarchism, in so far as anarchism theorises a form of communal living that does not need authority and punishment.

The main brand of legal theory is legal positivism, and this is more or less related to a vision of sovereignty equated with that of a powerful state, that is, an institution conceived as produced through a radical divide between rulers and ruled and endowed with monopoly on violence. This is usually meant as the capacity to overcome whatever other violence could be manifest or operative in society. Legal positivism, so interpreted, cannot but be rejected within an anarchist form of sociality in which violence is impermissible.

Much closer to anarchism would seem to be the traditional opponent of legal positivism, that is, natural law, which claims an intrinsic relationship between morality and law. According to this view, law is not just sheer force or authority, but it is a guarantee of a just order and of human rights or basic human goods. This view could be much more sympathetic towards a non-authoritarian sociality, and, indeed, in the canon of classical anarchism, there is a version of natural law, reflected, for instance, in Godwin's rationalism or in Bakunin's distinction between the laws of nature and the laws of man. However, as we have seen, natural law doctrines very often share with legal positivists the view of law as being based on coercion and force, while only adding a moral point to qualify such authoritarian social ontology. To anarchism, however, adding morality and justice to a concept of law that is still strongly imperativistic or coercive is simply an attempt to hide the violence of the law. If the visage and the practice of the law is still the one of a king or of a gaoler, the claim to justice makes the whole picture even more repugnant. Anarchism does not demand a moral justification for the law's violence, but, rather, a concept of law where coercion is not predominant and where violence is not presupposed as a necessary component. Its main interest lies first in the ontology – the 'is', not in the deontology, the 'ought to be' – of law.

A more civilised approach to law is possibly offered by Herbert Hart and his view of law as focused on a practice and a rule of recognition. Here indeed we could find hints of a promise of an anti-authoritarian notion of law. We might remember that Hart refuses sanction as a defining element of the concept of law. We could thus say that punishment is not the core of law and legal practice. Law, according to him, is made not of commands or prescriptions, but of rules, and these are not in any case reduced to orders of a superior to an inferior, commands, or to sanctions or threats of pains (a route on the contrary taken both by Jeremy Bentham's and his disciple, John Austin's, 'analytical jurisprudence' and by Hans Kelsen's 'pure theory'). Rules, for Hart, are prior to sanctions, and receive their meaning or sense only through rules that either give capacity for adjudicating disputes or that confer normative, not instrumental or coercive, powers, or else that are standards of validity and recognition for all other rules. Violence and coercion here do not seem to be central or even relevant. One might then conclude that a Hartian concept of law could be integrated within some form of anarchist sociality without too much difficulty.

The test of the anarchist is also used by Peter Winch in his study on the idea of social science and the relevance of rules to understand social life. Rules are intrinsic to social conduct – this is his main thesis. And rules are not causes, or motives, for action; they are reasons for it. In this sense, even the anarchist follows rules, and there is no conceptual obstacle to thinking of a law that applies to anarchists too. 'In the sense in which I am speaking of rules,' Peter Winch writes,

> it is just as true to speak of the anarchist following rules in what he does as it is to say the same thing of the monk. The difference between these two kinds of men is not that the one follows rules and the other does not; it lies in the diverse *kinds* of rule which each respectively follows.[28]

Legal and political obligation

It is possible to distinguish between an *obligation of law* and an *obligation to the law*. The first notion addresses the question about what we conceive a legal obligation to be, where the second asks whether there is a specific source of normativity for law that could fully preempt individual judgement and moral autonomy.

When dealing with the issue of the obligation *of law* we are confronted with three competing theories: (i) one relating an obligation of law to the liability or probability to be subject to a sanction or punishment; (ii) one that is connected to the idea of an independent reason for action that could derogate the individual's considerations and interests; and (iii) one that sees a legal obligation as a duty arising from a special social practice endowed with strong communitarian pressure. While the first and the second are hardly congruent with an anarchist approach to sociality, the practice or social pressure thesis could be integrated into a conception of anarchy as a community held together through informal agreements and a practice of mutual aid. Whenever classical anarchism has to deal with the issue of deviance and criminal acts, its usual response is replacing legal punishment with widespread social control exercised through groups of neighbours or workers' and citizens' councils. One could thus defend the view that a legal obligation, in the form produced through a communitarian practice, could still be conceivable within an anarchist society. Anarchism and law could accordingly be reconciled, at least insofar as we face the issue of an obligation *of law*.

More difficult is the attempt to reconcile anarchism with the obligation *to law*. One could plausibly argue that, when speaking of an obligation concerning law, 'law' is quite an ambiguous concept, in so far as it can be taken to mean both a 'legal system', the system of laws, and a concrete law or legal provision. The issue of the legal obligation could thus be considered as concerning the whole legal system or a single legal prescription. However, in several reconstructions of the question of legal obligation, the obligation to the system of laws seems to imply an unconditional obligation to the single law. Once the system of laws is considered justified, it would thus seem that each and every law in that legal order (morally) deserves to be obeyed. Once the conditions of justifications apply to the legal order as a system, consent is no longer again required for the observance of, or compliance with, a concrete rule in the system. This conclusion could nonetheless be challenged. One could plausibly consider a legal system as *prima facie* legitimate, but then might regard a particular law, in a particular situation, to not be applicable. The legitimacy of the system would not be fully transparent or equivalent to the legitimacy of the concrete legal rule.

On the one hand, one could argue that the legitimacy of the system (the state, for instance) does not relate at all to the overall justification of the concrete legal obligation, but is, rather, dependent on the merits of the case. This is the radical conclusion of philosophical anarchism, while political anarchism, which does not deny the need for social cooperation and a corresponding order of general rules or agreements, would claim a necessary connection between the legitimacy of a general legal order and the justification of an individual legal rule. A scheme of agreement freely undertaken by citizens might be sufficient to give legitimacy to the concrete rule and its application, provided specific procedural conditions are met – for instance, unanimity when deliberating the rule.

On the other hand, if the legitimacy of the totality of rules does not imply at least a weak justification of individual rules, it is difficult to understand what would be the point of such indiscriminate legitimacy and of reaching a consensus on a general scheme of cooperation. There is indeed a strategy that tries to find a way out from philosophical anarchism by denying the necessary connection between the two distinct levels of justification, that of the system of rules and that of the single rule. It has thus been claimed that one may affirm that law is entitled to coerce while denying that all of law's subjects have a duty to obey it. But how could an agency be entitled to coerce if the people its provisions apply to, or are addressed to, are not obliged to follow its instructions and directives? What could such entitlement possibly mean? An entitlement to coerce, to be meaningful, would imply a right to do so and a correlative duty to submit to the entitled conduct. To be entitled to coerce should be presupposed by a prior obligation or a normative situation, according to which the one who is coerced is an actual holder of a duty of obedience. A command presupposes a commander, and this presupposes that the one who is commanded acknowledge him or her as such. 'An act of obedience itself', as it is stressed by Peter Winch, 'contains, as an essential element, a recognition of what went before as an order'.[29]

However, for the political anarchist, authority cannot imply coercion in the same way that is natural for that particular form of authority that is the state, in so far as this is understood as a monopoly of violence, and a rigid hierarchical structure, a chain of commands. Here again we face the real issue that political anarchism is concerned with: the nature of political authority, and of social power in general, and its possible reform or abolition. Much of the discussion of legal obligation takes for granted that the law to be obeyed is the one imperatively issued by the state and enforced through the use of violent means. Political anarchism, in all its versions, would deny this. The necessary connection of the legitimacy of the general legal order with the justification of particular legal rule, and the acknowledgment of an operative endorsement by citizens and rule addressees, makes it no longer viable to uphold a notion of legal authority that bases itself on coercion and violence. Coercion and violence have to be questioned as such, and their use must again be submitted to a justificatory moment. And anarchism is inclined to deny any such justification.

Political anarchism will still be related to philosophical anarchism, but its programme is much more radical, in so far as it might be a project for an alternative model of law based on autonomy. The difficult issue here is not whether we as individuals ought to obey the law, but whether we as society could collectively shape the law in a way that reduces coercion and violence, and which guarantees that autonomy remains the ultimate condition of political obligation.

Political anarchism, in short, generalises and socialises the question posed by philosophical anarchism about the law. While the latter believes that there is no obedience without individual autonomy, the former raises a point that is later idiosyncratically articulated by Hannah Arendt: that no 'authority' is viable without 'power', that is, without an exercise of collective initiative and mutual concert among the people.

Law as institution

Legal institutionalism as a theory is meant to challenge the narrow conception of law championed by legal positivism, especially in its legalistic form of a body of explicit legal orders. The basic tenets of this theory were first developed by the Italian jurist Santi Romano, who described the legal order as an organised social form. Another variant of this theory is that of Maurice Hauriou, a French public lawyer, who distinguished between institutions as 'persons' and institutions as 'things', and equated the former with the state as a representative body. A further proponent of this theory is the German jurist Carl Schmitt, whose variant might nonetheless be labelled as 'illegitimate,' forming part of an anti-Enlightenment, irrationalist, and antiliberal perspective. Institutionalism has been later revived within the analytical legal theory by the work of Ota Weinberger and Neil MacCormick, as well as in social philosophy of Cornelius Castoriadis.[30] In opposition to legal positivism – with its insistence on bracketing out any strong normative (moral or political) arguments and on discounting the social context in which legal norms operate – institutionalism asserts the normative, and hence legal, bearing of social facts.

Santi Romano offers an initial, fully fleshed out account of institutionalism as a legal theory.[31] This account rests on two main tenets, one equating the legal system with an 'institution,' and the other an institution with an organised social form. This is tantamount to breaking with one of the main dogmas of legal positivism, namely, the unity of the sources of law, all of which are embodied in the form of the state. Romano's institutionalism thus posits a *plurality* of legal systems, all of which are open-textured and indeed 'contextured': they are not sealed off from society but, rather, woven into it, tracking its every movement. But this paradigm shift comes at some cost to the concept of a rule, with which the concept of an institution might be set in sharp contrast. In such an approach there is also a dissatisfaction with the usual positivist identification of law with state law. Institutionalism, already in its initial forms, programmatically intends to go beyond the state and enlarge the scope of application of the concept of law also to material, informal, or even anti-state or subversive social formations such as, for instance, workers' unions, political parties, or churches and mafias.

The approach Romano takes in dealing with the sources of law is anti-voluntarist, and it could even be qualified as anti-creationist. Which is to say that Romano sees the law not as a rule that is willed into existence, and thus created by an enacting authority, but rather as something that comes into being by spontaneous production, by customary intercourse, and is therefore always in effect wherever there is a sphere of social relations. As he puts it, statutory enactment is never the beginning of law: it is, on the contrary, an addition to pre-existing law or a modification of it. In this sense, the law-maker or legislator cannot properly be described as a 'maker' or 'creator' of law.

There is a different version of institutionalism which is offered by Maurice Hauriou.[32] Here we find a re-engineering of Romano's approach in three main ways. First, Hauriou introduces a somewhat idiosyncratic ontology of legal objects, distinguishing between 'institutions as persons' and 'institutions as things'. Second, he relocates the notion of institution as person into the realm of the political by making it roughly coextensive with the notion of the state as a representative body. And third, he gives representation an irrationalist slant, introducing the interesting concept of an 'idée directrice', a 'guiding idea'. Representative will be the one that best embodies that guiding idea or myth. It is this idea, or myth, that forms the core of an institution, giving it force and accounting for its existence. The institution is thus construed in existential terms, in the sense that it owes its very existence to the guiding idea lying at its core, an idea of which it is the essential embodiment. This makes for a conception that might lend itself to genuinely illiberal outcomes, once the 'idée direectrice' is interpreted in terms of a 'myth' no longer interrogated by 'logos', by reason and reflexivity. In fact, it is to Hauriou, and especially his conception of political representation, disconnected from a direct and explicit emanation from people's deliberation and will, that we can trace later theories of the authoritarian state.

The same can be said of the spurious German institutionalism of the Weimar Republic, whose chief proponent is

Carl Schmitt. Indeed, Schmitt conceptualises rules and institutions in opposition to each other (moreover by dramatising such opposition). This is so partly because in the notion of a rule he makes out a principle of equality that cannot be reconciled with his radically antidemocratic vision of law and politics. A law, as a general rule, is directed to a group of subjects treated as a logical class of individuals who are given the same qualities or properties, that is, who are equals.[33] A rule also has an intrinsic consequence that makes it possible for it to be judged right and wrong: 'The notion of following a rule is logically inseparable from the notion of *making a mistake*'.[34] In contrast, a decision as such without a prior foundational reference – and this is the decision cherished by Schmittian decisionism – cannot be wrong; it is existentially ever right.

On the other hand, an institution is free from a logical dependence on equality and can be shaped in whatever discriminatory and hierarchical way is thought to be appropriate. There is no justification required by an institution, not even the basic logical one that, instead, is to be present in the form of a general rule. This is because the institution is not to be transcended in a justificatory way; there is no question it cannot stop by pointing out that the question itself can only be raised within the scope and the normative validity of the institution interrogated or challenged. An institution here is immediately referred to as a 'form of life', beyond which any quest for justification or further 'sense' would be circular.

Schmitt's constitutional theory, particularly in the period from the early 1930s to the mid-1940s, came to be known as *konkretes Ordnungsdenken* ('concrete-order thinking') – an openly Nazified legal doctrine. Here institutionalism plays the role of an ideological support to what is indeed assumed as the real concept of law, one that is rooted in the extreme creationism of a radical and charismatic decider. 'Der Führer schützt das Recht', 'The Leader protects the Law', is the revealing title of a well-known and influential article by Schmitt, written to justify Hitler's killings during the infamous 'night of the long knives'.[35]

For all the diversity that sets them apart, however, institutional theories could all be seen to share an understanding of law as marked by three features. Law is conceived as 'societal', 'ordinative' and 'plural.' This means that, in the first place, law is closely bound up with society, so much so that the two terms are sometimes seen as synonymous. In the second place, law serves an ordering or organising function. Law is matter of an 'organisation', in general hierarchically structured, for instance, a corporative state. And, in the third place, law is not a monolith: far from being a single, coherent, self-enclosed system of rules that govern across a territory, law is actually a plurality of interconnected legal systems that interact with one another on various levels and in different areas of social life.

Having said this, we can now go back to the two 'legitimate' institutionalist theories – those of Hauriou and Romano – and point out several differences between them. First, for Hauriou, an institution is in a sense *prior to* law. An institution, he says, is an idea of a work or enterprise that is realised and endures juridically in a social milieu. For Romano, by contrast, the concepts of law and institution are one and the same thing. Every legal order, in his view, is an institution and, vice versa, every institution is a legal order: the equation between the two concepts is necessary and absolute. Second, while Hauriou argues that institutions must have a constitutional and representative form if they are to properly qualify as such, and that they must therefore realise a kind of rule of law, even if only on a minimal scale, Romano is deeply critical of that idea, arguing that to invoke the rule of law is to conflate two descriptive planes: that of the 'scientist,' and so of legal theory proper, and that of the moralist or politician, whose view is instead foreign to 'legal science'. Third, what counts as constitutive elements of an institution are one thing for Hauriou and another for Romano. Hauriou identifies these elements as consisting of: (i) an idea of social action that is to be realised; (ii) an organised power through which that idea is realised; and (iii) the social acceptance of the same idea. Romano, by contrast, identifies these elements as consisting of: (i) a plurality of subjects; (ii) the organising structure that links them to one another; and (iii) the regulating or governing power exerted though this ordering. Finally, while Hauriou's view, influenced by Bergson's vitalism, is sometimes presented as a political philosophy, Romano's view crosses into sociology. Indeed, for Hauriou, an institution is essentially *normative*, for at its core we find the ideal element, consisting not in the idea of the project or enterprise around which the institution is built, but in the principles of the rule of law or of political representation. Romano, on the other hand, is more realistic or, if you will, more cynical, considering that even the mafia, on his conception, is an institution: what matters, then, is not so much the underlying ideal element as the degree to which the institution is developed (its evolutionary stage) and how effective it is at doing what it does.

As for the 'illegitimate' variant of institutionalism, whose outlines are paradigmatically sketched out in a paper that Schmitt wrote in 1934 titled 'Über die drei Arten des rechtswissenschaftlichen Denkens' (*On the Three Types of Juristic Thought*), what is distinctive here is that, on the one hand, as noted, institutions are clearly set in contrast to norms, but on the other, they are akin to decisions. In Schmitt's *konkretes Ordnungsdenken*, an institution is an organic community, not bound by any set of standards or conventions, in which individuals are embedded as parts of a whole that they cannot transcend. This is a spontaneously self-regulating community that, accordingly, does not need any norms (always abstract and general) but rather owes its regulation to the vital manifestations that arise out of the mutual engagement of the members of the community. But what the community's regulation *ultimately* rests on is the decision-making of individuals who can establish a privileged position of contact with the same community, and in fact this is the *best*, most effective mode of regulation. Such institutionalism, then, rejects normativism on account of the suspicion with which it views the latter's reliance on conventional rules understood as universalisable provisions: so construed, rules can only rely on a minimal set of factual assumptions and so cannot serve as explicit reasons for action; they cannot stand in for the capacity of subjects to think through the practical decisions that need to be made.

Schmitt thus – as already anticipated – uses institutionalism as a hidden ideological justification for decisionism, which is the practical upshot of *konkretes Ordnungsdenken*. Obviously, neither Hauriou nor Romano are decisionists, and the latter even defends the normativist stance, which, unlike Schmitt, he does not understand to be inconsistent with the institutionalist stance. 'Legitimate' institutionalism remains linked to a rationalist worldview, and one that, in the case of Hauriou, in a sense remains wedded to the Enlightenment. Not so with Schmitt, whose entire thrust is anti-Enlightenment, irrationalist and illiberal.

An altogether different development is the neo-institutionalism that many years later would be advanced by Ota Weinberger and Neil MacCormick,[36] two legal philosophers who start out not from an anti-formalist outlook but rather from analytical philosophy, especially in the version of the Wittgeinsteinian 'ordinary language' approach, and referring to the notion of 'institutional facts' developed in the framework of analytical philosophy of language.[37] What most fundamentally sets this new institutionalism apart from the earlier conceptions is that it recovers the notion of a norm, which is now brought back into full operation.

Legal neo-institutionalism comes out of two converging traditions of thought: analytical jurisprudence in the renewed form advanced by Hart (of whom MacCormick was a colleague and disciple at Oxford)[38] and Kelsen's 'pure theory of law' in a critical and heterodox version constructed in Central Europe between Vienna and Prague. Even if the philosophical positions staked out by MacCormick and Weinberger in places differ in significant ways, the differences are outweighed by the similarities. Hence the neo-institutionalist label that can be applied to both theories, whose common features can be described as follows.

To begin with, the two theories are both broadly *anti-reductionist*. We can see this in the first place in the two theories' social ontology, under which the social reality cannot be completely reduced to the material spatiotemporal reality (as the Scandinavian realists *à la* Olivecrona claimed) and, accordingly, following the philosopher John Searle, a distinction is drawn between 'brute facts' and 'institutional facts'. Thus, law cannot be reduced to a set of rules, no matter how systematised they may be, for this does not account for the whole of law: in defining its concept, we need to also take other elements into account. These include the spheres of action made possible by the rules, as well as the principles of action at work in different social contexts. These principles inform the rules making up the legal system, and they form the basis on which judgements of right and wrong are made. So, too, coherently with this antireductionism, neo-institutionalism also moves away from an obsessively prescriptivist view of norms, which are now understood not only as strictures but also as ways of shaping the social space. So conceived, they not only conventionally *restrict* spheres of action but also *expand* them. Law, in this view, does not mainly constrain human conduct; it is first and foremost what makes it possible, what constitutes it. Indeed, as MacCormick points out, institutions (such as contract, property and marriage) enable human beings to increase the number of (institutional) facts existing in the world without necessarily increasing the number of physically existing objects.

Nonetheless, neo-institutionalist antireductionism is primarily *methodological* rather than ontological. This means that, on this conception, legal concepts cannot be reduced to the normative or prescriptive structures through which they are implemented, that is, to mere instruments in the hands of the legal scientist (as legal realists in the manner of Alf Ross would have it).[39] Legal concepts are not just devices for collecting data, but are something productive of data themselves.

Two other common traits of the main neo-institutionalist theories are their *anti-prescriptivism* – under which norms cannot be reduced to imperatives, mandates, or rules prescribing a course of conduct – and a tempered or *moderate legal positivism*, which on the one hand, conceives of law as a human-made construct (an artefact, the product of a deliberate design), but at the same time recognises that not everything that is law can be expressly intentional (there may be norms that are law and yet have not been expressly enacted by a legislator or established by a judge). Law is thus better seen as a practice that might also not be fully explicitly intended or constructed, but that is, however, open to its making explicit by both conceptual and justificatory reflexivity and reasoning. There is also a fourth common trait: despite some reservations expressed by MacCormick, neo-institutionalism could be described as embracing (or at least as consistent with) *metaethical noncognitivism* – for on the one hand, it asserts that law can be known (once the rules and principles have been established), but on the other hand, it denies this to be the case for (critical) morality, which is understood as a sphere that is clearly separate from law. This approach is strongly vindicated by Weinberger.

Although neo-institutionalism is methodologically much more refined than 'classical' institutionalism, there is significant overlap to be found here. Romano, for example, would welcome neo-institutionalist antireductionism (both the ontological and the methodological kind), would not have too many qualms about embracing a non-prescriptivist conception of law, and would not hold back from defending the separation of law and morals. And he, too, can be described as a 'moderate legal positivist'. No less significant, however, are the differences, of which at least two can be pointed out.

Now, what is the relevance of legal institutionalism in a discussion of the relationship between anarchism and law? To answer this question a short list of the classical legal theories should be summarised. There are essentially four doctrines. (i) *Command theory* – imperativism – which is a rigid form of prescriptivism, according to which law consists of a sum of commands supported by the threat of a sanction, of a use of violence, and the corresponding pain for the addressee. This of course presupposes a starkly hierarchical societal structure: here there should be a commander-in-chief who is master of the law. Law is the master's business, and it is used to give orders and inflict punishment. (ii) *Normativism*. Here law is a body of rules. But these are usually conceived again in a prescriptive sense, as directives given to a subject. Normativism, however, dilutes the traditional prescriptivism of command theory and might make it compatible with a nonhierarchical structure of law. Rules do not always presuppose a commander. They could be the outcome of a practice built in time through an evolution of habits. Such possible compatibility between a rule theory of law and a non-hierarchical view of society might be implied in Hart's philosophy of law; it might even be one of his originary promises.[40] (iii) *Realism*. This has assumed different forms and has been presented in various versions. There is the American realism that depicts law as only the decision of a judge. Law is what the judge says it is, and that all there is to it. Such a theory leads to a radical judicial decisionism. The application of the rule decides on the meaning of the rule and its scope. In this way it is the judge, not the legislator, who is the master of the laws. To explain what law is, Scandinavian realism uses the metaphor of an electric plant.[41] Law here is just like an electric plant providing a permanent discharge of energy that directs people's conduct in a strictly causal, mechanical way. This theory of realism, in both its versions, is hardly compatible with a notion of an anti-authoritarian law close to anarchism. But it might be nonetheless adopted in an anarchist perspective, if, from an anarchist perspective, one would first assume that law in general, in all its forms, is irredeemable in a free society, and then propose a social order without any form of law whatsoever.

The fourth grand theory is *natural law*, which presupposes a strong connection with morality and justice. As we have seen, this is a theory of law which may or may not be compatible with anarchism, depending on the form it takes. Incompatible would be a traditional form of natural law that presupposes a hierarchical and immutable order of nature that could not be in any way modified by reflective conducts and deliberations. However, natural law has not been foreign to the story of anarchism, and it is still present in the contemporary debate on anarchism and law, where we find interesting contributions that combine a strong natural law approach with a refusal of authority and domination.[42] William Godwin might also be considered a natural lawyer if one focuses on his extreme normative cognitivism. Natural law, however, according to all versions of anarchism, should at least be disposed to the re-elaboration of the concrete rule for the political community. For the anarchist, rules cannot be just shadows of the brilliant values and 'forms' encrusted in the sky of the natural law; they should be referable to individual and societal autonomy.

Now, the point of institutionalism and its relevance for anarchism is that it is hostile to all four versions of legal doctrine that we find in the tradition. It cannot accept the command theory, especially because this is too rooted in an individualist conception of society and law. In this way, imperativism seems to need some sort of methodological individualism, whereby society can never be approaching a specific dimension and a particular source of sense and meaning. Society and sociality seem to escape from the command theory's observation. But anarchism usually sees individuals interconnected through strong social bonds and a principle of solidarity. Institutionalism, then, is somehow suspicious of rules, or it cannot clearly see the ontological legitimacy of rules as distinct from practice. Normativism is too idealised and too formal an approach to law and societal structures. Institutionalism, by contrast, opposes to rules a certain practice, and it reduces the level of idealisation, and consequently the abstract, alienated form, given to the law. But institutionalism, being antireductionist, cannot accept the simple mechanical ontology of realism.

Moreover, legal realism presupposes an anthropology whereby human beings are moved specifically by causal and physical contact, in a way that makes coercion or constraint the basic motor of social coordination. This is not the way institutionalism generally conceives social intercourse, for institutions are not the outcome of constraint but rather of powers, of competences, or capacities, opened to the subject by rules, whose nature is mostly constitutive, not merely prescriptive. Finally, natural law cannot be accepted by institutionalism, especially if natural law is meant as the projection of normative 'forms' or 'basic goods' that are fixed and therefore not open to self-certification by their holders, people, citizens, human beings. All these differences within the tradition of legal theory and its four main expressions could also be found in the anarchist interrogation of the law. The reasons mentioned as to why institutionalism refuses imperativism, normativism, realism, and natural law are all congruent with the anarchist approach to law. This also explains why several anarchist versions of institutionalism, such as the one developed by Cornelius Castoriadis, or before that the one projected in the work by George Gurvitch,[43] are openly anarchist in tenor. Thus, we might perhaps conclude that it is the idea of institution that better fits with an anarchist concept of law. This is so because institutionalism's basic feature is its anti-prescriptivism. Law here is not essentially a command. Nor is a legal rule necessarily a prescriptive statement. For institutionalism's basic rules are 'constitutive', producing, not reducing chances and scope for actions. Now, the step forward from 'regulative rules', rule-imposing duties, to 'constitutive' ones, rules enabling capacities, for the contemporary anarchist David Graeber, is just what marks a transformation that we could call the 'anarchist moment': 'So at some moment along the way, rules-as-constraining pass over to rules-as-enabling, even if it's impossible to say exactly where'.[44]

Institutions in political and legal theory, however, can assume a conservative role. This can happen in a number of ways. They can be opposed to normativity, and found rules instead on facticity. Transcendental and reflective practice is thus denied. They can be opposed to rules, so that, for instance, law is no longer the business of individuals and something that, being referred to a generality of cases and addresses, implies a principle of equality. They can used to stop the quest of justification, barring the move beyond the institution and the positive community of values this gives shape to. It is the bedrock that cannot be interrogated, because any interrogation would imply the validity of the institution itself.

It can mark the predominance of a collective force, of society as a whole, to individuals, where these do not find any place for resistance. This means a reduction of complexity for an originally wide range of action options. Institutions reduce such a range, and in this way reduce complexity and provide certainty. And they can be equated with *auctoritas* and *gravitas* projected beyond the single human life. Institutions are permanent entities that allow human life to project itself beyond contingency. They curb human primitive instincts, making it possible for a Freudian Id to become a rational Ego, through the institutional Superego. So here we cannot, of course, forget that there are two basic paths for the notion of institution to follow.

On one path, an institution is a structure that reduces complexity and gives discipline to human needs, eliminating many of these. Institutions in this way act as big collective Superegos, controlling the anarchic movement of the Id, the unconscious desires of people. In this sense – a road taken, among others by Arnold Gehlen, a German conservative sociologist – institutions serve as devices, *dispositifs*, for sublimation and repression, stabilising the materiality of human and social desires.[45] But there is a different option, the one *inter alia* defended by Castoriadis and, we would claim, by legal neo-institutionalists, whereby institutions and law, as an institutional fact, mark and signify the emergence of a novel social reality expanding the range of possible actions granted to human beings.[46] Through the law as institution our freedom is increased, not diminished. A similar view is the one proposed by Hannah Arendt, which makes a clear distinction between 'violence' and 'power'[47] – power being people acting in concert – and law is included in this dimension of 'power'.

In summary, we are confronted with two main kinds of institutionalism and, accordingly, two basic notions of law as institution. One is a return to tradition, to common legal theory, and an anthropology where a human being's destiny is discipline and obedience. But there is a different option for law as institution, where law as an institutional fact is seen as a public domain for people and individuals to expand their power and capacity and to take care of themselves without denying each other the dignity of their desires. This latter is an anarchist solution, and this is the position we seek to defend.

In an introduction to a short collection of writings on institutions, Gilles Deleuze interestingly thematised the notion of institution as an alternative to the notion of the law as the prescription of a lawgiver. While the latter – the law – is a limitation for human conducts, the former – the institution – is 'a positive model of action'.[48] This means that an institution does not operate by threat and constraint, but by persuasion and empowerment. While the model of the law considers sociality as a negative dimension to be controlled and tamed, the model of institution sees sociality as the very core of the institutional dimension. So Deleuze concludes that a tyranny is a regime where there are many laws and very few institutions, while democracy is a legal order where you find lots of institutions and very few laws. Here, democracy, so conceived, might possibly also be a blueprint for an anarchist legal regime.[49]

Notes

1. Cf. W. B. Gallie, 'Essentially Contested Concepts', *Proceedings of the Aristotelian Society*, Vol. 56, (1956), pp. 167–198.

2. See W. Benjamin, 'Zur Kritik der Gewalt', in Id., *Sprache und Geschichte: Philosophische Essays*, ed. by R. Tiedemann, Reclam, Stuttgart 1992, pp. 104 ff.
3. Cf. M. La Torre, 'On Two Distinct and Opposed Version of Natural Law: Inclusive versus Exclusive', *Ratio Juris*, Vol. 19, 2006, pp. 197 ff.
4. See H. L. A. Hart, *The Concept of Law*, Clarendon, Oxford 1961.
5. See Hannah Arendt, *The Human Condition*, University of Chicago Press, Chicago 1958.
6. See Joseph Raz, *Ethics in the Public Domain*, Oxford University Press, Oxford 1995, chapters 9 and 10.
7. See, for instance, Niklas Luhmann, *Das Recht der Gesellschaft*, Suhrkamp, Frankfurt am Main 1990.
8. See H. Kelsen, *Reine Rechtslehre*, I ed., Deuticke, Wien 1934.
9. See, for instance, T. Campbell, *The Legal Theory of Ethical Positivism*, Routledge, London 1996, anticipated by U. Scarpelli, *Cos'è il positivismo giuridico*, Comunità, Milano 1965.
10. H. L. A. Hart, 'Problems of the Philosophy of Law', in Id., *Essays in Jurisprudence and Philosophy*, Clarendon, Oxford 1983, p. 106.
11. See, for instance, L. Wittgenstein, *Philosophische Untersuchungen*, Suhrkamp, Freankfurt am Main 1977, I, § 68, p. 58.
12. Cf. M. La Torre, *La justicia de la tortura,. Sobre Derecho y fuerza*, Trotta, Madrid 2022.
13. K. E. Himma, *Coercion and the Nature of Law*, Oxford University Press, Oxford 2020, p. 23.
14. See H. Kelsen, 'Gleichheit vor dem Gesetz', *Veroffentlichung der Deutschen Staatsrechtslehrer*, Vol. 3, Walther de Gruyter, Berlin 1927, p. 55.
15. Cf. C. Castoriadis, 'La découverte de l'imagination', *Libre*, Vol. 3. 1978, pp. 151 ff.
16. Cf. P. M. S. Hacker, 'Sanction Theories of Duty', in *Oxford Essays on Jurisprudence*, ed. by A. W. B. Simpson, Clarendon, Oxford 1973, pp. 131 ff.
17. See R. Dworkin, *Law's Empire*, Hart, Oxford 1998, chapter 7.
18. See R. Dworkin, *Justice for Hedgehogs*, The Belknap Press, Cambridge, Mass. 2011, pp. 400 ff.
19. R. Dworkin, *Law's Empire*, p. 110.
20. See. I Kant, 'Das Ende aller Dinge', in Id., *Ausgewählte Kleine Schriften*, Felix Meiner, Hamburg 1965, pp. 89 ff.
21. Indeed, Feyerabend makes it clear that his epistemological anarchism does not have direct political implications

and is to be distinguished from political anarchism – the anarchism of Kropotkin for instance – which, he argues, is contradictory in still obeying scientific authority. See Paul Feyerabend, *Against Method: Outline of an Anarchist Theory of Knowledge*, London: Verso, 1993, 12–13.

22. See Abensour, *Democracy Against the State*.
23. See Simmons, *Moral Principles and Moral Obligations*.
24. Wolff, *In Defense of Anarchism*, p. 57.
25. This is the case, paradigmatically, of Joseph Raz's philosophy of law. See J. Raz, *The Authority of Law*, 2nd ed., Oxford University Press, Oxford 2009.
26. See also M. La Torre, *Nostra legge è la libertà: Anarchismo dei Moderni*, Derive Approdi, Roma 2017.
27. See J. Finnis, *Natural Law and Natural Rights*, Clarendon, Oxford 1980.
28. P. Winch, *The Idea of Social Science and Its Relation to Philosophy*, Routledge & Kegan Paul, London 1985, p. 52.
29. P. Winch, *The Idea of Social Science and Its Relation to Philosophy*, p. 125.
30. See Cornelius Castoriadis, *L'institution imaginaire de la société*, Seuil, Parois 1975.
31. See Santi Romano, *The Legal Order*, Routledge, London 2017, first ed. in Italian *L'ordinamento giuridico*, Pisa 1917.
32. See, paradigmatically, M. Hauriou, Aux sources du droit. Le pouvoir, l'ordre et la liberté, Cahiers de la Nouvelle Journée, Paris 1933.
33. Cf. I. Berlin, 'Equality', In Id., *Concepts and Categories*, ed. by Th. Hardy, 2nd ed., Princeton University Press, Princeton, N.J. 2013.
34. P. Winch, *The Idea of Social Science and Its Relation to Philosophy*, p. 32.
35. See C. Schmitt. 'Der Führer schützt das Recht: Zur Reichstagsrede Adolf Hitlers vom. 13. Juli 1934', *Deutsche Juristen-Zeitung*, 20 July 1934.
36. See their *An Institutional Theory of Law*, Springer, Berlin 1986.
37. See J. Searle, *Speech Acts: An Essay in the Philosophy of Language*, New ed., Cambridge University Press, Cambridge 1970.
38. Still the best book on Hart's legal philosophy is a sympathetic work written by MacCormick and published in 1980: *H. L. Hart*, Arnold, London 1980.
39. See A. Ross, *On Law and Justice*, University of California Press, Los Angeles 1958.

40. Cf. M. La Torre, 'The Hierarchical Model and H. L. A. Hart's Concept of Law', *Revus – Journal for Constitutional Theory and Philosophy of Law*, 21, 2013, pp. 141–162.
41. See K. Olivecrona, *Law as Fact*, I ed., Mugrave, Copenhagen 1939.
42. See, for instance, G. Chartier, *Anarchy and Legal Order: Law and Politics for a Stateless Society*, Cambridge University Press. Cambridge 2013.
43. See his magnum opus *L'idée du droit social: notion et système du droit social*. Sirey, Paris 1932.
44. D. Graeber, *The Utopia of Rules: On Technology, Stupidity and the Secret Joys of Bureaucracy*, Melville House, Brooklyn, N.Y. 2015, p. 199.
45. See, for instance, A. Gehlen, *Urmensch und Spätkultur: Philosophische Ergebnisse und Aussagen*, 6th ed., ed. by K. S. Rehberg, Vittorio Klostermann, Frankfurt am Main 2004.
46. A similar point is made by Roberto Esposito. See *Institution*, trans. Z. Hanafi, Cambridge: Polity Press, 2022.
47. See H. Arendt, *On Violence*, Harvest: New York 1970.
48. G. Deleuze, *Introduction*, in *Instincts & Institutions*, ed. by G. Deleuze, Hachette, Paris 1953, p. ix.
49. A similar point is made by Christos Marneros, who uses Deleuze's notion of institutions as a way of theorising an anarchist concept of law without an *arché* or commanding principle. See '"It is a Nomos Very Different from the Law": On Anarchy and the Law', *Acta Universitatis Lodziensis: Folia Juridica* 92 (2021): 125–139.

Three

The Long Arc of Anarchy: A Source of Modernity

A possible genealogy

In the following, a genealogy of anarchist and anti-authoritarian thought is attempted. Here the thesis we defend is that modernity and anarchism are strongly intertwined. Anarchism might be considered the wellspring of modernity, in the sense that it mobilises the central idea of autonomy and self-empowerment. The notion of rights is also essential to give legal form to autonomy and thus construct modernity. This fracture of the traditional, hierarchical social world has been historically and intellectually experienced in various forms, not all of them congruent. In particular, there have been two declinations, one emancipatory, the other concerned with mastering the world, leading to capitalism and the bureaucratisation of society. The latter has prevailed over the former, vampirising the experience and the desire for autonomy, making it instrumental to a programme of domination and exploitation. This two-sidedness of modernity is well manifested in the notion of sovereignty. Sovereignty can, on the one hand, be understood in terms of individual freedom and autonomy. But it can also be understood in terms of political or state sovereignty, which implies obedience to authority and the subjection of the individual to an institutionalised order of power. We encounter a similar ambiguity with the notion of rights. Rights can be emancipatory and can engender new forms of sociality and freedom; but they can also, as we show in a later chapter, reproduce relations of domination, particularly in the form of property rights and the notion, deriving from Roman law, of the absolute possession over objects to the exclusion of everyone else: 'ius utendi fruendi et abutendi res sua quatenus juris ratio patitur'. Anarchism is the most coherent expression of the positive, inclusive, emancipatory side of modernity. From an anarchist perspective, rights are no longer possessive, and their corresponding duties are activated only by the condition of reciprocity.

A genealogy of anarchism can serve to illuminate this emancipatory side of modernity. In this chapter an anarchist genealogy is proposed in three steps, respectively by presenting and discussing three philosophical doctrines – those of Baruch Spinoza, William Godwin and Pierre-Joseph Proudhon. Godwin and Proudhon are key figures in the anarchist canon. Spinoza is less obviously part of this tradition.[1] However, as we endeavour to show in this chapter, Spinoza's ontology forms one possible way of conceptualising an anarchist notion of autonomy.

A baroque ontology

The connection we are attempting to draw between Spinoza's thought and anarchism would be regarded as controversial. Most interpretations of the Dutch philosopher have tended to see him as a proponent of a republican communitarianism or, alternatively, of an absolute state, following an approach not too distant from Hobbesian political doctrine.[2] However, this interpretation can be challenged once Spinoza's conception of sovereignty and his theory of individual rights are properly interrogated. This can only be adequately approached through an investigation into his ontology; for Spinoza's theory politics is the ultimate outcome of an ontological movement. Politics, on such view, consists of an excess of sovereignty that, on the one hand, is connected with the idea of 'multitude' – people gathering in the public space driven by their need for action and by their desires and emotions. On the other hand, there is no possible way of containing this sovereignty within safe or manageable limits; the 'multitude' is rebellious and its demands are insatiable. The institutional dimension, the *civitas*, the 'city' and its powers, are not defined once and for all by a contract that empowers authority and disempowers citizens. This open nature of the political space is outlined by Spinoza in his famous letter number 50, clarifying the difference of his view of the social contract from Hobbes' doctrine. There is no possible contract that transfers rights and powers from subjects to political authority. By establishing a republican contractual authority, citizens get more power than they had before the foundation of the republic. Power is permanently in the hands of the people and flows from their natural rights, which exceed political institutions and the limits of legal authority. Therefore, there is never any possible closure of the political instituting moment.

Spinoza's political (and legal) thought is to be found in his three main works, *Tractatus Theologico-Politicus, Ethica, Ordine Geometrico Demonstrata,* and the unfinished *Tractatus Politicus.* His *Tractatus Theologico-Politicus* proposes a reinterpretation of both the Jewish and Christian traditions, through a philological critique of the canonical texts, especially of the Bible. However, politics rather than religion is really Spinoza's main concern here, and one could claim that all his efforts are directed at devising a political and, indeed, legal philosophy.

The starting point for Spinoza's rather obscure ontology is that there is only one substance in the world: mind and matter are intrinsically connected. Such strong ontological monism cannot really be understood without considering the philosophy which is the permanent reference and the background against which the Dutch philosopher develops his theorising: Descartes' revolution in metaphysics. Descartes' strategy is to reinterpret basic ontological questions as queries about knowledge competences, and these are tested against self-interrogation and self-assessment. The experience of the self, its presence, is the starting point of the whole of Descartes' mode of inquiry. Spinoza's great merit lies in attempting to extend the Cartesian radical scepticism to the entire territory of the human condition and, in particular, to the very sensitive domains of religion, politics and law. Cartesian freedom of thought is taken beyond the individual search for truth and turned into a social right, reshaping it as free speech and thus paving the way to a separation between religion and the public sphere. But this is first undertaken through a reform of Descartes' philosophy.

Unlike Descartes, Spinoza does not proceed from a position of doubt. In thinking logically, we cannot doubt. This we find in proposition 4 of his *Principia Cartesianae Philosophiae*

'Principles of Cartesian Philosophy' (the only book published with his name during his life): *I think, ergo sum,* can be the first known truth, only insofar as '*we* think', *nos cogitamus.* The radical subjectivity of doubt is thus downplayed in the collective practice of thinking. The *I, Ego,* is absorbed by a *We, Nos,* and indeed from the start there is no room for an independent self in Spinoza's system. Reasoning is a general enterprise, not just an individual endeavour. The analytical or existentialist pace of Descartes' probing of an undisputable truth is replaced by a synthetic and geometrical presentation where we proceed not from a radical existential experience of the self, but from the objective evidence of a clear and distinct first principle – which is God – approached through rationality. While in Descartes' philosophy, God is encountered after the self, in Spinoza's system we first encounter God and then we forever forget the self. The dissolution of doubt is achieved through intuition. Once we have clear and distinct ideas, this is enough to dissolve any possible doubt. Spinoza's ontology offers a solution to the gaps left open in Descartes' construction. We do not need to find a link between body and mind, according to Spinoza, since the mind and body form one entity.

This is also reflected in his notion of causality where a material cause is conceived as a logical condition. From the vantage point of such coincidence there would be no need to exclude a *génie malin,* an evil demon, making our perception and rationality a depository of mistakes and delusions, since minds are ideas of bodies, and individual human minds are *modi,* modes, expressions of the divine mind, reflecting all that *is;* this *is* cannot by definition be mistaken. God is the only possible substance in the world, if we assume that a substance is that entity that does not need any other substance to be. And God cannot be malevolent, that is imperfect, again by definition, by the very force of the evidence of His existing.

God is the entity that contains all positive properties, including existence itself. 'Existence' is considered a special quality of a being. Such a divine entity endowed with all possible qualities, in so far as it is by definition perfect, can then be considered and conceptualised by means of infinite perspectives and points of view. However, human minds are able to see only two of such attributes of the divine substance, cogitation and extension. This means that minds, *res cogitans*, and bodies, *res extensa*, are not really two distinct *res*, two diverse entities, but only two alternative ways of considering one and the same substance. This then deploys its power along infinite modes, *modi*, which however in themselves are finite entities.

Once we acknowledge that there is only one substance, there will be no possibility of a God that is distinct from creation. Creator and creation here are consubstantial, which is not the case in Descartes's ontology, where God is still the absolute creator, and to be such He is given full free will. On the contrary, in Spinoza's system where creator and creation are united, and collapse into one another, there is no need for free will. Everything that happens had to happen in that precise way, since it was already contained in the substance itself and its power. This scheme of course has a strong impact on the concept of freedom and that of laws and rights. According to Spinoza, freedom is but a *causa sui*, a condition experienced by an entity whose actions are intrinsic to its nature. Freedom, according to a formula that will be later employed by Hegel among others, is the recognition of necessity; it is necessity itself reflected and acknowledged. Will and intellect are therefore considered one and the same thing (see *Ethics*, Part 2, corollarium to proposition 49). This is especially true, insofar as God is concerned. In the same vein a law is not an imperative, but simply the manifestation of the power intrinsic in the substance, in the nature of the legislator. A law is the deployment of only one substance – power.

Subversive sovereignty

In the Appendix to the first book of Spinoza's *Ethics*, which is devoted to explaining the nature of God, we find the following statement: 'All the prejudices I here undertake to expose depend on this one: that men commonly suppose that all natural things act, as men do, on account of an end, indeed they maintain as certain that God himself directs all things to some certain end'. But this is, as is stressed, just a prejudice. Nature, that is God – since for Spinoza the two entities fully coincide – 'natura seu Deus' (Preface to the Fourth Part of *Ethics*), is not moved by any end, by any final cause, but only from determinative conditions. To claim that God could have designs, or ends, would imply that He has needs or desires. But having a need or a desire means striving for something one does not yet have. However, God, who is the highest possible perfection, by definition has everything He needs.

Nor does God have a will. Since a will once more indicates wanting something that one does not yet possess or enjoy. But God already has and enjoys all that is. This implies that the world is the only possible one. God could not have made a different one, for all He does is by necessity implicated in His nature. There is no contingency in God's affairs, and therefore nor in nature: 'There is nothing contingent' (*Ethics*, Part 1, proposition 26). Within nature, that is God, we can distinguish a *natura naturans*, 'nature becoming nature', and a *natura naturata*, 'nature that has become nature'. The former is 'what is in itself and is conceived through itself', that is, 'God, insofar as he is considered as a free cause' (*Ethics*, Part 1, scholium to proposition 29). By *natura naturans* we should understand 'whatever follows from the necessity of God's nature' (ibid.). *Natura naturans* is God's essence considered as such, in all its power, while *natura naturata* is God seen as the sum of all His acts, all of His 'modes'.

To better understand such fundamental distinction, we should refer to Spinoza's theory of knowledge. This consists of a hierarchical structure of sources of knowledge. We have first perception and opinion, whereby we get blurred and confused ideas about the world. We then have *notiones communes*, universal concepts, operated by the intellect, whereby we get clear and distinct ideas of individual entities in the world. Finally, we have intuitive knowledge, reason, whereby we attain a cognition, a clear and distinct idea of God and its essence. *Natura naturata* is then God understood through the intellect and the ideas of *modi*, of individuals, while *natura naturans* is the highest form of cognition offered by the intuitive apprehension of God as cause of itself, *causa sui*. The difference is more an epistemological than an ontological one. There is but one nature or God. In such world there is no possible contingency; facts are the logical development of the essence of God, and laws are the logical notation of its attributes. There is no power distinguishable from act: 'God's power is nothing except God's active essence' (*Ethics*,

Part 1, scholium to proposition 3). Now, this picture excludes the possibility of a God as a legislator, issuing laws that are discrete imperatives backed by sanctions. We should 'take great care not to confuse God's power with the human power or right of kings' (ibid.). Calling Him a king would mean diminishing His real nature, and to belittle us that are His free emanations.

The place where we find in distilled form Spinoza's concept of law is chapter 4 of his *Tractatus Theologico-Politicus*, dealing with God's law, *De lege divina*. This chapter begins with a clear distinction between, on the on the one hand, *human* and, on the other, *divine and natural* law. Human law is not assimilated into natural law, which is considered equivalent to divine law. However, there is a common meaning of law, and that is a principle whereby individuals, human or not, follow a common standard or reason. This could happen by the necessity rooted in nature ('a necessitate naturae'); and we have a natural (or divine) law, or by human convention or decision ('ab hominum placito'), a human construct, and thus we get a human law. In the case of natural law, the law is a necessary conceptual derivation from the definition or essence of that particular thing ('ex ipsa rei natura sive definitione necessario sequitur'). The human law, that Spinoza says should better be called *jus*, is a precept that human beings lay down for their good life, a more secure and comfortable living ('ad tutius, et commodius vivendum'), or for other reasons ('ob alias causas'). In both cases, laws are not imperatives, or commands, but rather *rules*, general standards, and are not necessarily sanctioned by an appended penalty or reward, though this might occasionally happen. Natural or divine law cannot be broken or violated, while human law can easily be disregarded. The production of human law is a matter of human will, as is following it. But how could human beings, who are part of nature necessarily ruled by natural law, establish rules that are contingent and conventional? How could we have conventions if everything in the world is determined by nature? How could we, on the one hand, defend a strong determinist concept of what happens in the world (where humans are not a special jurisdiction, 'imperio in imperio', but are indeed subject as every other entity to necessary determination) *and*, on the other hand, conceive of human affairs as ruled by law based on the consent and will of their producers and users?

Spinoza does not try to evade this question, and, in order to deal with it, he proposes two arguments. First, human law can be seen as a decision of human beings, insofar as these are driven by their internal power, that is their internal faculties. Whatever they do is their powers' making. This means that their laws, as common deliberations, are properly understood as human, and conventional. The second argument is that human laws are seen as such, as conventional, from the limited epistemological point that is given to human beings. These cannot follow causality in all its steps and relations. For human beings properly define causality in terms of close causality, of vicinity, 'quia res per proximas suas causas definire, et explicare debemus'.

Now, there is no doubt that those laws of human practice are determined through human deliberation, and therefore this can, or should, be considered (from our limited gnoseological, internal point of view) their source. The fact of decision and deliberation, and the corresponding conventional conduct, are sufficient to explain such laws. What is preeminent in human laws, understood in this way, is not sanctions but rather their rationale and aim. However, the problem is that human beings are not always rational. They are moved ('obnoxiati') by passions and affects, causes that originate from their natural environment or from external impulses, and they are often not masters of themselves. They are not always able to perceive the force of the rules' rationale, and are reluctant to follow them. This is why these rules sometimes need to be reinforced through sanctions, punishments and rewards. Consequently, one can describe individuals as 'subjects' of the law, or 'slaves' of the law. But this is only meant metaphorically, since the law is nothing but a series of rules and norms human beings collectively decide to give themselves or others: 'Cum itaque Lex nihil aliud sit, quam ratio vivendi, quam homines ob aliquem finem sibi, vel aliis prescribunt'. Law is far from involving a decisionist imperative with whatever possible content, as it is supposed in the legal positivist *vulgata* (by Kelsen, for instance). Law is its own rationale, and thus a sense and a reason for acting together. Moreover, positive law is not conceptually a result of coercion or force. It might be so contingently and occasionally. But it can never be so fully. Human beings, Spinoza maintains, are not brutes and animals to be directed through violence. They think for themselves and have the capacity to behave as self-directed agents.

Spinoza's metaphysics thus entails a revision of the modern doctrine of natural law. The great founding father of such doctrine is the Dutch lawyer and philosopher Hugo Grotius, but its most powerful thinker is Thomas Hobbes, who turns natural law theory into a justification for a stable and absolutely legitimate political order. Now, it is by reading and discussing Hobbes' contract theory that Spinoza develops his views. The first question he has to face here is how to combine the notion of a right, that is a liberty, with a strong negation of free will and a radical determinist worldview. This is mostly elaborated in chapter 2 of his *Tractatus politicus*.

As we have seen from his concept of law, normativity is reinterpreted by Spinoza in terms of natural necessity – the 'ought' is reabsorbed into the 'is' – but this 'is', however, is conceived in terms of power, that is, an expression of the essence of things, their drive to self-conservation. This theoretical constellation, essentially borrowed from Machiavelli, leads to the equation of power and right, *potentia* and *jus*, where *potentia* is to be understood in terms of material power, of might. Accordingly, natural law is the same as natural right; however, the latter is a specification and individual determination of the latter, signifying the portion of God's force or natural necessity/power allotted to each and every individual thing, and in particular to human beings (*Tractatus politicus*, 2, 4). Whatever one *can* do, one has the *right* to. There is no other limitation to natural rights than power. Therefore, in the state of nature natural rights are destined to clash with one another; human beings will exist in relations of mutual enmity, 'sunt enim homines ... natura hostes' (*Tractatus politicus*, 8, 12). This means that human designs and actions are permanently endangered by others' designs and actions. In such a state, natural right counts for little. To make it stronger and more meaningful, we need the cooperation and sum of others' natural rights. In fact, 'when each man most seeks his own advantage for himself, then men are most useful to one another' (*Ethics*, Part 4, corollary 2 to proposition 35). Therefore, the principle that holds is not 'homo homini lupus', as is claimed in Hobbes' pessimistic anthropology. Rather, for Spinoza: 'Man is a God to man' (*Ethics*, part 4, scholium to proposition 35). This suggests the possibility of mutual aid, and of a political order whereby individual natural rights are pooled and instituted as a collective capacity. However, to achieve this result, Spinoza says that individuals should give up their rights in full to a supreme collective authority. This point, however, is an additional source of contradiction in his philosophy.

As a matter of fact, we are told, on the one hand, that, to have a body politic, individuals must give up their rights and grant them to a sovereign, be this an individual or a collective body. On the other hand, when asked where lies the difference between his theory and Hobbes' one, he says explicitly (see Letter 50) that while in Hobbes' system human beings permanently lose their rights by transferring them to the sovereign, in his own version of the social contract, individuals keep, even intensify, their rights and powers. Here Spinoza's argument is somewhat oblique, according to a style that he usually employs when dealing with thorny, politically sensitive issues. This is a style that Leo Strauss has misinterpreted as a form of esoterism, while correctly perceiving that it is a form of writing deployed against the background of possible persecution.[3] First, an argument is presented, but then in the following, its force is attenuated by a different, indeed opposite, argument, to finally take the sting out of the first argument. By not grasping the obliquity of his argumentation, more than one commentator has been led astray. For instance, there is a widespread interpretation of Spinoza as a defender of an absolute state.[4] Yet, Spinoza never argues for absolute political sovereignty over citizens and a full subjection of citizens to the sovereign.

We have seen that, for Spinoza, we can have a political order and positive law only if individual natural rights are fully transferred to the sovereign. However, in chapter 20 of *Tractatus theologico-politicus*, we find a dissonant thesis: the natural right of freely thinking and judging can never be transferred to anyone (20, 1). Now, this thesis fundamentally alters the doctrine of absolute sovereign power. Since the natural right to freely think and judge can never be given up, the absolute power of sovereigns should stop before the freedom of opinion and the free speech of subjects. But Spinoza makes a step beyond the vindication of free speech. Free speech means that citizens can judge the sovereign's laws and declare them unjust and unreasonable, which means that an unreasonable sovereign decree will only be enforced by extreme violence and with the opposition of citizens, which will render public security and harmony fragile. The conclusion to draw is then the following: the supreme power of the sovereign cannot trespass the limit of reasonableness and collective freedom of judgement (ibid., 20, 1). There is in the end no absolute power of sovereigns (ibid., 17, 1), and positive law cannot have whatever content is decided by public authorities. This is also why Spinoza explicitly states that the true end of a body politic, of a *respublica,* is not public security but, indeed, freedom. Freedom as power and as capacity of self-preservation and self-affirmation is an internal ontological quality of human beings. Sovereignty cannot but at its own peril be built upon a denial of human beings as free agents (ibid.).

Anarchism explicitly vindicated

William Godwin's political thought is concentrated in his main theoretical work, *An Enquiry Concerning Political Justice,* first published in 1793. Here he develops a form of radical individualism and philosophical anarchism which becomes the basis for a critique of legal and political obligation. Unlike in traditional justifications of the law – which see it as supplementing morality and directing human conduct according to its dictates – Godwin believes that law, as command, cannot have a cognitive content. This was also claimed by Spinoza. Cognition is offered through arguments, not through force and punishment. A command is not a reason for action, not even a secondary one, since it cannot as such act as reason. For the command to be treated as a reason depends on the private judgement, identification and assessment. On the other hand, a motivational gap, if filled through force, will deny normativity its meaningful core: a conduct would be performed not because it is right, but only out of fear of sanction. In this way, the very idea of moral action is distorted, and there can be no hope of moral progress.

Moreover, the bulk of doctrines trying to offer legitimacy to political order are incapable of justifying obedience. There are three main doctrines in this area: (i) appeal to divine authority; (ii) appeal to the factual force of the powerful, or the normativity of the factual; and finally (iii) contractarianism. All three are faulty, according to Godwin. Divine authority theories are still silent about the criteria according to which God would grant a specific norm or power its legitimacy. They do not specify what should be their own merits beyond a generic reference to the value of obedience, thus remaining hopelessly vague and indeterminate. The normativity of the factual confuses might with right, leading again to a generic justification of citizens' passivity to authority, and severing the necessary connection between politics and morality. Eventually, a social contract has necessarily to be assessed and confirmed through private judgement, and it could not impose more than what private judgement accepts: 'No consent of ours can divest us of our moral capacity.' (*Political Justice*, III. ii). Contractarianism, in this way, is permanently open to individual contestation.

Godwin then attempts to develop a legal theory coherent with this ultimate finding, and he does this through a declarative notion of the legal rule. A law is a declaration of what is made evident through moral judgement. Legislation thus cannot be considered as prescriptive capacity. Executive and judicial powers will strictly follow the legislative deliberations, and mostly operate in a deductive and instrumental manner. Power, in this way, will be minimised. *Philosophical* anarchism thus opens the door to *political* anarchism, and to a legal order and a political programme in which authority would never become rigidified, since it would be permanently accountable and open to ongoing interrogation by individuals. This sceptical position is not necessarily incompatible with the building of political institutions, as long as they keep coercion and command to a minimum. Instead, they would derive their legitimacy from private judgement and from collective deliberation between individuals: the 'unrestrained communication of men's thoughts and discoveries to each other', as Godwin puts it (*Political Justice*, II.v). Private judgement only becomes meaningful when exercised through mutual recognition and cooperation, which Godwin sees as an essential feature of human life.

This is why it is not strictly correct to view Godwin's anarchism as a form of liberal individualism. Liberal individualism – in which we can include the more radical forms of libertarianism and anarcho-capitalism – privileges the idea of the market, private life and 'civil society' as a sphere of individual freedom, and confines its critique of power and authority, in varying degrees, to the political sphere, to the sphere of the state. However, such a limitation could not be justified from an anarchist perspective. To the anarchist, and especially to Godwin, the requirement of giving and asking for reasons – the ethical interrogation of authority – is not limited to the political sphere but encompasses all social domains, the private as well as the public. Neither families nor labour nor the market can escape the search for justification and the strict claim of autonomy and private judgement. Classical liberalism can never live up to the radical principle of anarchism. While liberalism accepts property as a matter of course, or a historical *fait accompli* that does not need justification, anarchism will finally conclude – particularly with Proudhon – that such form of property is equivalent to theft, and to the loss of autonomy.

Anarchy as collective power

Pierre-Joseph Proudhon's political philosophy pays special attention to the sphere of law. This is already apparent from his seminal work, *Qu'est-ce que la propriété?*, where the central issue discussed is the right of property and its legitimacy. Property is challenged from various angles, normatively and conceptually, but mostly from a legal philosophical standpoint. In traditional legal doctrine, rights are seen as 'absolute', independent of any social relationship. Property is considered as the 'absolute' right *par excellence*, *jus utendi ac abutendi*, right to use and abuse, a sovereignty that does not need recognition by any other subject. However, Proudhon believes that such absolute sovereignty is the remnant of a mythical, religious worldview. It is a residual fragment of a political theology that aimed to first justify political sovereignty, and then extended to the sovereignty of the individual.

Property, as a relation of absolute power, flows from the king to private proprietor: 'If goods are property, why should not the proprietors be kings, and indeed despotic kings, kings in proportion to their acquisitive faculties?'[5] A property owner is thus an absolute king in miniature.

According to Proudhon, there is no fact whatsoever that could legitimise absolute private power over things, that is property, without assuming history or simply facts as normative reasons. In other words, the fact that someone temporarily possesses property – a relation that Proudhon equates with the occupation of a theatre seat – does not in itself justify the absolute right to property. Facts cannot assume this normative function without a traditionalist or positivist doctrine behind them, a doctrine that is, moreover, philosophically and socially unjustifiable: 'This is the method of the ancients: the fact exists, therefore it is necessary, therefore it is just, therefore its antecedents are also just'.[6] We could call this a legal positivist fallacy. Facts, however, do not have justificatory force, especially as far as rights are concerned: 'Every right must be justifiable in itself, or by some right prior to it, and property in no exception'.[7] The mere fact of property is no more than force without justification. Nor can property be justified from the alternative position of natural law. We do not find anything like the institution of property in nature. Rather, land is a common good: 'The land is indispensable to our existence, thus a common thing and insusceptible of appropriation'.[8]

Furthermore, human beings leave the natural state through a social contract and enter into a civil state. Power is a form of popular sovereignty created by citizens building a political community, a common public space. No private entitlement can preempt this common space. Popular sovereignty is thus opposed to private property: 'Popular sovereignty opposed to private property! Might not that be called a prophecy of equality, a republican oracle?'[9] But suppose that natural law could be based just on normative terms, and we could claim a natural right of property. This is, however, impracticable, argues Proudhon, because such a right could not meet the strict requirement of universality that natural rights are said to embody. Property cannot be universalised; therefore it cannot be a natural right. Universality here means the possibility of mutual agreement and the promise of sociality. A universalisable right is a right that can be socialised, that is, it is open to social communication amongst subjects. But this is not the case with property: 'Property, in its etymological sense and by the definition of law, is a right outside of society ... If we were associated for the sake of liberty, equality, and security, we are not associated for the sake of property.'[10] If a man was drowning, and to save himself, he landed on someone's private land, the proprietor could not legitimately throw him back into the sea. He has a right to refuge on this land. This shows that to make property compatible with sociality, the commonsensical basis of morality, the absolute power of property should be reneged. There is indeed an 'invisible hand' in society, but it is normative, not merely functional. It is communication guided by justice and equity, not a self-regulating market driven by profit and accumulation.

From this perspective, property, as an egocentric sphere of autonomy, cannot be the condition for liberty, as it is in classical liberalism. Quite the opposite. The absolute right to property is hostile to freedom, since one's freedom is a capacity that is always intensified, rather than limited and threatened, by the freedom of others. The freedom of the liberal proprietor is the impotent, solitary freedom of the isolated monad. The capacity to act, to exercise one's freedom, depends on acting in cooperation with others; liberty thus cannot but be social and cooperative: 'From the social point of view, freedom and solidarity are identical terms: the freedom of everyone being no longer a limit ..., but a support, the human being that is mostly free is the one that has the most of relations with the other human beings.'[11] We find a similar way of thinking about freedom in Spinoza.

Through this critique of property, Proudhon develops a more general concept of society, political power, and law. But he does not eschew the necessity for a more general philosophy. Indeed, he even tries to develop his own ontology and philosophy of history, based on the idea that reality is composed of a series of entities, or 'things' – a notion that derives from Charles Fourier, the French Utopian Socialist. All the points in this 'series' are of equal importance – there is no hierarchy between them. This is an alternative to the Aristotelian view of causes that start from an unmoved prime mover that moves a second mover and then a third, as part of a triadic schema. This Aristotelian scheme is revised by Louis de Bonald, one of the main philosophers of the French Counter-Revolution, who interprets society, and reality in general, as mirroring the hierarchical structure of a family, where there is a prime mover – the father and husband – then a means, a 'ministry', the wife and mother, and then just a 'moved', the child. Society reflects this in its triple formation of a king, a government of ministers, and then 'subjects' who simply obey the father's rules and the mother's instructions. Proudhon rejects this reactionary political metaphysics and reinterprets the triad as a 'series', in which each of the elements can react to any other, without any sort of hierarchical arrangement.[12]

This is also why Proudhon's philosophy of history is starkly opposed to the Hegelian phenomenology of Spirit and its providential ordering of events. Proudhon sees history as an evolutionary trajectory, that is as 'progress', but this is not a seamless movement. There are struggles, contradictions, antagonisms, ruptures, without reconciliation, without a final destination. There is a thesis and an antithesis, but without a synthesis.[13] The following moment in the historical process is at best the outcome of a compromise, of a balancing between two previously opposed forces; forces which constitute this new situation are maintained in their identity, rather than being and absorbed ('aufgehoben') into a new totality. There is only a partial, rather than a total, reconciliation of forces.

Proudhon does not deny the possibility and the activation of collective social forces: 'Collective beings are as much realities as individual ones are' – we read in his *Justice in the Revolution and in the Church*.[14] He is no methodological individualist. Individuals, that are a socially produced form of subjectivity from the start, interact and are connected through communicative acts, both linguistic and material. Communication is the existential mode of the social being, and it means not only discourse, but also commerce and the exchange of goods. In this sense, a market is a form of communication, and its nature is similar to discourse. Political power should be understood in the same way; it is 'immanent to society',[15] and might be considered, in almost Arendtian terms, as acting in concert. Whenever people act in concert – something that is intrinsic to their social nature – they produce political power. Power, in this perspective, is not a voluntarist experience, an act of will and monocratic self-affirmation. Rather, it is a product of mutual aid and recognition, of a relation between plural actors. Pluralism is a fact of nature and society. And it will also be a definitional condition of law.

Proudhon's concept of law cannot thus be the one of a command issued by a political superior, a sovereign. Nor is law a product of the spirit of time progressing in a dialectical fashion. Command, history, and tradition belie the seriality of the social practice that is the source of law. Law is a relationship, something that is better expressed by the idea of a contract. This is why justice, according to Proudhon, is mostly commutative, not distributive. A distribution, it is assumed, needs a hierarchically superior actor capable of distributing, but superiority is contrary to the nature of law. The only form of legal justice is the commutative one, the one presiding in mutual recognition and agreement. This is also why the form of the state should be reshaped and replaced by that of a federation, or better of a confederation, where central authority acts as a coordinating agency in the service of plural, horizontal political actors, and entities.

In one of his later and more mature works, *Du principe fédératif*, Proudhon explicitly deals with the concept of law.[16] He lists three basic doctrines. The first is based on the idea of command, directly deriving from Christian theology. Secondly, there is a relationship theory – the one basically defended by Montesquieu – seeing the law as an intrinsic rule of societal phenomena, and as a guiding standard for institutional arrangements. Finally, the doctrine based on the idea of arbitration, where a rule is set as a balancing criterion for human interests and deliberations. Only this third notion can refer justice to a reflexive practice of citizenship, while the first is imbued with the monarchical principle and an authoritarian morality, and the second cannot reflect the normativity of the claim for justice that presides in human communication. In conclusion, law, according to Proudhon, is to be considered the result of relations made accessible to deliberation through a practice of agreement and arbitration that is, moreover, supported by the evidence of relevant needs. Thus, law is both a normative and a cognitive practice in a way that allows for commands to be eschewed and for sanctions and coercion to be minimised: 'The rule of reason will replace the despotism of will'.[17]

This is the fundamental point, the crossroad, where liberalism and anarchism part company. Liberalism challenges authority and power only in its political form, without, moreover, putting in question its necessity or its ontology. The substance of power and authority, as submission and derogation to an alien will and as inevitably accompanied by force and violence, are not contested in liberal theory. When John Rawls, at the beginning of *A Theory of Justice*, tells us that justice is a virtue of institutions, he does not question the nature of these political bodies; they are simply presupposed, taken as given. The only issue is how to give them legitimacy. We see the same in Bruce Ackerman's *Social Justice in the Liberal State*, where the notion of power assumed is the traditional one of command and ruling; the argument developed presupposes a commander of a space shuttle who needs to justify his orders, and thus the relationship of command, obedience and punishment that this entails. No practicable alternative is envisaged. In any case, justification is only required in the political sphere, while the private sphere – the sphere of family, the market, society at large – can still be determined by power relations that are free of justification and control. In such a perspective, freedom is mostly conceived as non-interference, and this is fully compatible with the experience of dependence and domination.

Anarchism can be considered a radicalisation of liberalism.[18] Justification is required for every form of authority and power, from that of government to that found in the family and in economic relationships. And the claim for justification is not just normative. It does not take as given social institutions as such. Justification claims penetrate the very essence and practice of the institution considered. The question is no longer when specific forms of coercion are justified, but whether coercion in general is legitimate. And this second query implies a search for possible alternatives. Freedom is no longer the mere lack of interference, or a mere monocratic autonomy; it must be able to be collectively experienced and articulated. One's freedom is not a limit to the other's liberty; they refer mutually one to the other, and in such mutual recognition is to be found their true guarantee. Freedom becomes a mutual interaction between independence and collective participation. In this sense, anarchism is republicanism made secure and self-sufficient.

In Proudhon the long path that proceeds from Spinoza reaches full circle. Society is seen as a body imbued with the multiple desires of people and made coherent through their explicit reflexivity. Law is no longer a question of command, obedience, and punishment. Rather it is a civilising moment of mutual recognition and deliberation. A law of the multitude that asks for reasons and justifications cannot be cruel, inhuman and alienating. The space for mutual recognition and deliberation can only be nurtured by the energy given through active and subversive acts of individual, existential anarchy.

Epilogue

From Spinoza through Godwin and eventually to Proudhon, a line of thought is developed that is based on a new materialist and rationalist worldview. Normativity becomes a matter of force relations and sociality. The traditional doctrine of free will is questioned by all three thinkers and there is no rehabilitation of a metaphysical absolute freedom. Nor is freedom understood as the negative capacity of limiting others' interactions, as in the liberal sense. Rather, freedom is related to empowerment and human flourishing, and, accordingly, rights are conceptualised as powers, not just as legal entitlements or protected areas of private liberty and enjoyment. The body politic is reshaped as a community of citizens who collectively deliberate about their destiny and a common way of life. It is a fully secularised public space; here theological concepts do not apply, or if they do, this happens only *a contrario*, by contrast and opposition, in terms of their negation or full reconsideration – as occurs in Spinoza's philosophy, where God is finally equated with nature ('Deus sive natura') and nature is seen as a sum of forces ('conati') that individually drive people to use their capacities. Godwin adds to this a stronger element of reflexivity, which allows also for separation of individuals from the multitude in a sort of negative dialectical movement. Proudhon takes this anarchical line of thought a step further, extending anarchy to economic and family relations by completing Godwin's initial critique of capitalism and traditional styles of life. Law is criticised as a form of alienation, in the same terms as private property and the state. In all three thinkers we find a rejection of authoritarianism in all its forms, political, economic, and social.

In this anti-authoritarian paradigm, institutions are not the embodiment of an external sovereign will; rather, they are the expression of sociality and mutual deliberation. Rights are understood as individual powers and capacities. Morality is the procedural framework that makes capacities flourish – a kind of 'will to power', rather than an external standard of judgement. Here law is the constitutive act of a social space in which those capacities and powers can develop and expand. Law thus becomes a space of liberation rather than constraint and coercion, something that empowers individuals and fosters new forms of freedom. If there must be coercion, it is kept to a minimum. Regulative rules are contingent and always open to contestation, rather than fixed. Nor do they need sanctions and violence to be operative. Rather, they gain their binding force from the freedom they offer to actors to develop action and give a collective sense to their coordination. If there is an idea of sovereignty in this scheme, it is a form of sovereignty that comes from acting in concert.

All this, we argue, starts with Spinoza's seminal work. His contribution to anarchist modernity could thus be summarised in a few points. (i) Political order is an expression of a permanently active collective force springing from the multitude. Of course, this sovereignty could produce authoritarian regimes, an absolute monarchy, for instance. But the latter is only one possibility among several, and could just as easily take the form of a democratic republic, or a self-governing city. Sovereignty is not the outcome of a cession of rights of actors within a state of nature; rights are never given up in order to enter into the civil, condition. Obedience to authority is not natural for human beings; it is rather a cause of pain for them.[19]

Law is seen as a natural expression of sovereignty, that is, of the natural rights of people now collectively organised in a city after their overcoming a 'state of nature' where a good life was still fragile and uncertain. This is a second fundamental thesis. (ii) Law is based on might, on power, and this is equivalent to right. Laws and rights are not opposites, they mutually refer to one another. Law is not a constraint, a restriction of power or freedom, but rather a concretisation of power and freedom.

A third thesis concerns the practice of citizenship. (iii) Citizenship is not allegiance or subordination to a sovereign; it is another name for sovereignty. Citizenship is *the other side of sovereignty*, sovereignty, as it were, seen from below. Citizenship is a matter of rights more than duties, and citizenship rights are *fragments of sovereignty*.

Spinoza reactivates the idea of a virtuous circle of citizenship: a citizen is an individual who can be asked to follow a rule only if he or she has agreed to this rule and contributed to its issuing. However – and this is where Spinoza's theory may no longer be entirely compatible with anarchism – citizenship is considered as necessarily particular and exclusive. 'Cities' are limited jurisdictions in competition, or conflict, with one another. War is a natural condition between 'nations' or 'states'. There is no cosmopolitan horizon in Spinoza. Political rights cannot be universalised – a conclusion that anarchism could never accept. It will be the great merit of Bakunin's political theory to connect political freedom with a criticism of state borders and national particularism. Moreover, as we go on to argue, the paradigm of sovereignty – even the republican sovereignty of citizens that Spinoza invokes – may not be best way of conceiving of anarchist legal institutions.

Notes

1. But cf. D. Colson, 'Anarchist Readings of Spinoza', *Journal of French Philosophy*, Vol. 17, 2007, pp. 90 ff. A possible anarchist interpretation of Spinoza's philosophy is to be found in G. Deleuze, *Spinoza – philosophie pratique*, Éditions de Minuit, Paris 1981, and in E. Balibar, *Spinoza et le politique*, Presses universitaires de France, Paris 2011, and more recently E. Balibar, *Spinoza politique. Le transindividuel*, Presses universitaires de France, Paris 2018.
2. Cf., for instance, G. Tarello, *Storia della cultura giuridica moderna. Assolutismo e codificazione del diritto*, and G. Fassò, *Storia della filosofia del diritto*, Vol. 2, Il mulino, Bologna 1970.

3. See L. Strauss, *Spinoza's Critique of Religion*, Chicago: University of Chicago Press, 1997.
4. See, for instance, Justin Steinberg, 'Spinoza and Political Absolutism', eds. Yitzhak Melamed and Hasana Sharp, *Spinoza's Political Treatise: A Critical Guide*, Cambridge: Cambridge University Press, 2008, 175–189.
5. Pierre-Joseph Proudhon, *What is Property?*, ed. by Donald R. Kelley and Bonnie G. Smith, Cambridge University Press, Cambridge 1994, p. 211.
6. Ibid., p. 45.
7. Ibid., p. 55.
8. Ibid., p. 73.
9. Ibid., p. 73.
10. Ibid., p. 42.
11. Pierre-Joseph Proudhon, *De la création de l'ordre dans l'Humanité, ou Principe d'organisation politique*, ed. by C. Bouglé and H. Moysset, Marcel Rivière, Paris 1929.
12. Ibid.
13. See Pierre-Joseph Proudhon, *Système des contradictions économiques, ou philosophie de la misère*, 2 vols., Marcel Rivière, Paris 1923–1924.
14. Pierre-Joseph Proudhon, *Property is Theft!: A Pierre-Joseph Proudhon Anthology*, ed. by Iain McKay. California: AK Press, Edinburgh 2011, p. 655.
15. Ibid., p. 658.
16. Proudhon, *Du principe fédératif et oeuvres diverses sur les problems politiques européens*.
17. Proudhon, *What is Property?*, p. 214.
18. See Giampietro N. Berti, *Il pensiero anarchico dal Settecento al Novecento*, Lacaita, Manduria 1998; and Massimo La Torre, *Nostra legge è la libertà: Anarchismo dei Moderni*, DeriveApprodi, Roma 2017.
19. The same point would be made centuries later by Hans Kelsen, who said that obedience is painful.

Four
Carl Schmitt and the Anarchists

Over the previous chapters we have considered the anarchist critique of legal authority. As we have shown, what anarchists primarily object to is the principle of political obligation. In other words, what is rejected is the idea that insofar as one is a member of a particular political community one has a duty to obey the law and is to be coerced into doing so. This the anarchist considers to be a violation of one's moral autonomy and one's attitude as an independent person with her own life project. As we have seen, the law's absolute claim on our obedience is central to positive law theory, in which law is mostly viewed as a system of commands and sanctions. For Kelsen, the laws have *coercive* effects: 'They command a certain human behaviour by attaching a coercive act to the opposite behaviour'.[1] The law was a self-contained system of norms and sanctions with nothing beyond it, which means that the individual living under the jurisdiction of a particular legal system has no external normative order, no alternative 'natural' principle of justice or morality to appeal to; or alternatively that, if he has external normative standards of conducts, these are merely subjective and in any case are pre-empted and abrogated by positive law. He is bound to obey simply because the legal community, having a monopoly on the use of coercive force, deploys this to enforce certain forms of behaviour and to sanction others. The law, for Kelsen, is therefore a self-referential system based on relations of power. Law is self-contained also insofar as it is the only possible objective form of normativity, justified by a *Grundnorm*, a 'ground rule' that is, the master rule giving validity and existence to the other second-order rules that constitute the legal system.

But does the law have an *outside*? This is the question that guides this chapter. In responding to this question in the affirmative, anarchists, who contest the idea of legal authority, and the authoritarian conservative, Carl Schmitt, who seeks to uphold and bolster it, might seem to find themselves, paradoxically, on the same side. Anarchists appeal to an ethical horizon beyond the law – found in nature or in the principle of individual moral autonomy – as a way of reflecting on the law's limits and challenging its authority. The law, in other words, cannot capture or totalise every domain of human life. Coming from the very opposite position, Schmitt says something similar: there is, too, something outside the law, something the law cannot fully capture or grasp – and that is *sovereignty*. Unlike Kelsen, who wanted to rule out the exceptionality of sovereignty as being essentially incompatible with the law, or, better, make sovereignty a by-product of the legal order itself,[2] Schmitt saw it as the law's fundamental guarantee. Where the anarchist might seem to agree with Schmitt is in seeing sovereignty and its exceptional authority as being at the very heart of the law; yet Schmitt affirms it, while the anarchist condemns it.

Yet, how could we account for this strange affinity between Schmitt and the anarchists? What is it that binds together two absolute enemies: the radical conservative with fascistic tendencies, and the anti-authoritarian rebel, the revolutionary anarchist? Schmitt and the anarchists share an 'absolutism' on the question of legal-political authority: the former absolutely affirms it, the other absolutely repudiates it, but they would both agree on its absolute character. In this chapter, we intend to explore this subterranean dialogue between Schmitt and the anarchists, a dialogue that Schmitt carried on in a number of his key works throughout his career. Indeed, Schmitt remained haunted by the spectre of revolutionary anarchism, regarding this as much more dangerous to the legal-political order than liberalism. For the theorist of enmity, Schmitt's real enemy, his real ideological opponent, was not liberalism so much as anarchism. Or rather, Schmitt interprets anarchism as a radicalised form of liberalism, as the hard core of this ideology. In Schmitt's writings we encounter the ghosts of anarchists like Bakunin, Proudhon, and Stirner time and time again. It is by exploring this unusual encounter that we aim to reveal something important about the nature of legal authority and its relationship to sovereignty.

Political theology and the state of exception

Not much attention has been given to Schmitt's relationship with anarchism. Most of the commentary on Schmitt's legal theory focuses on his critique of liberalism.[3] As is generally recognised, Schmitt regards liberalism as a kind of anti-political rationality, one that seeks to mediate political conflict – to obscure the friend–enemy opposition that Schmitt saw as vital to political life – through deliberation and procedure, and to reign in the sovereign exception through constitutions and the rule of law. Liberalism, for Schmitt, was therefore a kind of political technics;[4] it imposes a series of institutional rules and procedures intended to regulate political life according to rational norms. Therein lay its nihilism. Indeed, Schmitt regarded liberalism as part of the condition of secular modernity, defined by the loss of traditional sources of legitimacy and moral and political authority once provided by the church and absolutist monarchs. The collapse of the theological world in the sixteenth century led, according to Schmitt, to a series of displacements of authority – from the deism of seventeenth century, to Enlightenment rationalism in the eighteenth century, the rise of industrial capitalism in the nineteenth century, and finally to the modern era defined by political liberalism, parliamentarianism, coupled with technological domination. Eventually, for Schmitt, liberalism coincides with the high point of political neutralisation. Liberalism turns political life into rational administration and endless debate without a genuine decision, and without friends or enemies. It is part of the nihilistic drift of modern secular societies.[5] For Schmitt, this nihilistic and secularising impulse is what liberalism shares with anarchism.

Schmitt's critique of liberalism is particularly pronounced in his early writings from the 1920s and 1930s, in which he is responding to the political instability and constitutional crises of the Weimar period in Germany. He regards liberalism as having weakened the constitutional order, and as failing to provide a stable foundation for political and legal authority. Schmitt's critical engagement with liberalism is part of a complex series of debates over constitutional law, political authority, and liberal culture with interlocutors like the aforementioned Kelsen,[6] and the conservative philosopher Leo Strauss.[7] The main thrust of Schmitt's charge against liberalism during this period was that it was an inadequate expression of democracy – liberal pluralism and parliamentarianism failed to represent the singular, unified identity of the people[8] – and that, in its insistence on the rule of law and constitutional limitations on executive authority, it failed to protect the constitutional order from existential threats.[9] Real authority – the kind sufficient to guarantee the constitution – could only come from a recognition of the constituting power of the people as a force external to it, and could only be only be achieved by giving exceptional powers to a sovereign dictator who would take emergency measures to enforce law and order.[10] As is well known, this increasingly anti-liberal position led Schmitt towards increasingly authoritarian solutions, including advocating the use of emergency legislation by the Chancellor to suspend the Weimar constitution altogether – under the infamous Article 48 – to strongly sympathise with Italian fascism, and to his later support of, and collaboration with, the National Socialist regime.

Schmitt's theory of sovereign dictatorship is fully developed in his *Politische Theologie* from 1922. The text begins with the famous lines, 'Sovereign is he who decides on the exception'.[11] For Schmitt, what really defines sovereignty, what is at its core as a political and legal concept, is the right to decide unilaterally on exceptional situations – that is, to determine what actually constitutes an emergency of the state (*Ausnahmezustand*) and to decide what to do about it. In response to serious emergencies the state must have the authority to suspend the constitutional order and rule by decree. The central claim here is that the sovereign state has to be able to act outside the normal constitutional rules and constraints if it is to protect the constitution from various threats. The very survival of the constitution depended on the sovereign right to suspend it. As a juridical category, sovereignty always inhabits the position of exception in relation to the norm – the normal legal order which it exceeds and, in exceeding it, also founds and determines it. The exception can never be wholly accounted for by the norm, nor can it be seen as deriving from it. According to Schmitt, the sovereign decision on the exception is defined in law and derives its authorisation from it, but at the same time exceeds it. The sovereign exception only has meaning in relation to the legal norm it transgresses. Sovereignty is a liminal concept: it inhabits a 'grey zone', being inside and outside the law at the same time. Sovereignty is, as he puts it, a 'borderline concept'.[12]

This paradoxical logic emerges as part of Schmitt's critique of liberal constitutionalism (Hugo Preuss and Otto von Gierke), which sought to rein in the sovereign exception through the rule of law; and, more specifically, in his debate with Kelsen (as well as Hugo Krabbe)[13] who sought to identify the state with the law and developed a theory of positive law as wholly derived from a self-contained, self-referential series of norms with nothing outside it. The problem with these theories, according to Schmitt, was that in trying to rule out the exception that would be legally relevant – to 'de-personalise' sovereignty – they failed to acknowledge the way in which legal norms and rules actually presuppose an exterior that grounds them, constitutes their limit and has the authority to apply them to specific situations; an authority to decide when and how a norm is applied. It is the sovereign exception that therefore guarantees the totality of the law. This is why, for Schmitt, the exception, while related to the legal rule, is nevertheless preeminent over it: 'The exception is more interesting than the rule. The rule proves nothing; the exception proves everything.'[14] In insisting on the supremacy of the exception over the norm, and in showing that the authority and efficacy of the legal order is reliant upon a sovereign decision that exceeds its limits, Schmitt is not only defining juridical and political concepts but actively defending the idea of strong, authoritarian sovereignty as a solution to the weakness of the existing constitutional order.

The need for strong sources of authority and legitimacy in the modern world is also reflected in another major theme of the text – that of political theology itself. In a secular world that lacks religious sources of authority, which no longer believes in God nor recognises the legitimacy of the church, new sources of order and authority must be established. However, if the political sovereign is to play this role, it must take on a kind of theological illumination. Schmitt is not advocating a theocracy or some kind of return to the old doctrine of divine right; such a return would be impossible. Yet, the political sovereign must fill the void, the place of the sacred left vacant by religion. It must have the transcendental properties of God. This is why Schmitt seeks to understand the modern secular state through theological categories.[15] There is a structural parallel between the God who transcends the world and the political sovereign that transcends social relations. And just as God can suspend the laws of the nature through the miracle, so the sovereign can suspend the constitutional order through the exception. The actions of God and the actions of the sovereign are a form of creation *ex-nihilo*; they are both self-founding, self-determining, autonomous concepts, producing themselves out of nothing. In drawing these analogies between theological and political categories, Schmitt is doing more than simply proposing, as he puts it, a 'sociology' of political and juridical concepts. Rather, the sovereign state, if it is to provide a source of legitimacy and stability, must be invested with God-like powers. As a radical Hobbesian, Schmitt wanted to create a modern Leviathan, a new mortal God that would tower over society and unilaterally determine law.[16] Central to Schmitt's political theology is a kind of secular political absolutism or even monotheism.[17]

Legal anarchy

Yet, if Schmitt's concern was to protect the constitutional order against external and internal threats, why did he support a form of sovereign dictatorship that was incompatible with it? Why did he come to the conclusion that the only way of protecting the rule of law was by invoking the sovereign state of exception that led ultimately to its destruction? The triggering of Article 48 and the Enabling Act of 1933 paved the way for the Nazi dictatorship and the eleven-years-long state of emergency in which, as Agamben points out, the constitutional order was never formally abolished but, rather, permanently suspended. Indeed, Agamben argues that the sovereign state of exception reveals the *anomie* or 'anarchy' at the heart of the law: that is, the way that the authority and enforcement of the law relies at the same time on a dimension of 'force' that is outside the law, that is unhinged from its normative structure: 'The state of exception is the anomic space in which what is at stake is a force of law without law (which should be therefore be written: force-of-X[law])'.[18] This is close to the idea of ontological anarchy that we have sought to explore at the heart of legal authority; in other words, the instability and undecidability of the law's foundations. In the case of the sovereign exception, which is always to be thought in relation to the law that it exceeds, the structure of the law becomes 'anarchic' – that is, it is unleashed from the system of rules, norms and constraints; that regulates and governs action.[19] This would be something approaching what Hannah Arendt called the 'anarchy of power' to characterise totalitarian regimes.[20] In Schmitt's reasoning, to be able to enforce order, the sovereign must be able to exceed its normal legal and constitutional constraints and have a certain freedom to act, to do what it could not otherwise do under normal conditions. We are of course familiar with this kind of refrain even from liberal democratic governments, who tell us that to respond to some crisis they need emergency powers; their hands must be untied. So, paradoxically, the sovereign state of exception, as theorised by Schmitt, resembles a form of 'anarchy'. However, Schmitt is quick to distinguish the exception from disorder and chaos: order in the juristic sense still prevails, even if it is, he says ominously, 'not of the ordinary kind'.[21] This is a kind of artificially induced 'anarchy' designed to preserve, rather than overthrow, the existing order, or – as we saw in Schmitt's welcoming of the Nazi seizure of power – overthrowing it in order to preserve it.[22] To borrow the concept of 'immunization' from the theorist Roberto Esposito,[23] the exception might be seen as the action in which, in order to protect oneself from a virus, one injects oneself with it so that the system's immune response is stimulated; in the same way, to immunise itself against the threat of anarchy, the state suspends the rule of law and becomes 'anarchic'. We will return to this theme of auto-immunity in the following chapter.

Could it be, then, that the real threat that Schmitt was responding to – the real cause of his political disquiet – was not liberalism, but revolutionary anarchism? As the Jewish philosopher and one of Schmitt's post-war interlocutors, Jacob Taubes, puts it, Schmitt is the 'apocalyptic prophet of the counterrevolution'.[24] Indeed, for Taubes, both he and Schmitt are apocalyptic thinkers, but Schmitt thinks 'from above', whereas he thinks 'from the bottom up'.[25] We have seen already what thinking the apocalypse 'from above' means for Schmitt – the counterrevolution, instigated by the sovereign exception, designed to preserve the state order from the threat of revolution, and yet which ultimately authorised the Nazi apocalypse that ended up destroying the German state. So, how should we understand the alternative apocalypse from below that Taubes talks about? Revolutions, in their destruction of the existing order, in their overturning of hierarchies, are of course apocalyptic events. In his interpretation of Pauline theology, Taubes explores the eschatological message of Paul's *Epistle to the Romans* – an address to the Jewish Christian congregations in Rome (circa 57–58 AD). Here he finds a political theology that operates as a direct revolutionary counterpoint to Schmitt's counterrevolutionary political theology. Schmitt's political theology, as we have seen, tries to prevent the revolution from occurring, even if it has to provoke a certain form of legal anarchy – the state of emergency – in order to capture and contain within the order of law the real anarchy of the revolution. In theological terms, the sovereign plays the role of the *katechon* – the restraining power that prevents the coming of the Anti-Christ, the event that precedes (as well as delays) the Apocalypse and the arrival of the Messiah.[26] Schmitt is one who, in Taubes' words, 'prays for the preservation of the state, since if, God forbid, it doesn't remain, chaos breaks loose, or even worse, the Kingdom of God!'[27] However, Taubes' interpretation of Paul offers a more revolutionary perspective. Not only is *Romans*, according to Taubes, a political declaration of war against the authority of Caesar, it is also the registering of an eschatological horizon, in which the end of world and the coming of the Messiah are imminent, and the transience and unimportance of this-worldly political power becomes apparent. For Paul, the coming of the Messiah who will redeem the world is concomitant with the destruction of the Roman Empire. In Taubes' hands, Paul's messianism is a kind of radical *hyper-political* theology 'from below', a revolutionary state of exception, in which the order of power crumbles away. In a similar vein – and again in reaction to Schmitt's conservative state of exception – Walter Benjamin talks about the need to bring about a real, revolutionary state of emergency to combat the rise of fascism, rather than clinging on to the existing order.[28]

For this reason, we can say that anarchism, in its rejection of legal authority, is the ethical and political counterpoint to Schmitt's sovereign state of exception. Anarchism, we argue, offers a more effective means of critically interrogating Schmitt's legal thought than liberalism. Indeed, it is precisely the uncanny proximity between Schmitt and the anarchists on this question of legal anarchy that allows this interrogation to take place.

The spectre of anarchism

A careful reading of Schmitt's key texts reveals the extent to which he was haunted by the threat of revolutionary anarchism, much more so than by liberalism. Liberalism was part of the background condition of modern secularism and nihilism, but anarchism was its clear and present danger. While Schmitt's references are mostly to historical figures of anarchism – like Bakunin, Proudhon and Stirner[29] – we also have to bear in mind that the time of the Weimar crisis in which Schmitt was writing, and to which he was responding, was characterised by actual revolutionary uprisings from the far left, notably the Spartacist uprising in 1919 led by figures like Rosa Luxembourg, who was in some ways much closer to anarchism than to Marxist-Leninism, as well as by the anarchist activist, Gustav Landauer. Furthermore, not only was anarchism a direct revolutionary challenge to sovereign authority and the legitimacy of the law; it was one of the philosophies of immanence – along with Marxist materialism – that essentially ruled out the idea of transcendence. In other words, anarchism is an inherently antinomian and atheistic philosophy based on material, usually biological, life forces, which is totally incompatible with metaphysical ideas of God. Not only was anarchism fiercely opposed to the authority of the clergy and to the mystifications of religion, but also to the concept of sovereign transcendence to which it was inherently linked. Anarchists wanted to destroy not only the state as a political and legal entity, but also the metaphysical and religious thinking upon which it was founded. The slogan of anarchism is, after all, No Gods, No Masters. Schmitt therefore saw anarchism as absolutely hostile to political theology, and as presenting a serious challenge not only to the political authority of the state, but to the very idea of sovereign transcendence that he sought to ground in theology. For Schmitt, as we have seen, in the flattened out modern secular world, bereft of a dimension of the sacred, new sources of legitimacy and authority needed to be found, namely a theologically charged conception of sovereignty that transcends social relations, just as God was once said to transcend the universe and the laws of nature. And it was precisely this way of thinking that anarchism so radically called into question.

It is important to recall here that the term political theology, at least in its modern usage, comes not from Schmitt, but from Bakunin in the nineteenth century. In a polemic against the Italian statesman Guiseppe Mazzini, 'La Théologie politique de Mazzini et l'Internationale' [1871], Bakunin deploys 'political theology' as a term of abuse. He accuses Mazzini of illegitimately mixing together religion and politics. Mazzini's republicanism and his revolutionary role in the formation of the Italian state were marred by his Christianity and religious idealism. In the eyes of Bakunin, Mazzini had fallen victim to a theological abstraction that led him to turn against the cause of human emancipation and revolutionary socialism. Thus, Bakunin charged Mazzini with being a 'political theologian' and the 'last high priest of religious, metaphysical, and political idealism which is disappearing'.[30] This was Bakunin's atheistic assault on political theology – that is, on the close relationship between religion and politics and between the church and state, as well as on all transcendental and idealist philosophies that were for him a disguised form of theology.

According to Bakunin, the idealist, whether of the religious, philosophical or political kind, is one who abstracts moral principles from the materiality of life, suspending them above the living forces of society, and turning them against humanity. That is why, for Bakunin, religion has usually been on the side of the state, why the theologian is also a political absolutist, and why sovereignty has wrapped itself up in religious ideology. Just as God transcends the world and nature, the state transcends and stands above society; the same principle of absolute sovereignty is at work in both. Moreover, the reason why religious idealists and political absolutists reach the same conclusions is that both proceed from the doctrine of original sin, which leads them to the same 'melancholy destiny': man is not to be trusted, and therefore needs the moral authority of religion and the political authority which can only come from a strong state. Schmitt reasons in exactly this way. It is this metaphysical abstraction from the real world that is intolerable to Bakunin: 'As a theologian, Mazzini must think, and he really does think, that all morality descends on human society from on high, by the revelation of a divine law; whence it follows that society has no inherent or immanent morality'.[31] It was his outrage at this that led Bakunin to declare himself on the side of Satan in his rebellion against God's authority. Satan was the first real humanist and anarchist. Modern revolutions – exemplified by the Paris Commune of 1871 – were thus the 'last the audacious realisation of the Satanic myth, a revolt against God; and today as always the two opposing parties are ranged, the one under the standard of Satan or of liberty, the other under the divine banner of authority'.[32] For Bakunin, we are confronted with a great conflict between the forces of idealism and political reaction (the church, state and capital, shrouded in phantasms, with its ideologues, metaphysicians and political theologians); and the progressive forces of materialism, atheism, internationalism and revolutionary socialism.[33]

Bakunin's implacable critique of political theology is a major concern for Schmitt. Indeed, Bakunin is revealed as one of Schmitt's chief antagonists, one who best represents modernity's assault on the sanctity of the state. In fact, we could go as far as to suggest that Schmitt's whole politico-legal-theological apparatus and his theory of the sovereign state of exception is mobilised precisely against the threat posed by the kind of atheistic and materialist revolutionary politics that Bakunin represents. If there is a relationship of enmity at work Schmitt's in political theology, Bakunin, and the anti-politico-theological gesture of revolutionary anarchism, emerges as the real enemy.[34]

An intense enmity for Bakunin – and indeed for the tradition of revolutionary anarchism and materialism that Bakunin represents – is evident in a number of Schmitt's texts, including in *Roman Catholicism and the Political Form* [1923].[35] However, nowhere is the politico-theological war between Schmitt and the anarchists expressed more clearly and explicitly than in *Political Theology I* itself. In the final chapter of this text, Schmitt sets up a dialogue between counter-revolutionary conservatives – Catholic traditionalists and legitimists like Joseph de Maistre, Louis de Bonald, and Juan Donoso Cortés – and revolutionary anarchists, the usual suspects being Proudhon and Bakunin. Schmitt clearly admires the former and detests the latter. Indeed, Schmitt in a sense speaks through Donoso Cortés in affirming the counter-revolutionary position of sovereign dictatorship. Like Schmitt, Donoso Cortés, writing in the wake of the 1848 revolutions, also believed that sovereignty was necessarily absolutist. The old monarchical order was threatened on all sides by atheism, liberalism and revolution, and, for Donoso Cortés the only way to preserve moral authority and political legitimacy was through dictatorship. Also, in a similar way to Schmitt, Donoso Cortés saw this struggle in quasi-theological terms: he saw 'only the theology of the foe'.[36] Who was Donoso Cortés' (Schmitt's) foe? Unlike liberals, for whom he had nothing but contempt, Donoso Cortés regarded the anarchist as his true enemy, one for whom he at the same time had a certain sort of respect, even admiration, as if recognising his own reverse mirror image:

> That extremist cast of mind explains why he was contemptuous of the liberals while he respected atheist-anarchist socialism as his deadly foe and endowed it with a diabolical stature. In Proudhon he claimed to see a demon. Proudhon laughed about it, and alluding to the Inquisition as if he were already on the funeral pyre, he called out to Donoso Cortes: Ignite it![37]

Therefore, while Schmitt saw liberalism as an empty, nihilistic philosophy, based on endless equivocation and deliberation – one that sought to neutralise the political domain by pretending it did not exist or imagining that political conflicts could be resolved through rational dialogue – he saw in anarchism a political extremism that was implacably opposed to political authority. If liberalism occupied the middle ground in the ideological (and politico-theological) conflict, Schmitt's radical conservatism, and Bakunin's and Proudhon's revolutionary anarchism and atheism, were at the extreme opposite ends.

What the counterrevolutionary conservative and the revolutionary anarchist shared was a certain extremism and absolutism, particularly with regard to the sovereign state. The reactionary defended the principle of state absolutism *absolutely*, while the anarchist – who also regards the state as absolutist in principle – *absolutely* rejected it and sought to abolish it. In other words, for the reactionary, the sovereign state, which can only ever be absolutist, is an absolute good, or at least an absolute necessity; while for the anarchist, for whom it can *also* only ever be absolute, the sovereign state is an absolute evil and an unnecessary encumbrance upon otherwise freely formed social relations. 'To him, [Donoso Cortés] every sovereignty acted as if it were infallible, every government was absolute – a sentence that the anarchist could pronounce verbatim, even if his intention was an entirely different one.'[38] Both Schmitt and the anarchists engage in a certain demystification of legal authority: coming from opposite angles, they unmask the sovereign absolutism that lies behind the legal order.

Central to this debate is the question of human nature. For the conservative, including Schmitt, man is inherently evil, or at least morally flawed and in need of strong government; whereas for the anarchist, man is inherently good, or at least has the capacity for self-government, and is therefore without need of the sovereign state. The opposition on the question of human nature is further emphasised in Schmitt's *Concept of the Political* [1932] in which a genuinely theological and conservative vision of man's fallen nature is contrasted with anarchism's much more benign conception. This is an opposition that has direct political consequences:

> Ingenuous anarchism reveals that the belief in the natural goodness of man is closely tied to the radical denial of state and government. One follows from the other, and both

> foment each other. For the liberals, on the other hand, the goodness of man signifies nothing more than an argument with whose aid the state is made to serve society. This means that society determines its own order and that state and government are subordinate and must be distrustingly controlled and bound to precise limits.[39]

We can see here, once again, the ideological schema Schmitt establishes: conservatism – liberalism – anarchism. Unlike conservatism, both liberalism and anarchism affirm the natural goodness of man, and this leads to a certain anti-statism. However, the anarchist position is much more radical. While the liberal distrusts the state and believes it must be restrained, kept within precise legal limits, the anarchist wants to do away with the state altogether. In more general terms, while liberalism is concerned about power and domination only in the specific and limited area of public institutions, anarchism expanded this liberal anti-authoritarian suspicion of power. Power and the risk of domination were now to be found in all areas of human relations, including in particular private, labour and family relationships. It is not just political power, but power in all its expressions, that is criticised and rejected by anarchism.

So, central to Schmitt's politico-theological thinking is a war over the very meaning and survival of politics; a war between two kinds of 'extremisms' or 'absolutisms'; a war between a radical conservatism that affirms absolute sovereignty and a strong, authoritarian state, and an atheistic revolutionary anarchism that seeks to overthrow the state in the name of the materialism, nature and the immanence of life. These antagonistic positions, as we have seen, are united in their shared absolutism, something that leads to paradoxical conclusions, particularly for the anarchist. Because the anarchist must absolutely reject the sovereign decision, as it interferes with the immanence of life, Schmitt says that 'this antithesis forces him of course to decide against the decision; and this results in an odd paradox whereby Bakunin, the greatest anarchist of the nineteenth century, had become in theory the theologian of the antitheological and in practice the dictator of the antidictatorship'.[40] According to Schmitt, the absolute hostility of the anarchist to both God and the state would lead him into another kind of absolutism; his materialism becomes another kind of anti-theological theology.

Schmitt's curious and rather too easy dismissal of anarchism as another kind of theology does not of course end the matter. Anarchism is by no means an easy target for Schmitt. Unlike liberalism, which Schmitt can identify as an anti-political rationality, anarchism, in its 'absolute' hostility to political and legal authority, and to domination in general, is much harder to pin down, much more intensely 'political', although not in the authoritarian sense that Schmitt is promoting. As we have seen, in its radical opposition to the state, and to authoritarian decisionism, anarchism constitutes the ultimate enemy for Schmitt. Anarchism is also the enemy to him because of the internal connection it establishes between radical freedom and equality. And equality, even more than freedom, is the privileged target of Schmitt's counterrevolutionary theory. And yet Schmitt also recognises, in this relationship of enmity to anarchism, a shared absolutism on the question of sovereignty. Anarchism confronts Schmitt with his own question in an inverted form: how does the law account for the political dimension that exceeds it? Even though they come from completely opposite directions, both Schmitt and the revolutionary anarchists reveal the limitations of the law in controlling political power. The anarchist critique also reveals the dangerous truth of political authority – its inherently anarchic, violent nature that Schmitt wanted to conceal, or at least contain, by maintaining its relation to the law in the form of legal exception, thus giving it the dignity of a guardian of the law, eventually bestowing upon it a form of legal legitimacy.

Notes

1. Hans Kelsen, *Pure Theory of Law*, trans., Max Knight, Berkely and Los Angeles: University of California Press, 1967, p. 33.
2. As Kelsen says, 'As a political organization, the state is a legal order'. Ibid, p. 286.
3. See, for instance, David Dyzenhaus ed., *Law as Politics: Schmitt's Critique of Liberalism*, Durham NC.: Duke University Press, 1998.

4. See John McCormick, *Carl Schmitt's Critique of Liberalism: Against Politics as Technology*, Cambridge: Cambridge University Press, 1997.
5. Carl Schmitt, 'The Age of Neutralizations and Depoliticizations', trans., Matthias Konzen and John P. McCormick, in *The Concept of the Political*, trans. by G. Schwab. Chicago, IL: University of Chicago Press, 2007, 80–96.
6. See Lars Vinx, *The Guardian of the Constitution: Hans Kelsen and Carl Schmitt on the Limits of Constitutional Law*, Cambridge: Cambridge University Press, 2015. See also David Dyzenhaus, *Legality and Legitimacy: Carl Schmitt, Hans Kelsen and Herman Heller in Weimar*, Oxford: Oxford University Press, 2000.
7. See Heinrich Meier, *Carl Schmitt and Leo Strauss: The Hidden Dialogue*, trans. by J. Harvey Lomax. Chicago, IL: University of Chicago Press, 1995.
8. See Carl Schmitt, *The Crisis of Parliamentary Democracy*, trans. by E. Kennedy. Cambridge, MA: MIT Press, 2000.
9. Carl Schmitt, *Constitutional Theory*, trans. by J. Seitzer. Durham, NC: Duke University Press, 2008.
10. See Carl Schmitt, *Dictatorship: From the Origin of the Modern Concept of Sovereignty to the Proletarian Class Struggle*, Cambridge: Polity 2013.
11. Schmitt, *Political Theology*, p. 1.
12. Ibid., p. 5.
13. Like Kelsen, upon whom he was a major influence, Krabbe affirmed the idea that the state is identical to the legal order and is nothing other than the binding force of the law. What Schmitt objected to in these two theorists was their attempt to 'de-personalise' sovereignty, to reduce it to a function of the law. See Heinz H. F. Eulau, 'The Depersonalization of the Concept of Sovereignty', *The Journal of Politics*, Vol. 4, No. 1 (Feb., 1942), pp. 3–19.
14. Schmitt, *Political Theology*, p. 15.
15. Ibid., p. 36.
16. This is made clear in Schmitt's discussion of the political theology of Hobbes' Leviathan, in which it is argued that Hobbes gives us a decisionist theory of sovereignty (see Carl Schmitt, *The Leviathan in the State Theory of Thomas Hobbes: The Meaning and Failure of a Political Symbol*, trans. by G. Schwab and E. Hilfstein. Westport, CT: Greenwood Press, 1996.
17. This was the basis of Erik Peterson's critique of Schmitt, who queried the theological basis for Schmitt's monotheistic account of sovereignty, arguing that it was incompatible

with the Christian Trinitarian doctrine, and accusing Schmitt of a kind of political heresy (see Erik Peterson, *Theological Tractates*, ed. and trans. by M. J. Hollerich, Stanford, CA: Stanford University Press, 2011).

18. Agamben, *State of Exception*, p. 39.
19. See also William E. Scheuermann's discussion of Schmitt's early theory of legal indeterminacy, to which he attributes Schmitt's later endorsement of the legal anarchy of the Nazi regime. *The End of Law: Carl Schmitt in the Twenty-First Century*, Second Edition, London: Rowman and Littlefield International, 2020.
20. Here she largely follows Franz Neumann's analysis of the Nazi totalitarian state which embodied an 'anarchic' and highly dysfunctional structure of power. See *Behemoth: The Structure and Practice of National Socialism 1933–1944*, Chicago: Ivan R. Dee, 2009.
21. Schmitt, *Political Theology*, 12.
22. The state of exception that exceeds the law is a specific reference to the notorious Article 48 of the Weimar Constitution, which gave the President, in times of crisis, the authority to issue 'emergency decrees'. This was used by the Nazis in 1933 to assume absolute power and remained in place throughout their reign, thus effectively authorising a permanent state of emergency.
23. See Roberto Esposito, *Immunitas: the Protection and Negation of Life* (Cambridge: Polity Press, 2011).
24. See Jacob Taubes, 'Carl Schmitt: Apocalyptic Prophet of the Counterrevolution', in Taubes, *To Carl Schmitt: Letters and Reflections*, trans., Keith Tribe (New York: Columbia University Press, 2013), 1–18.
25. Ibid., p. 13.
26. This is why, as Massimo Cacciari points out, the katechon is always identified with law: 'Thus the *katechon* cannot be conceived otherwise than in the spirit of law (*nomos*).' *The Withholding Power: an Essay on Political Theology*, trans., Edi Pucci, London: Bloomsbury, 2018, 14.
27. Jacob Taubes, *The Political Theology of Paul*. Stanford, CA: Stanford University Press, 2003, pp. 69–70.
28. W. Benjamin, 'On the Concept of History', Selected Writings, Vol. 4: 1938–1940, ed. by H. Eiland and M. W. Jennings, trans. by E. Jephcott. Cambridge, MA: Harvard University Press, 2003, pp. 389–400.
29. In his prison writings, Schmitt discusses his long acquaintanceship with Stirner's philosophy, crediting him with

being one in a line of key thinkers who laid the groundwork for the destruction of the philosophical and theological tradition after 1848, and with its replacement by a sort of contemporary 'paganism' or Pan-ism. *Ex Captivitate Salus*, ed., Andreas Kalyvas and Federico Finchelstein, trans., Matthew Hannah, Cambridge: Polity Press, 2017, pp. 64–65.

30. Bakunin, 'The Political Theology of Mazzini and the International' [1871].
31. Ibid.
32. Ibid.
33. Bakunin's critical diagnosis and fierce assault on political theology is found throughout his writings, including his later work, 'God and the State' [1882].
34. This is the point emphasised by Heinrich Meier, one of the more perceptive commentators on Schmitt. See *The Lesson of Carl Schmitt: Four Chapters on the Distinction between Political Theology and Political Philosophy*, trans., Marcus Brainard (Chicago & London: University of Chicago Press, 1998), 5.
35. According to Schmitt, 'He [Bakunin] swept away all metaphysical and ideological obstacles, then turned with Scythian might against religion and politics, theology, and jurisprudence'. *Roman Catholicism and Political Form*, trans. by G. L. Ulmen. Westport, CT: Greenwood Press, 1996, p. 36.
36. Schmitt, *Political Theology*, 62.
37. Ibid., p. 63.
38. Ibid., p. 55.
39. Carl Schmitt, *The Concept of the Political*, trans. by G. Schwab. Chicago, IL: University of Chicago Press, 2007, pp. 60–61.
40. Schmitt, *Political Theology*, p. 66.

Five

Autoimmunity and the Problem of Legal Foundation

The previous chapter explored an unexpected encounter between Carl Schmitt and the anarchists. It was argued that both are engaged in a certain demystification of legal authority. In spite of attempts by legal positivist theorists, like Kelsen, to reduce the state to a system of legal norms, and despite the attempt, central to the liberal political theory tradition, to rein in sovereignty through the rule of law and constitutional checks and balances, the absolutist dimension of sovereignty reveals itself, particularly in 'states of emergency' in which the distinction between liberal democracies and authoritarian regimes seems to become opaque or to fall away entirely. We have, in recent times, seen clear instances of this: during the pandemic, governments, democratic and authoritarian alike, were able to consign millions of their citizens to a form of house arrest and impose severe and unprecedented restrictions on public gatherings and normal social interactions, with very little legislative scrutiny. While perhaps not a 'state of exception' or a sovereign dictatorship in the precise Schmittian sense,[1] the response of governments around the world to a public health emergency made visible the authoritarian core of state sovereignty that ultimately underpins any political regime.

In bringing to light the extra-legal dimension of sovereignty, Schmitt and the anarchists are concerned – albeit in different ways and to different, indeed opposite ends – with the problem of political theology. In other words, they aim to show that the authority of the law is not derived from its own internal system of norms and rules, but rests on other foundations – foundations that could, for better or worse, have theological sources. This takes us back to the problem of legal obligation and its seemingly impossible justification.

Why should one obey the law? Is there a normative reason for it? We have already discussed this question that is at the core of philosophical anarchism. If, as Montaigne said, law has a 'mystical foundation' – in other words the expectation that the law be obeyed *simply because it is the law* and for no other exterior reason – then we need to understand why this is so. Yet, any investigation of these 'mystical foundations' is likely to take us down dead ends and raise endless ambiguities and contradictions. If the law is based ultimately on power, or *force*, or the fear of punishment, then in what sense does it bind us *morally*? If, on the other hand, the law is founded on some pre-legal or natural conception of justice, or *right*, then how can this be articulated other than through the law itself; what meaning does it have outside the law?

As we have seen, Kelsen himself was forced to presuppose some hypothetical 'basic norm' as a kind of founding original principle that would form the underlying basis of the legal system; the law, as a supposedly self-referential system of norms, at the same time relied for its overall legitimacy on a grounding *Ur-norm* that was at once part of this order, yet also transcendent and determinative of it. However, for Kelsen *Grundnorm*, Ground-rule, is only a sort of transcendental epistemic category: it is just a determination, better a prefiguration of meaning, not of an existential source of justification or normative power. It is a rule the practising lawyer, and the legal scientist, had to presuppose if they want to give meaning to legal practice as legal. It is a presupposed, not a posed, rule – that is, a cognitive device, something close to Otto Vahinger's requirement of 'als ob', an 'as if', a fictive hypothesis.[2]

Considering the question of legal authority therefore immediately throws up a paradox. What is this authority based upon? Who actually founds the legal system and by what authority do they do so, given that the initial act of founding logically precedes any legal authorisation? The establishment of a legal order is therefore an act of sovereignty; it is a form of *self*-institution, or *autopoiesis*, a kind of creation *ex nihilo* that cannot, logically speaking, be authorised by the rules of the system it brings into being. Cornelius Castoriadis shares a similar ontology: there is no norm of the norm ('il n'est pas de norme de la norme'),[3] be it a preceding, prior positive rule or a strong normative, moral standard of justice. However, for Castoriadis, the self-creation of law is not the same as Schmittian decisionism; rather it is a collective enterprise that is, moreover, permanently open to being collectively contested and reviewed through the social imagination of citizens. It is not an *avant-garde*, or a strong leadership, that produces the law, as is the case for Schmitt. For Castoriadis, the production of law is a social adventure of the community as a whole.

The problem of foundation, in any case, points to the way that sovereignty can never be fully contained or captured within law, but always inhabits a place outside it. In this sense, sovereignty embodies a certain violence, or potential violence, an action outside the law, what Walter Benjamin would call 'law-making violence' (*rechtsetzend Gewalt*) – an issue that we will explore in greater detail in a later chapter. However, it is clear that this extra-legal dimension of sovereignty, which becomes present in founding or constituting moments of lawmaking, poses a major problem for legal theory. This chapter aims to explore this problem inherent in legal foundation. In doing so, it will consider two interrelated issues. First, the (auto)immunising function of the law – in other words, the way that the law is intended to protect individuals and communities from certain threats, yet, in doing so, ends up violating its own principles and risks destroying what it is intended to preserve. Secondly, we explore the problem of the revolutionary founding of a new legal-political order, or what is called constituting power; and the way that, in overthrowing one legal-political order and instituting a new one in its place, every revolution risks instantiating new forms of domination. Here we explore the specific anarchist response to this problem: a revolution that aims at the *dismantling* of the order of power and authority, and the creation of autonomous spaces and relations outside it, rather than its seizure and control.

(Auto)immunity

What is the function of the law? Within the liberal tradition, going at least back to Hobbes, the law, enforced by the sovereign ('covenants without the sword are but words, with no strength to secure a man at all'), protects the body politic and the individuals within it, securing them against violence. Indeed, law – determined by a sovereign who is at the same time above the law – is the conceptual border that separates the civil state from the state of nature, the condition of lawless anarchy where laws of nature exist but have no binding effect. The law, for Hobbes, guarantees the freedom of individuals from excessive interference by the actions of others.[4] For Locke, the law has a two-fold function: it protects individuals from one another, as well protecting the freedom of individuals and their natural rights from arbitrary incursions by government. Law thus imposed a constraint not only on the behaviour of individuals in relation to one another, but also on the power of the executive. That is why, for Locke, political absolutism, characterised by the absence of the rule of law, always veered towards tyranny and left the individual and the community defenceless against the arbitrary will of the sovereign: 'for if it be asked, what security, *what fence* is there, in such a state, against the violence and oppression of this absolute ruler? The very question can scarce be borne. They are ready to tell you, that it deserves death only to ask after safety.'[5] The law is thus a protective border, a 'fence' between individuals, and between the individual and the sovereign; in limiting and regulating behaviour, it also guaranteed freedom and indeed human survival itself.

Law thus immunises life against certain threats; it contains individuals and the community within a protective boundary, guaranteeing peaceful coexistence and the enjoyment of certain rights and freedoms. However, as it has been recently outlined, the paradox of this immunising function is that, just as a body's immune system protects itself against biological threats like viruses by incorporating these contaminants into its defence mechanisms, so the law 'contains an element of the same substance it is intended to defend against'.[6] This is why the law always bears an intimate relationship with violence: why the law has to in a sense incorporate violence, or potential violence, in order to ward it off; why Leviathan is only a concentration and accumulation of the anarchic violence that was once in the hands of individuals. We should not be surprised, then, that the enforcement of the law at times seems to exceed its legitimate boundaries and violate its own proclaimed principles; when the legal system, in liberal states, persecutes certain minorities and groups, protecting the rights of some while denying them to others. This shows us that in protecting us the law is also, at times, obliged to be predatory, to sacrifice the very rights and freedoms it is intended to preserve. This tension between the principles of the law and its actual effects is crystallised in the moment of exception where, as we saw, the application of the law in concrete situations is ultimately dependent upon the sovereign decision to suspend the legal order altogether in times of emergency, or upon an application of law that requires exceeding its formal boundaries and procedural constraints.

It may be that the gap between normal legal order and the sovereign exception is becoming more visible, that the gulf between law and power is widening – and this is perhaps what accounts for the crisis of legitimacy afflicting liberal democracies today. Increasingly violent protests and police response to protests, government lying, the violation of procedural norms, the bypassing of legislative checks and balances, and populist challenges to the independence of the judiciary are all signs of the waning of the symbolic authority of the law. This is an aspect of the condition we have referred to as ontological anarchy. Liberal democracies, defined by the rule of law, find themselves unable to manage their internal tensions and inconsistencies without at the same time violating their own principles and norms. Perhaps, as Derrida has argued, democracies have always been subject to autoimmune crises. Perhaps democracy's very nature as an open-ended, undetermined, 'anarchic' system of rule has a tendency towards its own self-destruction. After all, democracy must, if it is to remain a democracy, leave itself open to the risk of anti-democratic and authoritarian forces using the electoral system to get into power. Yet, if democracies try to protect themselves from their enemies with enhanced security measures, they risk shutting down the very thing they intend to protect.[7] The problem of autoimmunity is symptomatic of the paradoxical relationship between democracy and sovereignty. According to Derrida, democracy and sovereignty, while in some ways antithetical, are necessarily hinged together. While democracy is, on the one hand, a free regime in which anyone has the right to rule, it is at the same time a form of government (*kratos*). Democracy is, on the one hand, pluralistic and, on the other hand, an expression of the unified, singular sovereign 'will of the people' – a notion which, as we see today in the case of right-wing populism, has distinctly authoritarian connotations. This is the internal tension or *aporia* that democracy has, according to Derrida, always to reckon with. Our claim, as we will elaborate in a later chapter, is that democracy is not irretrievably attached to sovereignty; that it is possible to have forms of democratic decision-making without centralised authority, as we have seen in many political experiments in recent times, such as Occupy and other public assemblies and radical movements. Perhaps these can be seen as examples of what Derrida called the 'democracy to come' (*avenir*), whereby, in constantly radicalising itself, the practice of democracy 'deconstructs' sovereignty. Such democratic innovation is what we call anarchism.

Just as, for Derrida, democracy has an undecidable relationship with sovereignty, so the law has an undecidable relationship with *force*. The law, if it is to be applied, has to be enforced, something that implies a *potential* coercion or violence; and yet, this force is also what is at odds with the law, and which threatens to undermine its legitimacy and claims to justice. For Derrida, then, the difficulty that any critical analysis of the law must come to terms with is: 'What difference is there between, *on the one hand*, the force that can be just, or in any case deemed legitimate (not only an instrument in the service of law but the practice and even the realisation, the essence of *droit*) and, *on the other hand* the violence that one always deems unjust'.[8] In other words, how is it possible to distinguish between legitimate and illegitimate force?[9] Is it the law itself that determines the justness or legitimacy of certain types of force, and, if this is the case, then what is it that gives the law this 'monopoly', given that the law is itself is founded on a form of force which, insofar as it precedes the law, is neither legal nor illegal?[10] Derrida tries to disentangle these aporias between law and violence, and law and justice, through a reading of Benjamin's 'Critique of Violence'. As is clear, any critical questioning of legal authority – including and especially anarchism – must start with the enigma of the law's foundations. As Derrida says: 'For there is an authority – and so a legitimate force in the questioning form of which one might ask oneself whence it derives such great force in our tradition'.[11]

Revolution and the problem of foundations

Like deconstruction, the anarchist analysis of legal authority reveals the originary violence at the basis of the law. The state monopoly of violence does not mean a reduction of violence, its definitive or substantial taming, but an extreme concentration of the capacity of using violence in a way that it would overwhelm whatever private use of force. The mystifications of the social contract tradition only serve to obscure the violent accumulation of state power and the domination of social forces upon which all state-based legal systems are ultimately founded. Law acts to conceal and retroactively authorise this founding act of violence, incorporating it into its mechanisms of enforcement. In its critique of legal authority, anarchist theory seeks to make visible, as Foucault put it, 'the blood that has dried in the codes'.[12] This genealogical analysis of the law characteristic of anarchist theory thus renders the principle of legal authority at the very least undecidable and therefore open to legitimate ethical and political interrogation.

The indeterminacy of legal foundations becomes particularly acute in revolutionary situations, in which one legal order is uprooted and replaced by another. Revolutions, at least in the classical sense, are about wiping the slate clean, effacing all remnants of the previous social order and constructing legal and political institutions from the ground up. Arendt once said that revolutions confront us with the question of new beginnings.[13] Yet it is here, in this foundational moment between the old world and the new, that the authority of the law is revealed in all its ambiguity. After all, who actually has the authority to constitute the new legal order? On what legal basis does a revolutionary party or leadership remove one system of law, one constitution, and replace it with another? This is an act of sovereign self-authorisation which is only later authorised by the new constitution. Moreover, in whose authority does this revolutionary leadership claim to speak: is it in the name of the laws of nature, or the sovereign 'will of the people', and, if so, in what sense does it legitimately represent the people, given that 'the people' do not pre-exist the revolutionary constitution but are an *effect* of it? Anarchism has always regarded as problematic the idea of political representation: if 'the people' can only be represented or spoken for by another, this only reproduces hierarchy and domination. Even in a post-revolutionary society, the people are just as likely to be alienated by a new elite which claims to speak in their name while, in reality, serving its own interests. This is why anarchism has always had a preference for direct action and participation over political leadership and representation. The anarchist critique of representation applies to all forms of political organisation, from democratic political parties to revolutionary vanguards. However, the problem of representation goes deeper than simply the question of leadership. As Derrida asked, who actually signed the US Declaration of Independence in 1776: was it the framers of the document, like Jefferson, and those who claimed to be signing on behalf of 'the people'; or was it 'the people' themselves ['We the people" as the Declaration states]? Yet 'the people' in this sovereign, political sense were only brought into being by the Declaration:

> But these people do not exist. They do not exist as an entity, the entity does not exist before this declaration, not as such. If it gives birth to itself, as free and independent subject, as possible signer, this can hold only in the act of the signature. The signature invents the signer. This signer can only authorize him- or herself to sign once he or she has come to the end – if one can say this of his or her own signature in a sort of fabulous retroactivity.[14]

These ambiguities and difficulties refer to the question of *constituting* power: who or what has the authority to create a new political and legal order? The concept is central to the revolutionary tradition, and has been invoked by thinkers as diverse as Carl Schmitt and Antonio Negri.[15] According to its original formulation by Abbe Sieyès on the eve of the French Revolution, the *pouvoir constitutent* – which referred to the constitution-making authority of the people – was to be distinguished from the *pouvoir constitué* – referring to the established legal order. Because 'the people', existing as a pre-political 'nation', derived its authority from sources outside the legal order – namely from nature – it therefore had the legitimate power to change this order, to abolish it and to establish a new one in its place.[16] This idea is taken up by Schmitt in his understanding of constitutions. A constitution, he says, 'is not based on a norm, whose justness would be the foundation of its validity. It is based on a political decision concerning the type and form of its own being, which stems from its political being'.[17]

Once again in opposition to positive law theory, Schmitt argues that the legal order derives its authority not from its own internal norms, but from a force or will exterior to it, and which therefore has the authority to amend and even revoke and replace it. This constituting decision is the expression of the sovereign will of the people, although, in Schmitt's hands, this takes on decidedly anti-democratic and even theological connotations, essentially being modelled on the *potestas constituens* of God.[18] Moreover, as Schmitt argues, the constitution-making 'will of the people' is always unified and homogeneous, and is expressed not through deliberation and debate, but through simple endorsement, or *acclamation*: 'The people's constitution-making will always expresses itself only in a fundamental yes or no and thereby reaches the political decision that constitutes the content of the constitution'.[19]

This notion of acclamation is reminiscent not only of the rituals of Italian fascism in the 1920s, but, in more recent times, the Brexit referendum, in which the 'will of the people' – which was expressed purely in a binary decision ('a fundamental yes or no') – was seen to carry absolute political authority and had to be obeyed at all costs.[20] This notion of constituent power, as formulated by Schmitt, is strongly resonant today of the politics of authoritarian right-wing populism, in which the sovereign 'will of the people' – always seen as unified and homogeneous – is pitted against not only 'the elites' and minorities, but also against the very idea that democracy should represent a plurality of interests and uphold the rule of law. Indeed, Schmitt's conception of democracy – based on a rejection of parliamentary politics and liberal constitutional norms and procedures – is highly authoritarian and exclusionary; for Schmitt, democratic equality is premised on inequality, on the privileging of one group over others. In other words, democracy is reduced to the representation of 'the people' as a narrow, exclusionary identity; other groups and minorities (immigrants, cultural, religious or sexual minorities, for instance) are not, in the eyes of populists, genuinely part of the people.[21] Moreover, despite the claim made by Schmitt and other proponents of constituting power that 'the people' should be the sovereign and determining force, its political will is seen as best articulated through the singular figure of a leader who stands outside the established political system and challenges it.[22] In the contemporary politics of populism, the leader is strongly identified with 'the people'; he (or she) is of the people and yet transcends them, becoming, in this position of exceptionality, a pure and unmediated expression of their will. The constituent power represented – even if only in a superficial and highly manipulative way – by today's populisms, both right *and* left (notwithstanding their significant differences), contains an authoritarian dimension centred on a politics of sovereignty: the people (usually defined as the nation) as sovereign, constructed around the decisive will of the sovereign leader who, once in power, takes a wrecking ball to the rule of law.

Destituent power

We would suggest that the idea of the constitution-making will of the people – whether of the revolutionary or weaker populist variety – only reaffirms the order of power and authority that it apparently contests. This sort of politics is always a project of hegemony; its aim is not to dismantle power and authority but to either control the existing mechanisms of the state and executive authority, or to replace one order of power and authority with another. It falls into the trap of the *place of power* – or sovereignty – replicating its structures and its principle of authority. This is not to say, of course, that revolutions have not introduced important and worthwhile innovations, like individual rights, democratic citizenship, and forms of political, legal and social equality. However, they have also led, on other occasions, to new forms of domination and tyranny. At the very least, revolutions, even as they grant new rights and freedoms, lead to the inscription of the individual into a new order of power and law.

Is there another way to think about revolution? Can we imagine a form of radical transformation that does not seek to create a new sovereign political order but, rather, to radically decentralise power? What makes anarchism unique in the revolutionary tradition is that it proposes a form of political action that does not seek to capture state authority – as if such a thing can really be 'captured' – but rather to radically decentralise and democratise the social order, so that there is no more command-and-control structure. Of all the revolutionary political philosophies and movements, anarchism is the one that remains the most sensitive to the dangers of power. Power, particularly state power, is not simply a neutral instrument that can be used to transform and emancipate society if the right group or class is in control of it. Rather, power has its own logic, its own rationality, which always tends towards greater concentration and centralisation, and which is often beyond the means of individuals to control it. Of course, power is not an object or a 'thing' but merely a social relationship; however, *as* a social relationship, it forms and changes the subjectivity of those who participate in it.[23] This is especially the case with more hierarchically instituted structures of power, which tend to reproduce and intensify authoritarian desires – as well as submissive behaviours – in those caught within their networks. Thus, the revolutionary who seeks to capture power, to control the state, even though he or she aims to emancipate society, will inevitably become caught up in the state's rationality. As Bakunin put it: 'We of course are all sincere socialists and revolutionists and still, were we to be endowed with power ... we would not be where we are now'.[24]

This, of course, was the main point of contention between the anarchist and Marxist revolutionary traditions, a disagreement on revolutionary tactics that caused the split in the First International in 1876 and has divided radical politics ever since. While the Marxist and later, Marxist-Leninist, side of the proletarian movement believed that the state could be a tool of social transformation, at least in the 'transitional phase', if controlled by the working class led by the revolutionary vanguard, the anarchists (Bakunin, Kropotkin and many others) argued that the state itself, as a structure and mechanism of power, as a principle of authority, was the main obstacle to revolutionary progress and that it had to be dismantled. If it was not, state power would only reproduce itself in a revolution and would become entrenched, creating new class divisions and new forms of domination. Bakunin, for instance, argued that the Marxist program of the 'people's state' or the 'dictatorship of the proletariat' would only lead to new forms of dictatorship – to a new class of scientists, experts and technocrats governing the masses.[25] As he put it: 'They [Marxists] do not know that despotism resides not so much in the form of the State but in the very principle of the state and political power'.[26] And, in the words of Kropotkin, 'there are those who, like us, see in the State, not only its actual form and in all forms of domination that it might assume, but in its very essence, an obstacle to the social revolution'.[27]

Central to anarchism and to its critique of revolutionary theory is the notion of *prefiguration*. This is the idea that there is a direct relationship between the ends that one pursues and the means by which one pursues them. As the anarchist Errico Malatesta's used to say, if to win we have to set up the gallows in the public square, I would prefer to lose. In other words, if one wants to avoid instituting new forms of domination and violence – if one aims for an emancipated and free society – then one should not use authoritarian or violent means to achieve this. A highly centralised revolutionary party, prepared to seize power through violence, would only replicate the structure of power and would only lead to further violence. Rather, the form of society the revolutionary hopes to achieve should already be prefigured in the means, tactics and organisational structures employed to achieve it. Prefiguration is a rejection of all 'strategic' thinking; it is an ethical rejection of the idea that the means can be sacrificed to the ends, simply because the means become inseparable from the ends. Related to this is the emphasis, in anarchism, on the revolution in the *here and now*. In other words, rather than thinking of the revolution as a great, singular Event to come, that would transform the totality of social relations, we should pay attention to the myriad ways in which social relations are transformed in the immediate sense, in localised spaces and moments – at times dramatic and at other times seemingly mundane – and which can be found not only in political upheavals but in everyday interactions, relationships and organisations, involving voluntary agreements and cooperation between individuals at the community level. It is through attending to the these 'micro-political' events – which go on everywhere, all the time – that we might understand the anarchist concept of the social revolution, as opposed to the political revolution. Bakunin therefore talks about the revolution, not in terms of the seizure of the apparatus of power – which is what the political revolution aims at – but rather as the organisation of autonomous social forces 'outside and against the state'.

A solution to the seemingly intractable question of constituent power and its strong authoritarian implications is William Godwin's critique and re-elaboration of the concept of 'nation'. This – we know – was the substantive reference of constituent power already at the beginning of its theory and practice in the French Revolution. Nation is a pre-political entity that politics would find already formed and could assume as existentially valid: a homogeneous community capable of expressing a strong identity and subjectivity and its own conception of the good. Godwin criticises the idea of nation conceived in such terms, because he sees it as too arbitrary. According to such a romantic idea, nearly every possible social group could be a nation once it is able to be expressed in a myth of unity. This need not be agreed or discussed, but only emotively projected. And to do so, it must be presented as opposing or contrasting some outside, an eternal subject identified as a counterpart, as an alien, actually and finally as an enemy. Schmitt's doctrine of 'the political' – based on the friend – enemy opposition – radicalises this approach. The romantic idea of the nation – the one Sieyès refers to – would be, from Godwin's point of view, a sovereignty that is projected as the power of one group over another. In this perspective, the nation is in itself a project of domination. Against this approach Godwin proposes a different view of the nation: a constitution that explicitly rejects hierarchy and exclusion – an anarchist 'constituent' power. A nation is built, says the English philosopher, in so far as

> any number of persons who are able to establish and maintain a system of mutual regulation for themselves comfortable to their own opinions, without imposing a system of regulation upon a considerable number of others inconsistent with the opinions of these others, have a right, or, more properly speaking, a duty obliging them to adopt that measure.[28]

Here a political community is not formed by centring itself on the project of a state as a monopoly of violence, but rather on scheme of cooperation that is inclusive and that does not impose rules on people that they themselves have not made.

Today, in the time of the collapse of the revolutionary grand narrative, we need to rethink the classical idea of revolutionary action and what it aims to achieve. The state in advanced 'communicative' capitalist societies is no longer a completely centralised entity but rather a complex, hybrid, networked form of organisation, which penetrates into the depths of civil society, which is both localised and globalised, in which sovereignty is shared between political and economic bodies, and whose domain of operation is neither identifiably public nor private but somewhere in between. Here, the legal system plays an important role in redefining the state's field of operation and its relationship to society. Laws are shaped not only by legislators and the judiciary, but by a myriad of legal advocacy organisations, policy networks, NGOs and private sector organisations. This is not to say, of course, that this 'pluralisation' of the neoliberal state has meant that its repressive functions and coercive capacities have in any way been diminished; indeed, we could say that where the state recedes – particularly in terms of its traditional welfare functions – its policing and surveillance role expands and becomes more pervasive. Yet, sovereignty is much less clearly demarcated today. Moreover, revolutionary theory has for a long time had to grapple with the breakdown of traditional mass workers' movements and organisations. At the same time, after decades of neoliberal 'consensus' politics, we seem to have entered into a new crisis of legitimacy and a new period of hyper-politicisation, in which the political space, particularly in liberal democracies, is increasingly contested. Yet, this era of re-politicisation at the same time lacks any clear organising principle or even a coherent vision of a possible future, beyond simply reacting to an ever-growing sense of crisis.

This context makes it interesting to consider what a revolution might actually look like today. Can it still be thought of in terms of constituting power, in other words, the power to create a new constitution, a new legal-political order? Certainly, while some contemporary radical theorists like Negri invoke this idea, to refer to the self-authorising power of the 'multitude' – which at the same time would remain autonomous from any constituted legal order – this idea seems increasingly difficult to sustain. Rather, the types of movements and convergences we have been witness to in recent times – from democratic public assemblies,[29] to online digital dissidence,[30] to new 'viral' forms of protest against police violence, racism, ecological destruction, and Coronavirus restrictions[31] – necessitates a different way of thinking about political action. We will discuss some of these new forms of dissent, and their relation to legal authority, in a forthcoming chapter on civil disobedience – but it seems clear that they do not conform to the classical revolutionary model of politics. They are often leaderless, characterised by the absence of formal, centralised organisational structures – even though they have 'spokespeople' of various kinds – and they often have no fixed political programme, apart from a vague set of demands. Moreover, they are not hegemonic political projects in the sense that they do not seek to gain power, and indeed, they eschew the formal channels of political representation. In other words, in their decentralised, 'horizontal', even anonymous modes of interaction, communication and organisation, insofar they do not seek to capture the apparatus of power but to challenge it from the outside, they might be considered non-sovereign, 'anarchic' forms of politics.[32]

One way to understand these new forms of dissent is through an alternative notion of 'destituent' power.[33] Agamben draws a distinction between constituent and destituent power:

> If the fundamental ontological question today is not work but inoperativity, and if this inoperativity can, however, be deployed only through a work, then the corresponding

> political concept can no longer be that of 'constituent power' [potere constituente], but something that could be called 'destituent power' [potenza destituente] … A power that was only just overthrown by violence will rise again in another form, in the incessant, inevitable dialectic between constituent power and constituted power, violence which makes the law and violence that preserves it.[34]

For Agamben, the challenge of radical politics today is to think *beyond* the idea of projects or ends – a certain goal or telos that we should work towards – and rather in terms of a politics of *pure means*. This emphasis on means is in some ways close to the anarchist ethics of prefiguration, as discussed above, although we would suggest that prefiguration does not, at the same time, neglect the question of ends; on the contrary, it regards means and ends as inhering to one another. Agamben also makes the distinctly anarchist point that the violent revolution will only recreate the order of power, law and violence that it sought to overthrow; thus, constituent power always remains within the order of constituted power, that is, of legal authority. So, if destituent power is neither a politics of pure construction, nor pure destruction – which comes to the same thing – then what is it?

Destituent power is not the desire to change particular laws or government policies, but instead refuses the very legitimacy of the political-legal order by withdrawing support from it. Yet, as Raffaele Laudani argues, destituent power is also distinct from revolutionary action and cannot be seen simply anti-institutional:

> Despite carrying clear libertarian instances, destituent power is not anti-institutional per se, because, on the contrary, it makes the assumption of the nonartificial and ineradicable presence of power and its institutions. Its action is instead extrainstitutional, in the sense that unlike revolution and other forms of modern political action inspired by constituent power, it is not primarily motivated by an institutionalizing end.[35]

Destituent power, or action, is therefore neither institutional nor anti-institutional, but, rather, *extra*-institutional.

What does this mean exactly? The way we might interpret this is as a form of political and ethical action that is no longer enthralled to the logic of institutions. That is to say, it is *autonomous* from institutions, rather than simply being opposed to them. To simply reject institutions is, at the same time, to be caught within their grasp; it is to be dominated by institutional thinking, even in opposition to them. When he was once asked about what sort of alternative there could be to the current system – the eternal question of 'what replaces the system?' – Foucault replied: 'I think that to imagine another system is to extend our participation in the present system'.[36] We could also say that to imagine a form of society without 'institutions' – or to simply be opposed to institutions and to imagine that one can do away with them, which comes to the same thing – means that one remains enthralled to them. All forms of society, even anarchist societies, will have institutions of various kinds – that is to say, they will have rules, norms and systems for regulating behaviour. The question is how these institutions are designed, how coercive or otherwise they might be, how much autonomy and plurality they allow, and the degree to which they are genuinely open to modification, experimentation, and democratic control. In other words, anarchism – as opposed to some kind of naïve libertarianism – is not against institutions per se, even legal institutions, but simply against the sovereign and authoritarian principle that they are usually based on. Moreover, anarchists interact with institutions – including legal institutions – all the time. Anarchists become lawyers and legal and human rights activists; they work within current legal institutions to reform law, to ameliorate its effects, to try to make it less violent and punitive, to defend those who are its victims – all the while retaining a critical distance from the principle of legal authority and subjecting it to an ongoing ethical critique in the name of a greater sense of justice. So, being *extra-institutional*, as opposed to simply anti-institutional, means operating in liminal spaces, at the interstices of institutions and laws, using them in a pragmatic way while retaining an ethical distance from them; using the law against the state, even turning the law against itself.

Perhaps another way to think about this relationship of autonomy implied by this extra-institutional position, is through Max Stirner's notion of the 'insurrection' or 'uprising' [*Empörung*]. We usually associate 'insurrection' with a wild, disordered, spontaneous revolt or even with a violent campaign of resistance. However, Stirner has in mind here something very different. The insurrection is a form of ethical-political action which is, once again, neither about capturing political power, nor about destroying it, but rather about becoming *autonomous* from it, not being captivated by it. Here he draws an important distinction between insurrection and revolution:

> The Revolution aimed at new arrangements; insurrection leads us no longer to *let* ourselves be arranged, but to arrange ourselves, and sets no glittering hopes on 'institutions'. It is not a fight against the established, since, if it prospers, the established collapses of itself; it is only a working forth of me out of the established.[37]

Where the revolution works to transform external social and political conditions and institutions, the insurrection is aimed at the transformation of the *self*. It involves placing oneself *above* external conditions and constraints, whereupon these constraints disintegrate. It starts from the affirmation of the self, and the political consequences flow from this. The insurrection, unlike the revolution, works against the sovereign principle – but not necessarily in the sense of seeking to get rid of institutions, as this would lead simply to different kinds of institutions – but rather in the sense of asserting one's power over institutions. It suggests a way of unbinding ourselves from systems of power and our dependency on them, even our desire for them (it is a 'working forth of me out of the established'). We can see that this notion of insurrection is radically different from most understandings of political action. It eschews the idea of an overarching project of emancipation; freedom is not so much the end goal of the insurrection – although it often results in freer institutions – but, rather, its starting point, its ontological ground. In this sense, it is *ontologically anarchic*; it emanates from a radical indeterminacy that characterises subjectivity. So, rather than a revolutionary project which sets itself the goal of liberating people from institutionalised power – and which risks merely imposing upon them another kind of power in its place – the insurrection allows people to institute their own freedom by first reclaiming their own self. It has first of all an existential, or ethical, not a political meaning.

Anarchic foundations

It is at this point that we return to the question of foundations. Is there a way to think about political action, and even political and legal institutions, that avoids the problem of foundations – in other words, that avoids the sovereign principle of authority that grounds the idea of a legal order? Can we imagine forms of politics and law that are ontologically anarchic? In his reading of Claude Lefort's notion of 'savage democracy', philosopher Miguel Abensour relates this idea to Reiner Schürmann's 'anarchy principle', which, as we mentioned in the Preface, emerges out of Heidegger's deconstruction of Western metaphysics. For Schürmann, if we recall, the implication of Heidegger's notion of the 'closure of metaphysics' – the withering away of ontological foundations and first principles – is that action is no longer determined by an *arché*. Action becomes freed from the authority of a foundation that pre-determines its goals and telos; action, in other words, becomes contingent, anarchic. While, as Schürmann insists, this anarchic principle – action without a 'why' – is different from anarchism as a political ideology, we have endeavoured to show how ontological anarchy might be applied to a rethinking of all political categories, including that of anarchism itself. While once again expressing reservations about a direct political translation of the 'anarchy principle', Abensour seeks to develop, on the basis of this, an ontologically anarchic (we would say *anarch-istic*) conception of democracy, which he understands as 'democracy against the state'; in other words, a form of democracy which is contingent, undetermined by fixed principles, always reinventing itself, and which resists the sovereign principle of the One. He says: 'In its very movement, in its dynamic, does not savage democracy have something in common with anarchy, understood in the sense of action from the hold of foundations – from an *arché* – in the sense of a manifestation of an action 'without a why'?[38]

If democracy is 'against the state' in this sense, does this also mean that it is necessarily against laws, against legal institutions? Here, according to Abensour, anarchic democracy can actually be reconciled with a certain conception of law and legal institution. In reference to Lefort's reading of Machiavelli and the importance he attributes to social conflict in protecting and promoting liberty in the republic, Abensour says that 'one quickly discovers how a certain conception of law can cohere with a libertarian idea of democracy and in this way belong to an anarchic constellation, particularly considering that the laws in favour of liberty are not laws like others'.[39] Nor is it incompatible with a connection to a substantive idea of justice as equal concern among free and equal subjects. Abensour even goes as far as to suggest that 'law is "anarchic", devoid of an *arché* in the sense of having no origin or beginning'.[40] Anarchist legal theory, we would argue, needs to consider the possibility that not all laws are the same: that certain laws, deployed in certain ways, can actually be used to promote freedom, to protect the rights of individuals, to open up new spaces of autonomy and new anarchist forms of life. Taking the idea that the law itself is 'anarchic' – and thus that legal thinking and practice need not be bound to a sovereign principle or founding *arché* that determines their meaning and application – we might instead see legal institution as an ongoing form of experimentation, as a certain practice of freedom. The anarchic, or anti-foundational, principle that we see as central to anarchist legal practice is not therefore incompatible with institutions and laws. On the contrary, it entails a continual and ongoing project of autonomous and democratic institutional design. Abensour says about democracy that

> it is a particular form of political experience that gives itself political institutions, so that it may endure with efficiency. Yet, it simultaneously never ceases to rise against the State, and in such a way that its effervescent opposition has less to do with negating the political realm than with embodying, in a most powerful and paradoxical fashion, an incessant 'new disorder' that reinvents the political realm beyond the State, and even against it.[41]

We would make exactly the same point about legal anarchy. The anarchist revolution (or better insurrection) needs to create legal and political institutions if it is to sustain itself. Yet it is precisely in creating new legal institutions that it forms and maintains itself as an autonomous politics and an insurrectionary space. Anarchism is a theory and practice of *law against state sovereignty*.

Notes

1. While Agamben's initial reaction to restrictions imposed by the Italian government in response to the pandemic in early 2020 was perhaps somewhat exaggerated – provoking the allegation from critics that he was indulging in conspiracy theories – he nevertheless drew attention to the way that crises of various kinds are used to authorise unprecedented emergency measures and powers that would not normally be acceptable. See *Where are We Now?*
2. See O. Vahinger, *Die Philosophie des Als Ob*, Felix Meiner, Hamburg 1920.
3. See C. Castoriadis, 'La "polis" grecque et la création de la démocratie', in Id., *Domaines de l'homme*, Seuil, Paris 1999, p. 371.
4. This also has authoritarian consequences. For the German anarchist, Rudolf Rocker, 'According to Hobbes law and right are concepts which make their appearance only with the formation of political society, meaning the state. Hence the state can never transgress against law, because all law originates with itself' ('Nationalism and Culture' [1933] The Anarchist Library, https://theanarchistlibrary.org/library/rudolf-rocker-nationalism-and-culture).
5. John Locke, *Two Treatises of Government*, ed. P. Laslett, Cambridge: Cambridge University Press, 1988, p. 328.
6. Esposito, *Immunitas*.
7. See Jacques Derrida, *Rogues. Two Essays on Reason*, Stanford: Stanford University Press, 2005.
8. Jacques Derrida, 'Force of Law: The "Mystical Foundation of Authority"', in Drucilla Cornell et al. (eds.), *Deconstruction and the Possibility of Justice*, New York: Routledge, 1992, p. 6.
9. This was already Blaise Pascal's dilemma when thinking about the force of justice. 'Il faut, dit-on, recourrir aux lois fondamentaux et primitives de l'État, qu'une coutume

injuste a abolies. C'est un jeu sûr pour tout perdre; rien ne sera juste à cette balance.'

10. Derrida, 'Force of Law', p. 6.
11. Derrida, 'Force of Law', p. 6.
12. Michel Foucault, *Society must be Defended: Lectures at the College de France*, 1975–76, ed., Mauro Bertani and Alessandro Fontana, trans., David Macey, New York: Picador,
13. See Hannah Arendt, *On Revolution*, London: Penguin 1990.
14. Jacques Derrida, *Negotiations. Interventions and Interviews, 1971–2001*, ed., and trans., E. Rottenberg, Stanford CA: Stanford University Press 2002, pp. 49–50.
15. A. Negri, *Insurgencies: Constituent Power and the Modern State* (trans. Boscagli M). Minneapolis, MN: University of Minnesota Press, 1999. See also Lucia Rubinelli, *Constituent Power: A History*, Cambridge: Cambridge University Press, 2020.
16. As Sieyès says: 'To imagine a legitimate society, we assumed that the purely natural individual will had enough moral power to form the association; how then can we refuse to recognize a similar power in the equally natural common will? A nation is always in a state of nature and, amidst so many dangers, it can never have too many possible methods of expressing its will. Let us not be afraid of repeating it: a nation is independent of any procedures; and no matter how it exercises its will, the mere fact of its doing so puts an end to positive law, because it is the source and the supreme master of positive law ...' *What is the Third Estate?* [1789], p. 13.
17. Schmitt, *Constitutional Theory*, p. 125.
18. Ibid., p. 126.
19. Ibid., p. 132.
20. So much so that members of the judiciary in the UK, who were seen to frustrating the results of the referendum, were branded as 'enemies of the people'.
21. As Schmitt puts it: 'Every actual democracy rests on the principle that not only are equals equal but unequals will not be treated equally. Democracy requires, therefore, first homogeneity and second – if the need arises – elimination or eradication of heterogeneity'. *The Crisis of Parliamentary Democracy*, p. 9.
22. Ibid., pp. 16–17.
23. This is why, as the anarchist Gustav Landauer put it, 'It [the state] can be destroyed by creating new social relationships'. See *Revolution and Other Writings: A Political Reader.*

Edited and Translated by Gabriel Kuhn. Oakland, CA: PM Press, 2010, p. 214.

24. Mikhail Bakunin, *Marxism, Freedom and the State*, trans. K. J. Kenafick (London: Freedom Press, 1950), 47.
25. Bakunin, *Political Philosophy*, p. 287.
26. Ibid., p. 221.
27. Kropotkin, *The State*, p. 9.
28. W. Godwin, *Enquiry Concerning Justice and Its Influence on Modern Morals and Happiness* (3rd ed., 1798), ed. I. Kramnick, Penguin, Harmondsworth 1985, pp. 262–263.
29. See, for instance, Judith Butler, *Notes Towards a Performative Theory of Assembly*, Cambridge Massachusetts and London: Harvard University Press, 2015.
30. Geoffroy de Lagasnerie, *The Art of Revolt: Snowden, Assange, Manning*, Stanford CA: Stanford University Press, 2017.
31. See Donatella di Cesare, *The Time of Revolt*, Cambridge: Polity Press, 2021.
32. We do not say, however, that they are 'anarchist' as such, mostly because they do not have a specific ideology; indeed, they might be considered 'post-ideological'.
33. The theme of destituent power or destituent action, as elaborated by a number of thinkers, is strongly influenced by the anarchist tradition. For a useful summary of different approaches to destituent power, see also Hostis, 'Destituent Power: An Incomplete Timeline', The Anarchist Library (November 1 2020): https://theanarchistlibrary.org/library/hostis-destituent-power-an-incomplete-timeline.
34. Giorgio Agamben, 'What is a Destituent Power (or Potentiality)?' trans., Stephanie Wakefield, *Environment and Planning D: Society and Space* 2014, volume 32, 65–74.
35. R. Laudani, *Disobedience in Western Political Thought: A Genealogy*, Cambridge: Cambridge University Press, 2013, pp. 4–5. See also Frédéric Gros, *Disobey! A Guide to Ethical Resistance*, trans., David Fernbach, London and New York: Verso, 2020.
36. See interview with Michel Foucault, 'Revolutionary Action: "Until Now"' in *Language, Counter-Memory, Practice*, ed., Donald Bouchard (Oxford: Basil Blackwell, 1977) pp. 218–233.
37. Stirner, *Ego and its Own*, pp. 279–280.
38. Abensour, *Democracy against the State*, p. 113.
39. Ibid., p. 122.
40. Ibid., p. 122.
41. Ibid., p. 123.

Six

Still a Cold Monster? On the Dual Nature of the State

An anarchistic rethinking of legal institutions – as discussed in the preceding chapter – might also lead us to a more careful reflection on the nature of the state as a political entity. What exactly do we mean by the state? Is it *only* an institution of sovereign domination, hierarchy and accumulation of violence, and therefore an entity to be destroyed, or can it take on a different connotation, as referring to a form of political community in which people freely determine their own rules and laws in the absence of sovereign authority? As we will seek to demonstrate in this chapter, there is a certain ambiguity on the meaning of the state, even within the anarchist tradition. Certainly, while most classical anarchists defined the state as a wholly oppressive institution, Proudhon, as we shall see, proposed an alternative account of the state as an institution of social solidarity and civic participation – a form of political community without sovereignty. Is it possible for anarchism to reclaim the meaning of the state, to redefine it in non-sovereign terms, as, instead, a political space – or series of spaces – that promotes free public deliberation, social justice and human autonomy and plurality? In broaching this question, anarchism distinguishes itself from libertarianism or 'anarcho-capitalism', which is defined simply in opposition to the state as a public space, and is not against other forms of domination and coercion that exist in the private sphere – for instance in the market and in relations of private property. In being simply 'anti-state', right-wing libertarians are concerned with limiting the capacity of public institutions to interfere with the private space of the market and the relations of exploitation that inhere within it.[1] By contrast, anarchism is much more attuned to the multiple forms of domination, violence, exclusion and structural hierarchy and inequality existing in *all* spheres of life, in both the private and public realms. It is therefore not entirely accurate to characterise anarchism as *simply* anti-state. Rather, anarchism is *anti-domination*.[2] This does not mean, of course, that anarchism is not concerned with the risk of domination inherent within the public space, in the realm of laws and institutions – quite the contrary – but this risk, it might be argued, results from the sovereign principle on which they are typically founded, rather than from the idea of a collective public space itself. This is why most anarchists would defend certain public institutions and state functions, such as the provision of welfare, publicly funded health care and public housing against their neoliberal rollback, while at the same time attacking the more coercive elements of the state, such as the police, the judicial and penal system, and the military. In other words, there is within anarchism a certain ambivalence on the question of the state in modern societies, thus inviting further reflection on its meaning and function.

The question of the state

The question of the state is central to political and philosophical anarchism. This is because it is an entity that claims to have a right to our obedience, a right that is absolute. Its commands should be obeyed without exception. Thus, a state is the form of social organisation that is seen to conflict with anarchist values and ideas. A state, as a structured and institutionalised organisation, is in tension with a form of life that projects itself as permanently changing and changeable. A political community is only really free, it is argued, if its members have a permanent right to redefine and modify the community's basic rules. Anarchism envisages a political community as the outcome of the mutual recognition of individuals and of the agreement about a common scheme of cooperation. Subjective autonomy here is the bedrock of political order, which can respond to people's evolving needs and circumstances. A different elaboration of this idea of autonomy conceives of institutions as only legitimate if they are not detached from their instituting moment, from their original, societal source. This instituting moment is the well-spring of autonomy, and cannot be captured by the established institution. In this way, what is institutional is constantly exposed to contingency and to the inventiveness of the social imagination, that is, collective autonomy.[3]

Contrary to this autonomous model of social relations, the state seems to embody a quite rigid form of institutionalisation that does not allow for adjustment and modifications according to the needs and will of people. It is based, it would seem, on domination, violence and hierarchy, such that freedom is permanently denied to citizens. It claims a value in itself superior to the dignity and autonomy of the individual. Individuals' basic goods, life, property, honour, respect, liberty, might all be sacrificed on the altar of the state. It is a 'person' in itself that is more than the association of its members and even of its officials or rulers. It can demand everything from its 'subjects', including their own death, be it in war or on a scaffold. As Nietzsche once characterised it, the state is a 'cold monster'.

However, the question of state, of its legitimacy and form, is not just a concern for anarchism, but might plausibly be considered as nearly the whole business of political and legal philosophy. Our entire life is experienced within the confines of the state. We are born and immediately we are registered as members, nationals of a state. Our everyday lives are determined by state rules and instructions. We live within state borders, we are brought up to sing a national anthem and salute a national flag. We are under state supervision and control from birth to death. If we infringe the state's rules and instructions, we are sent to state prisons or we have to pay state fines. A substantive part of our income is every year taken by the state in the form of taxes, which is spent in ways over which we have little or no control.

The nature of the state

What is the state? What is its nature? How could we define it? Max Weber famously defined the state as a monopoly of violence. In his *Politik als Beruf*, 'Politics as Vocation' (1922), we read that the state is 'that human community that (successfully) claims the *monopoly of the legitimate use of physical force* within a given territory'.[4] This does not mean that violence is the ordinary means by which the state acts; yet, according to Weber, it is what gives the state its specificity, what ultimately defines it in the last instance. It is what gives its nature.[5] Weber's idea is further developed by Carl Schmitt, according to whom a state is, rather, the monopoly of *decision*, meaning an exception to the 'normality' of rule of law.[6] This monopoly of decision refers to the sovereign's capacity to violate the law, a capacity that would potentially imply an exceptional use of force.

But the question remains: What is a state? Legal philosophy and legal theory have usually given two main answers to this question, once again testifying to the dual nature of the state, and the ambiguity of its grip on our society and imagination. The key to the understanding of the state here is seen in its connection to law. What is law for the state, or vice versa, what is the state for the law? Here two opposed visions are confronted. First, we have an approach according to which the state is an extralegal entity, a body able to act collectively, which is hierarchically structured with a commander-in-chief at its highest rank. A state, according to this account, is either a sovereign power that can impose obedience on others – a 'political superior' in John Austin's words – or else a kind of community, a historical society that is the expression of a specific national, cultural, or temporal context, an embodiment of an 'objective mind'. This is the account of Hegel and German Historicism. In both cases the state is prior to the law, it is the 'source' of law, and the efficacy of law is indeed limited in shaping the essentials of the state. The state operates legally by an act of self-limitation. This is the influential idea of George Jellinek, one of the founding fathers of European continental public law. This conception has relevant implications for the way we would then understand constitutionalism and the nature of a constitutional state. In this essentialist approach, the state is not the product of a constitution. The latter can only give some form to it; it offers formalisms of various kinds to its operation, formalisms, however, that can be dismissed when necessary. There is a continuity of the state that constitutions cannot alter – such is also the public international law conception of the state. The basic nature of the state remains the same whichever constitution is then adopted. Fundamental rights do not have constitutive validity, but serve rather as regulative rules. Fundamental rights here can never be rooted in original natural freedoms of citizens or in their basic moral dignity. Georg Jellinek understands public rights as being founded upon an individual's position of absolute subjection to authority, *status passivus*.[7] Fundamental rights are then negative rights, entitlements against state intervention. They cooperate vertically between authority and autonomy. In this view, however, a constitution could hardly claim *Drittwirkung* or 'efficacy towards third parties'; constitutional rights, being only active against the state, would not apply to private relationships and transactions. Constitutional law would only deal with the state's external conduct, without being able, for instance, to penetrate and impinge upon the market or on labour relations.

However, there is an alternative doctrine, according to which the state and the law are not of a different ontological quality. This is explicitly vindicated by Immanuel Kant, for whom the state is a collective entity that is structured through legal rules 'A state is … an association of a mass of people through rules of law'.[8] Kant's view is then radicalised by Hans Kelsen. A state, he claims, cannot be understood, nor can it act, without referring to rules. And within the state rules are equivalent to legal rules. There is no possibility of conceiving of a state from any other perspective once we assume the internal point of view of its agents. This is the legal perspective. The consequence of such approach is that every state is seen as a *Rechtsstaat*, a legal state.[9] The authority of the law and the authority of the state are one and the same thing. This thesis, however, does not have *prima facie* strong legal philosophical or political implications. In Kelsen's view, the ontology of state is based on force, not really on law. Nonetheless, the substantive emptiness, the radical formalism, of this approach contrasts with any attempt to offer an essentialist or naturalist picture of the state. This explains why Kelsen's picture of state was so strongly opposed by nationalists and communitarians, both on the right and the left.

On the other hand, the Austrian scholar's approach allows for the idea that sovereignty is simply another name for a valid legal order, and that law can be perfectly impersonated through supranational institutions. In the end, Kelsen's message is that law is independent of the state as a specific sociological formation, or alternatively that a state is just another name for any valid legal order. Here the duality of the state, its being, on the one hand, a historical community, a special sort of society, and on the other a formal, hierarchical structure defined by rules and procedures, is solved – as noted by Gustav Radbruch, the German legal philosopher – by simply denying that this is a problem. There is no solution to the dilemma of the dual nature of the state, only a denial of the problem, which is seen as arising from an unclear or mistaken epistemological strategy. The only cognitive point of view concerning a state is the internal, legal perspective. Beyond this, or without this, there is confusion and inappropriate essentialism or even mysticism – as happens, for instance, whenever the state is interpreted with reference to an impersonal soul or a collective destiny, and is filtered through a philosophy of history or a too thick social ontology.

But is Kelsen's thesis sufficient for understanding what a state really is? We have reason to doubt it. The Austrian scholar does not ignore the coercive side of the state practice, and, indeed, according to him, a legal order is a coercive system, and legal norms are ultimately about sanction and coercion. But the nature of the law cannot plausibly be reduced to coercion, nor can it explain the state and its operations and validity. Otherwise, a bandit's order, a rule by desperados, gangsters, or mafia, would be indistinguishable from law. Or we could envisage Auschwitz as an institution of law. Incidentally, according to Kelsen, validity, *Geltung*, is the specific form of the existence of both law and state. The state is more than just a monopoly of violence. There is a drive towards order and the structured regulation of conducts. The state thus is a *legal* monopoly of violence, where the legal attribute is what gives the state its specific nature and ontological justification.

However, is this reference to legality a sufficient guarantee for constraining the violence of state sovereignty? This is debatable. In the end here the factual prevails. This is explicit in Kelsen's admission that the basic ground rule of the legal order is the efficacy principle, one that is recurrent in public international law. Such an admission suggests that states are legitimate legal subjects of international law, ones that deserve recognition by the international community, in so far as they are powers that have full effective control within a specific territory. In this way we are taken back to Jellinek's idea of the 'normative force of the factual', *normative Kraft des Faktischen*,[10] so that the fact of authority is a sufficient condition for the claim to produce law; a claim quite close to the Pascal's recommendation that, since we cannot make justice powerful, we should aim to make the powerful just: 'Ne pouvant fortifier la justice, on a justifié la force'.[11]

Yet, is this coherent with the notion of the state as a civilising actor in society? This is not the view of the great legal historian Hermann Kantorowicz. According to the German scholar, to presuppose the state as prior to law would not necessarily allow us to give legal character to the rules, for instance, of international law or customary law. Constitutional law would also be impaired by this priority given to the state as the primordial source of law. As Kantorowicz says:

> We must not, as many do, consider the law a creation of the state, a theory, which would be incompatible with the existence of customary law, of canon law, and of international law. On the contrary, the State presupposes the law – international or national law – and this idea is borne out by the history of jurisprudence, which shows that no concept of the State has ever been formed that did not imply some legal elements.[12]

A self-limited power?

This was also the view of Gustav Radbruch, a friend and a colleague of Kantorowicz at the University of Kiel. Radbruch was a legal positivist and a strong legalist. He uses Jellinek's doctrine of the self-limitation of the state as a starting point. Law is the outcome of a self-limiting act. But law's efficacy is conditioned to an application of the rule that is universally undertaken. A self-limitation on the part of law means that law is applicable to the state itself. Of course, in this perspective, there is a state before a law. But the state's claim to make law – and this is a necessary evolutionary move for the state to develop its grip on society – is only possible under the condition of a law that is generally applicable, that is, applied to the state itself. Law does not provide an exception for the state. A state without a law is illegal and thus illegitimate. By contrast, a legal state, a *Rechtsstaat*, is, according to Radbruch, a state that raises a claim to justice. However, the question is intricate, and the legal positivism that Radbruch upholds makes things less clear and promising. Radbruch maintains the idea of a sovereign power that imposes, possibly by coercion, its own rules, with the justification that it has supreme authority, understood in factual terms as violence and the monopoly of force.

Legal positivism – the doctrine according to which the law's validity is not necessarily connected with justice, or morality – is a theory especially designed to justify the rise of the modern state. In the philosophy of law, legal positivism has been identified along three distinct versions. We have first a doctrine that claims the state is the only source of the law. This is sometimes also called the 'source thesis': the law is to be known just by looking at what an authority, that is a state, *says* the law is. This thesis is made plausible through the adoption of two more basic versions of positivism.

The first is the so-called 'methodological positivism': it is possible – according to this version – to know what valid law is in a descriptive, purely cognitive sense. This might be considered an epistemological rehearsing of the 'source theory'. There is somewhere a source of law. I approach it, I see it, I record it, and this is all I need to know what law is. I do not need to assume a normative attitude. I can be, I *should* be, neutral. I should only repeat the law. An Italian positivist legal philosopher, Uberto Scarpelli, used to say that legal rules are a reiteration of the sovereign's prescriptions.[13] A lawyer should only learn them, possibly by heart, indeed to 'sing' them ('cantar', as it is required for instance in Spain to pass the exam for judges), and repeat such rules over and over again. Why should the law be experienced in this way? There is a permanent conflict over what the rules of society should be. Such conflict is irresoluble from the point of view of a substantive morality. This is so, especially because notions of right and wrong are relative and cannot be cognitively approached. There is no right answer in an absolute moral sense. What is 'right', then, cannot but be the outcome of a decisionist action, undertaken by a figure that has the authority, the force, that can use the necessary violence, to impose the one solution that ends the controversy. And we need this authority if we want to live in peace and coordinate our conduct effectively.

A more oblique version of this normative positivism is offered by the 'service conception' of the authority developed by Joseph Raz,[14] whereby authority is justified in so far that it is of service to individuals' preferences and life plans. Authority rules are second-order reasons that replace first-order reasons – individual preferences generally – in so far as such preferences are better satisfied if those second-order reasons, authority rules, are followed. People would be better off, according to the claim of the 'service conception', by following authority rules than by trying to directly realise their individual preferences. Here the argument is presented as if it were a logical or even ontological claim. Since the law is something that claims authority, it does presuppose such authority, that is, a coercive power capable of imposing its prescriptions; this is the nature of law. It is a kind of ontological proof of the authoritarian nature of law. It reminds us of the medieval ontological proof of the existence of God: since God claims to be holding all properties, He should also have the property, the quality, of existence. 'Existence' is considered an adjectival quality such as 'goodness'. Now, in the same way as we assume that God is good, we should then also acknowledge that He owns 'existence', once we move from the basic idea that God is holder of all possible positive qualities. The authoritarian nature of law is deduced in a similar way. Behind such ontological proof of authority as the nature of law, there is a theory of the reason we have for action. In this case the argument runs more or less as follows: authority, issuing preemptive, second-order reasons for action, is able to give first-order reasons for action (individual preferences, and basic interests) greater satisfaction or a more effective realisation. First-order reasons are better placed to be realised if they are assisted by second-order reasons.[15]

But – and this is the gist of the argument – such assistance is equivalent to replacement, to preemption. Assisting individual preferences means authority replacing them through the authority prescriptions. Second-order reasons replace first-order reasons, and it is good that is so. To do that, however, there should be an authority issuing those second-order reasons, thus preempting first-order reasons. In order to follow and obey authority rules – second-order reasons – individuals should forget about their first-order reasons, in other words, their preferences, needs and desires. This, in a sense, is what also constitutes the state as such, its primordial 'coup d'état' – that is, the state's 'official' reasons supplanting citizens' 'private' reasons.[16] Authority makes people better off, and this is only possible if people, in following the authority of rules, give up the relevance and even the content of their first-order reasons, that is, their interests, needs, preferences. Before rules as second-order reasons – that is as authority commands – we are asked to forget the underlying good these reasons are supposed to assist and realise.

That a contemporary natural lawyer like John Finnis shares an analogous view of authority is evidence of the deep influence enjoyed by positivism over the whole of legal culture. Indeed, Finnis's view seems more radical than the one defended by Raz. According to the natural law thinker, legal validity at the end of the day is built upon the 'perhaps too stark principle' (Finnis' words)[17] of effective force. Once again, normativity is related here to the supreme capacity of a fact, *normative Kraft des Faktischen*. The state is a rule that is opaque in relation to people's desires and motives. This core thesis of positivism is also reflected and re-elaborated from different perspectives. Such is the case, for instance, of system theory, which thematises legal norms as expectations that are not open to disappointment – as is suggested by Niklas Luhmann.[18] Even disobedience to a rule, the fact that it is not followed, only affirms the existence of a rule. A state's legal rule therefore is valid, even if it is not repeatedly followed.

Not surprisingly, Radbruch, being a legal positivist, defends something of a similar tenor. His first move is recognising that legal positivism bases itself on a natural law assumption. He argues that if there is a supreme holder of force, whatever this prescribes ought to be followed.[19] But why? The answer here is given through an appeal to the highest value of legal security. It is only by obeying the supreme holder of violence and force that we can reach certainty about a common rule for society to follow. However, the same legal security principles oblige the state, the supreme force holder, to abide by the same law he has issued; the same intuition that connects legal certainty and state legislation leads to the idea of the rule of law binding the state.[20] Should the supreme legislator *not* be bound to his own commands and rules, his power would cease to be legitimate and would not be able to claim obedience. But law here is more than just any rule, statute, or command. Law is the only rule that can claim to be just.[21]

State as caring for the common good: an anarchist alternative

Legal positivism tends to obscure the dual nature of law and the state. From this perspective, authority is the core of law and the state. And behind authority lurks the experience of the monopoly of violence understood as the utmost possible force deployable. However, Radbruch, as we have seen, proposes a richer concept of law and legality, connected as this is to justice. He makes positivist reductionism less plausible, and opens up the possibility of an alternative theory. This alternative, surprisingly enough, was openly affirmed by the anarchist thinker, Proudhon.

We are used to thinking that anarchism is a doctrine that radically opposes the state. Indeed, for most anarchist thinkers the state is irremediably considered a form of violence and domination. This is certainly the position of contemporary anarchists like David Graeber. In his work on the history of debt, Graeber refers to the state not as a specific political form related to modernity, but rather as a notion to explain and name all forms of centralised power and authority in human history.[22] This approach is later confirmed in his general political anthropology of human societies, the *The Dawn of Everything*.[23] In this perspective there are states in Ancient Mesopotamia and Egypt, as well as in the Inca and Aztec societies in pre-Columbian America. The Roman city is here held to be a state, and so on. The qualifying character of a state is assumed to be its use of violence and the reduction of people in principle to slaves, to subjects who are fully disposable by power holders.

This is also the view of the anarchist Kropotkin, whose book on *The State* centres on the hypothesis of this political form as an outcome of sheer violence and oppression.[24] Kropotkin's view is that the roots of the state are to be found in war, and in the surrender and humiliation of the vanquished and conquered. Max Stirner had already declared that whoever has the power, will also have the right.[25] Thus, law is an accessory, a tool of the state for enforcing its power.

However, there is an anarchist thinker who has a more nuanced and sophisticated understanding of the state. Proudhon considers the state from two alternative perspectives. We can see the state simply in terms of the monopoly of violence, without any claim to justice, or if there is, it plays the role of mere ideological fiction. Here, force and violence are the definitional properties for a state. However, there is another sense of the state, which is both less formal and less purely empirical, and that is a state as the dimension of the public affairs, of common good, 'res publica'.[26] The common good is another name for the justice of political life, for the public morality of collective institutions. Politics is acting in concert not for its own sake, but in view of a general satisfaction of citizens, that is, of the common good. This makes politics different from private agreements, contracts, and market transactions. This is also what differentiates a political community whose aim is the good life of all concerned, and in a more general sense of human life as a whole, from companies or other associations, whose purpose is the realisation of a specific, particular aim. In this sense, a state, as a place where politics is performed as collective action, might be seen as a sphere where individuals are no longer considered isolated subjects, stripped of their social context, of their intersubjective attachments, of the reciprocity of commitments that makes up their identity. In this arena, the public is equivalent to reciprocity and solidarity. The state's *locus* is public morality, or the common good; in Hegel's jargon: the state, in itself and for itself, is the whole.[27]

Michael Oakeshott seems to follow Proudhon's suggestion when he proposes two possible declinations of the idea of state: one that he calls *societas*, the other *universitas*. *Universitas'* main character is its purposiveness, its instrumental strategic determination, whenever associates are driven by a uniform external target. *Societas*, on the other hand, refers to a mode of internal discursive recognition and conversation. Oakeshott then adds that modern states are at times an incoherent, mixture of both models.[28]

We could nonetheless hope that one model, the more civilised one, that of the state as public sphere and discourse, might eventually prevail. Here, in Proudhon's conception, the state is reshaped in terms of an institution of social solidarity and civil conversation, an expression of the participation of all citizens.[29] Here justice, moreover, assumes a strong redistributive turn by at the same time referring it to the citizen's sovereignty.[30] In this second view of the state, as an institution of public discourse and solidarity, there are no commands and subjection as original positions, and they do not have definitional character; rather, what is essential is engaging with commitments and agreements. Authority is here prompted by citizenship and participation. First-order reasons take the upper hand over the second-order state precepts. Law is referred back to considerations of justice, and thus to the collective solidarity of people that acknowledge each other's basic needs, rights, and virtues.

Now, what is the conception of the state most conducive to democracy and social justice? It is obvious that we are in need of a richer notion of state that might remain open to the question of its possible dual nature and the meeting of requirements that such duality mobilises. The COVID-19 pandemic has shown us the extent to which the common good is a question of care, and how effective care can only be provided by a public institution.[31] We might thus refer to the state as *a public institution of care*. We would then expect a concept of law, accompanying this civilised form of state, which is fully and permanently accountable to citizens' first-order reasons.[32]

In this way, we get an understanding of the state that anarchists could claim as their own. But this would be very different from our more familiar understanding of the state as an instantiation of sovereignty, of ultimate law-making authority and the unquestioned use of force. Rather, an 'anarchist state', if we can use such a term, refers to a dimension of the common good, a public sphere that is instrumental for individuals to make effective their personal projects of the good life and where they act in concert to experience the pleasure of participation in a common scheme and project. The good life would remain the business of each person. There is no other way to have a good life other than from the internal perspective of the person whose good life is the question. No one else can know what is really good for oneself. A good life is a life that one has the capacity and the means to project and conduct oneself. Pursuing a good life also means that one is ethically responsible for it. A public sphere cannot preempt this basic reference to the autonomy of the individual. Rather, it should protect and enable individual life plans. In this sense, a state could be reshaped as such a guarantee and eventually be considered as an institution that anarchism could reasonably and legitimately claim without denying its own normative core. This is maintained by the refusal of hierarchy, inequality and domination. An anarchist state – if that is not too paradoxical a term – would thus be a public sphere comprising persons endowed with equal dignity, each given the capacity to pursue their project of life, without submitting to any other rule than the one commonly and freely agreed.

Conclusion

A general criticism and rejection of the state seems to be the core of the anarchist theory of politics.[33] This – as we have tried to argue – might be reconsidered. In his lectures on the birth of biopolitics and neoliberal governance at the end of the 1970s Michel Foucault astutely observed how a general critique of the state was unsatisfactory.[34] This was based on several argumentative fallacies. One of these is a generalisation of the state's historical capacity for evil. Since there was Auschwitz, and the state was responsible for Auschwitz, the state is characterised by a permanent tendency towards totalitarian domination and violence; the permanent destiny of the state is the camp, as Giorgio Agamben rather hyperbolically maintains.[35] Yet, a national health system is also an aspect of the state, but this cannot be equated with a practice of extermination or even with coercion.[36] Such a position, according to Foucault, is only possible as a result of an insufficient, reductionist and totalising account of the state, one that was blind to its complexity and genealogy. Institutions are complex collective entities which obey distinct functional motives. To understand them properly we should be able to differentiate distinct institutional functions and modes of action. A general, unnuanced rejection of the state would not give us the best means for such an understanding. It would also oversimplify the critique of domination that is really at the heart of the anarchist position on the state. Adopting Proudhon's more nuanced approach to this question maintains, on the one hand, the anarchist critique of political sovereignty and domination, without at the same time sacrificing the collective good and the public functions instrumental to the flourishing of the good life.

Notes

1. The libertarian or 'anarcho-capitalist' approach to law regards law not as a public good but as a private good determined by the market. See, for instance, Bruce Benson, *The Enterprise of Law: Justice without the State*, Oakland, CA: The Independent Institute, 2011.
2. It is here that anarchism finds some resonance with a certain form of republicanism, a theory whereby the threat to freedom comes not so much – or not exclusively – from limitations and regulations imposed by public institutions but, more so, from the risk of domination and arbitrary interference inherent in all hierarchical power relationships, whether public or private. For an analysis of anarchism and republicanism, see Ruth Kinna and Alex Prichard, 'Anarchism and Non-Domination', *Journal of Political Ideologies*, 24(3) 2019: 221–240.
3. Cf. C. Castoriadis, *Pouvoir, politique, autonomie, in Id., Le monde morcelé*, Seuil, Paris 2000, pp. 137 ff.
4. M. Weber, *Gesammelte Politische Schriften*, ed. by J. Winckelmann, Mohr, Tubingen 1980, p. 506. Italics in the text.
5. 'Gewaltsamkeit ist natürlich nicht etwas das normale oder einzige Mittel des Staates: – davon ist keine Rede –, wohl das ihm spezifische' (ibid.).
6. Schmitt, *Political Theology*.
7. See G. Jellinek, *System der subjektiven öffentlichen Rechte*, Mohr, Tübingen 1905.

8. ('Ein Staat ... ist die Vereinigung einer Menge von Menschen unter Rechtsgesetzen'): I. Kant, *Metaphysik der Sitten*, ed. by H. Ebeling, Reclam, Stuttgart 1990, p. 169.
9. 'Er muss zu der Erkenntnis führen, daß *jeder Staat Rechtsstaat ist*', H. Kelsen, *Der soziologische und juristische Staatsbegriff*, II ed., Mohr, Tubingen 1929, p. 191.
10. See G. Jellinek, *Allgemeine Staatslehre*, III ed., Wissenschaftliche Buchgesellschaft, Darmstadt 1960, p. 337. Jellinek's thesis however is presented as a psychological finding, rather than as a normative argument (see ibid., pp. 339 ff.).
11. Pascal, *Pensées*, ed. by M. Le Guern, Gallimard, Paris 1977, p. 94.
12. H. Kantorowicz, 'The Concept of the State', *Economica*, No. 35, February 1932, pp. 5–6.
13. See U. Scarpelli, *Le 'proposizioni giuridiche' come precetti reiterati*, in 'Rivista internazionale di filosofia del diritto', Vol. 44., 1967, pp. 465–482.
14. See J. Raz, *The Morality of Freedom*, Oxford University Press, Oxford 1986.
15. See J. Raz, *The Authority of Law*, Oxford University Press, Oxford 1979.
16. Cf. P. Bourdieu, *Sur l'État. Cours au Collège de France 1989–1992*, Raisons d'agir/Seuil, Paris 2012, p. 123.
17. J. Finnis, *Natural Law and Natural Rights*, Clarendon, Oxford 1980, p. 250.
18. See N. Luhmann, *Rechtssoziologie*, II ed., Westdeutscher Verlag, Opladen 1983, p. 43.
19. G. Radbruch, *Rechtsphilosphie*, ed. by R. R. Dreier and S. L. Paulson, Heidelberg 1999, p. 172.
20. 'Der selbe Gedanke der Rechtsicherheit, der den Staat zur Gesetzgebung beruft, verlangt auch seine Bindung an die Gesetze', Ibid., p. 173.
21. 'Denn Recht ist nur, was den Sinn hat, Gerechtigkeit zu sein', Ibid.
22. See D. Graeber, *Debts*, Melville House, Brooklyn, New York 2011.
23. See D. Graeber and D. Wengrow, *The Dawn of Everything: A New History of Humanity*, London: Allen Lane, 2021.
24. Kropotkin, *The State*.
25. 'Wer die Gewalt hat, der hat das Recht'. M. Stirner, *Der Einzige und sein Eigentum*, ed. by A. Meyer, Reclam, Stuttgart 1981, p. 110.
26. 'Il existe en toute société, par cela seul qu'il ya société, une chose positive, réelle, qu'il est permis de nommer *l'État*.

Elle consiste, cette chose: 1. Dans une certaine force essentielle au groupe, et que nous appellerons force de collectivité; 2. dans la solidarité que cette force crée entre les membres du corps social; dans les proprietés et d'autres avantages communs qui la répresentent et qui en résultent.' P.-J. Proudhon, *De la Justice dans la Révolution et dans l'Église*, Vol. 2, Fayard, Paris 1988, p. 769.

27. 'Der Staat an und für sich ist das sittliche Ganze'. See G. W. F. Hegel, *Grundlinien der Philosophie des Rechts*, Suhrkamp, Frankfurt am Main 1986, p. 403.
28. M. Oakeshott, *On Human Conduct*.
29. '[S]i par l'État on entend la chose publique, la force collective, à la production et au benefice de la quelle participent tous les citoyens.' See P.-J. Proudhon, *De la Justice dans la Révolution et dans l'Église*, Vol. 2, p. 772.
30. This idea is reaffirmed by John Rawls, who says that 'The peculiar feature of the concept of justice – as is said by John Rawls – is that it treats each person as an equal sovereign'. J. Rawls, 'Constitutional Liberty and the Concept of Justice', in *Rights*, ed. by D. Lyons, Wadsworth, Belmont, Cal. 1979, p. 45.
31. See Esposito, *Institution*.
32. For a philosophical proposal pointing in such direction, see the recent book by Robert Alexy, *Law's Ideal Dimension*, Oxford University Press, Oxford 2021.
33. D. Loick, *Anarchismus zur Einfu*ehrung, Junius Verlag, Hamburg 2017, p. 119.
34. See Michel Foucault, *The Birth of Biopolitics: Lectures at the College de France, 1978–79*, ed., Michel Senellart, Basingstoke, Hampshire: Palgrave Macmillan, 2008.
35. See *Homo Sacer: Sovereign Power and Bare Life*.
36. Here Agamben's reflections on the public health measures imposed by the Italian state in the early stages of the COVID-19 pandemic in 2020, where he equated quarantining and social distancing with the imposition of the sovereign state of exception, sparked fierce controversy (see the series of exchanges with interlocutors such as Roberto Esposito and Sergio Benvenuto published under the title 'Coronavirus and Philosophers' in *European Journal of Psychoanalysis*, February to May 2020).

Seven
On Violence

The previous chapter considered the question of the state, and whether it was possible, as anarchists, to approach the state differently – analytically distinguishing between its benign and its more dominating and authoritarian *face*, and suggesting that the state could be rethought in terms of a public space, a community, composed of autonomous individuals who freely determine their own laws.

However, we are left with the problem of violence. Is it actually possible to envisage a legal community that does not at some level involve violence, or at least the threat of violence (coercion) in the enforcement of its own rules? As Kelsen reminds us, law is a *coercive* order: the authority of its norms necessarily depends upon the threat of sanctions, including the employment of physical force.[1] And certainly, according to most understandings of law, the threat, and actual use, of violence is regarded as central to legal authority and to the very principle of law-making. Locke, after all, defined political power as the '*right* of making laws with penalties of death, and consequently all less penalties, for the regulating and preserving of property, and of employing the force of the community, in the execution of such laws, and in the defence of the commonwealth from foreign injury; and all this only for the public good'.[2] The legitimate use of violence in law enforcement flowed from the natural right to punish once enjoyed by all individuals in their pre-civil state; a right which, according to the liberal social contract tradition, is relinquished and handed over to a legislative and executive power that reserves for itself the sole prerogative of judging and punishing.

Yet, violence is also something that disturbs and unsettles the boundaries of legal authority – particularly when the violence of law enforcement oversteps its constitutional limits. In recent times, we have seen numerous examples of excessive, and in some cases lethal, police violence in liberal democracies, particularly against racial minorities – for instance, against unarmed black men and women in the US and elsewhere – as well as against migrants and peaceful protestors. From an anarchist perspective, such egregious examples of violent policing should not be seen as outliers or exceptions but as the very core of legal authority; law *enforcement* is essentially a violent activity. Indeed, anarchist legal theory is concerned with unmasking this violence at the heart of the law. Unlike Schmitt, who reserves the expression of sovereign authority, and the violence it portends, to exceptional situations in which the constitutional order is suspended, anarchists point to the mundane nature of sovereign violence, seen in everyday acts of policing and border control. Thus, the 'exceptionality' of violence becomes for anarchists the analytical point of departure from which to interrogate legal authority.

However, if violence is intrinsic to the legal-political order – at least one based on the sovereign authority of the state – how do we resist and overcome it without the use of violence, and without instantiating an equally violent order in its place? We have already highlighted the dangers and pitfalls of the classical revolutionary model which, in overthrowing the existing state order, risks replicating its authoritarianism and institutionalising the same violence in a new revolutionary order. Anarchism, as we showed in the previous chapter, grapples with this problem, introducing important ethical considerations into radical politics: this is not simply a matter of imposing ethical limitations on political action but of questioning the whole means–ends rationality that characterises revolutionary strategy. However, can anarchism itself avoid the problem of violence? Historical and even contemporary experience has shown that anarchism is not immune to the temptations of violence. Violent actions against figures of authority – up to and including political assassinations and acts of terrorism – have been part of the history of anarchism and have been justified as necessary in the struggle for human (and non-human) liberation. Indeed, whether rightly or wrongly, anarchism has long been associated in the popular imagination with violent rebellion against the state. Will violence be an inevitable part of any serious campaign of resistance against state violence and domination, and, if so, is this ethically justifiable and consistent with anarchism's belief in the autonomy of the individual and the impermissibility of coercion? Is violence against violence legitimate? And, moreover, is it effective? Can a moral distinction be drawn between different forms of political violence: for instance, we might say that the destruction of property or of symbols of authority in acts of civil disobedience, or even violent confrontations with the police in mass demonstrations, are justified, whereas the assassination of political leaders or state functionaries, or the bombing of government buildings and corporate offices, is not. But why is this so? On what basis do we make this distinction? We might easily justify the use of such violence against tyrannical regimes. And how should we even define violence? Violence is a notoriously slippery concept, throwing up endless contradictions and ambiguities, especially when we consider its relation to politics and popular resistance.[3]

This chapter will address some of these ethical and political dilemmas. It will explore the relationship between violence and law, and it will do this through Walter Benjamin's famous essay, 'Critique of Violence', a text that we interpret in a distinctly anarchistic way. Benjamin's essay allows us to consider the ways in which legal authority, in its various manifestations, is intrinsically bound up with violence, whether at its foundations or in its everyday application. Furthermore, we will evaluate Benjamin's solution to the problem of legal violence in his enigmatic notion of 'divine violence', a form of revolutionary action that he associates with justice beyond law and the removal of law's hold over the individual. Here we suggest that this peculiar form of violence is close to the anarchist idea of prefiguration in collapsing the distinction between means and ends. We argue that 'divine violence', despite its difficulties and ambiguities, offers a different way of thinking about the relationship between violence and political action, and indeed, proposes an ethical transformation of the very idea of violence in terms of 'violence against violence'. Here we apply this to the debate in anarchist theory, and in revolutionary politics more broadly, over the meaning and efficacy of non-violence.

Violence and the law: Benjamin's 'Critique of Violence'

Central to any critical approach to the law – of which anarchism is the most radical example – is the exposure of the law's relationship with violence.[4] Law sees itself as different from violence and as offering a peaceful and rational way of resolving conflicts. Legal interpretation is therefore viewed as an essentially non-violent activity based on rational deliberation, and therefore as distinct from law-enforcement. In interpreting the law, in deliberating over its meaning and application, in adjudicating, in making legal decisions and determining verdicts, and even in pronouncing sentences, judges engage in an inherently different activity to that of police officers, prison authorities and executioners. The law is seen as a rarefied, pure sphere of activity – an autonomous world of legal codes and norms, of precedents and principles, of matters of justice and proportionality, and the weighing up of ethical questions – a sphere far removed from the violence of its application, and indeed from the broader structural violence of the political and economic system the law upholds.

To see the law in this way might be to mystify it to the point of abstraction. Robert Cover, an American legal scholar, argued that legal interpretation itself is an act of violence, a form of activity that cannot be separated from the violent sanctions and punishments it metes out. As he put it: 'Legal interpretation takes place in a field of pain and death'.[5] Legal interpretation – what judges do – is part of a broader social organisation of violence, encompassing the violence of the crime itself and the violence of its punishment. The judge is part of a collective apparatus of violence that includes many different voices, institutions, practices and actors, from the individual criminal him- or herself, to the jailor, to the executioner who awaits the decision from the judge. Yet, for Cover, this uncomfortable association between the 'word' of the law and the practice of violence is the only way things can be:

> So let us be explicit. If it seems a nasty thought that death and pain are at the center of legal interpretation, so be it. It would not be better were there only a community of argument, of readers and writers of texts, of interpreters.

> As long as death and pain are part of our political world, it is essential that they be at the center of the law. The alternative is truly unacceptable – that they be within our polity but outside the discipline of the *collective* decision rules and the individual efforts to achieve outcomes through those rules. The fact that we require many voices is not, then, an accident or peculiarity of our jurisdictional rules. It is intrinsic to whatever achievement is possible in the domesticating of violence.[6]

In other words, if we accept that violence is part of any political association – to the degree that the polity involves the collective determination of rules and therefore of legal sanctions – then legal interpretation has to take responsibility for its role in institutionalising this violence and it cannot imagine itself as autonomous from it. Law, politics, and violence are necessarily intertwined. All we can do to address this situation is to share responsibility for violence – to, in a sense, democratise its effects. But surely this is not an adequate solution to the problem of legal violence, and it would do nothing to reduce the level of violence embedded in the word of the law.

However, if violence contaminates law and politics in the way Cover claims, how is it possible to engage in a *critique* of violence? On what basis do we do so? The question would be not so much to find a legitimation or justification for violence, but more radically to exclude violence from social and legal practice. This is precisely the question Walter Benjamin poses in his celebrated and much commented on essay from 1921, 'Critique of Violence'. In exploring the grounds for a critique of violence, Benjamin considers the legal positivism and natural law traditions, coming to the conclusion that neither offers a sound basis for an ethical evaluation of violence on its *own* terms. While natural law theory evaluates violence according to the question of the justice of the *ends* to which it is put – violence is simply a means that can be put to either just or unjust ends – legal positivist theory, by contrast, sees violence only in terms of the legitimacy of the *means* employed, in other words, the degree to which they are legally sanctioned. At the end of the day, in determining things according to means and ends, neither perspective offers a way of considering violence as a distinct phenomenon with its own ethical criteria.

To really understand violence as a distinct moral concern, we need to step back from the perspective of the law altogether and regard violence on its own terms. This is, of course, very difficult – especially because it seems that it is the law itself that decides the very meaning of 'violence'. Insofar as the law is equated with the monopoly on violence, it claims the authority to determine what actually constitutes 'violent', thus illegitimate, action and what constitutes rational, just, and legitimate forms of action. Therefore, the law's problem with violence lies not so much in the injustice of ends to which it is employed but in the mere existence of violence outside its jurisdiction and control. This is what really constitutes a threat to legal authority, according to Benjamin. The law takes violence out of the hands of individuals and establishes its sole, sovereign jurisdiction over it. This is why Benjamin says, the figure of the 'great' criminal, regardless of his deeds, arouses a certain sympathy, or at least a fascination amongst the public, precisely because he embodies a violence outside the legal order, which, by its very nature challenges its authority.[7] In other words, the criminal, in breaking the social contract, reclaims his 'natural' rights to violence outside the sovereign order. The criminal symbolises a certain 'anarchy' – a return to a 'natural' condition of primeval freedom outside the authority of the law.

Anarchism does not for the most part romanticise criminality.[8] Crime, in its transgression of the law, only reaffirms its authority; any sympathy with the criminal that Benjamin detects amongst the masses is also accompanied by their demand for punishment. The desire for law and order, and sometimes for excessive punishment, is an equally popular sentiment. In this sense, criminal violence and legal violence are but two sides of the same coin. It is only at the level of fantasy that the criminal embodies the possibility of life beyond the law. Political sovereignty itself could be activated as a practice beyond the law or even against the law. Derrida, for instance, points to the close resemblance between the sovereign and the rogue (*voyous*): all states, he argues, insofar as they are governed by the principle of sovereignty that asserts itself as above the law, are 'rogue states'.[9]

By contrast, the anarchist life is not one of simple transgression of the law, but rather involves a transformation of our relationship to it, and prior to this, a reconceptualisation of law itself.[10]

Nevertheless, Benjamin's example of the 'great criminal' points to the way that the state jealously guards its own sovereign rights to violence while denying it to everyone else, and it is this legal monopoly on violence that he wants to question.[11] In this sense, the 'Critique of Violence' ['Zur Kritik de Gewalt'] is really a critique of *legal* violence. Here it should be noted that '*Gewalt*' in German means at once violence, power and authority. It is this ambivalence between legal authority and violence – their fundamental intertwining in the sovereign political order – that Benjamin explores throughout the essay. The law articulates itself through a violence that both preserves its boundaries and exceeds them; and violence in turn establishes a new law. Violence is present at the very founding of a new legal system, and this violence haunts its structures and institutional practices. Benjamin gives the example of military violence, which establishes a new legal system in the place of the old through the signing of a peace treaty following a conquest; as well as the death penalty, which signifies law's ultimate sovereignty over life,[12] and whose purpose is not so much the punishment of those who transgress the law, but the affirmation of law as life's inescapable fate. Benjamin's point here is that law always instantiates itself, founding and reaffirming itself, through violence. Violence brings law into being, breathes life into it, gives it vitality: 'violence, violence crowned by fate, is the origin of the law …'[13]

The law's intimate relationship with violence is explored through the antinomy introduced by Benjamin between 'law-making' (*rechtsetzend*) violence and 'law-preserving' (*rechtserhaltend*) violence, which might be understood in terms of the distinction between constituting and constituted power. There is the violence involved in the founding of a new legal order, which can even refer to the revolutionary violence that destroys one system and establishes another. And there is the violence involved in the enforcement of existing laws and guaranteeing the security of the political order. Benjamin's point, however, is to show how these two forms of violence ultimately collapse into one another, so that there is a continual oscillation between the two. The key example he gives here is that of the police, in which is combined, 'in a kind of spectral mixture', these two forms of violence.[14] The use of police violence for the purpose of law enforcement is obviously law-preserving. Yet, it is also *lawmaking*, because the police act at the very limits of the law and have the authority to determine how law is applied in particular situations. The police often act in an extra-legal capacity, outside the law or at its margins, in the liminal spaces between legality and illegality; police violence inhabits a kind of 'grey zone' or a space of exception. The case of the police shows how much law enforcement implies violence. There is a surplus of force in the executive power of action. Schmitt highlighted the way that the legal order relied on an external dimension of sovereign force that determines the application of laws in 'concrete situations'. Similarly, in enforcing the law, the police also make a sovereign decision, especially where the legal situation is unclear. In this sense, the actions of the police are also 'law-making', in so far as they exceed the law. This would be close to the idea of a sovereign state of exception – if only police violence were not so mundane, so 'unexceptional'. The policing of protests, and the decision to employ certain operational tactics, such as 'kettling', which do not have a sound legal basis, is a very clear example of this law-making power; as is the decision made by police about whether certain protests were in breach of COVID-19 restrictions, as we saw in the heavy-handed policing of a vigil held in the UK in 2021 for Sarah Everard, ironically herself also a victim of police violence.[15] The legal violence of the police rampages uncontrollably throughout the civil space, determining the law in those spaces of exception where its limits are unclear. As Benjamin puts it, the police intervene '"for security reasons" in countless situations where no clear legal situations exists, when they are not merely, without the slightest relation to legal ends, accompanying the citizen as a brutal encumbrance through a life regulated by ordinances, or simply supervising him'.[16]

The law articulates itself through a violent enforcement that at the same time it cannot control, and which exceeds its limits; a violent excess that both disturbs and constitutes the limits of the law. This continual blurring of the line, this legal ambiguity at the very core of police power, is why Benjamin describes the police as 'formless, like its nowhere-tangible, all-pervasive, ghostly presence in the life of civilized states'.[17] While certainly a matter of degree, police violence is the element that seems to blur the line between liberal democracies and authoritarian states. Indeed, Benjamin makes the important point that whereas the despotism of the police is a sort of hangover from absolutist regimes, to whom its presence was in a way appropriate, in liberal regimes, defined by the separation of powers, the rule of law and the guarantee of individual rights, its 'spirit' is more disturbing and devastating; police violence, while seemingly in contradiction with these principles and institutions, at the same time lives comfortably alongside them, at once upholding them and testifying to their weakness and decomposition.

Moreover, if the law is to be understood through its connection to violence, at the same time, violence might be understood through its connection to law. Benjamin's critical claim is that violence is violent *through its relation to law*, through its legal instantiation, whether it is the violence that preserves the legal system or the violence that overthrows the legal system only to establish a new one in its place. What establishes the link between law and violence – what binds them together in this continual oscillation – is the sovereign core of state authority, in other words, *power*. As Benjamin says: 'All law-making is power making and, to that extent, an immediate manifestation of violence'.[18] Benjamin refers to this violence that brings the law into being, and continually refreshes and revivifies it, as *mythic violence*. Just as Niobe, the figure from Greek mythology whose children are slaughtered by the gods in punishment for her hubris, is transformed into a petrified stone waterfall as a constant testament to her transgression, mythic violence transfixes us, holding us in its clasps and passing judgment over us. The law is our fate. Worse than the violence it inflicts is the eternal guilt which it imposes upon us; we are always positioned as guilty in the eyes of the law.[19]

'Divine violence' and the destruction of the state

How, then, to break out of this eternal cycle of law and violence? Benjamin's answer to this is with another kind of violence – what he calls *divine violence*. This is a form of violence that is irreducible to the law, that neither enforces the law nor founds a new legal system, but which strikes at the very heart of legal authority, deposing or abolishing it. Divine violence is a form of violence against the violence of the law. It releases life from the grasp of the law, saving us from this fate. Benjamin says:

> The dissolution of legal violence stems … from the guilt of more natural life, which consigns the living, innocent and unhappy, to a retribution that 'expiates' the guilt of mere life – and doubtless also purifies the guilty, not of guilt, however, but of law. For with mere life the rule of law over the living ceases.[20]

Yet, divine violence is more than just the destruction of the law, because, as we have seen, this always risks the establishment of a new legal system. Rather, divine violence affirms life's pre-eminence over law, thus expiating and removing the law's hold over us.

While divine violence is no doubt an enigmatic concept, with obvious theological and eschatological connotations[21] and a strong background of philosophy of history, it is possible to read it in anarchist terms.[22] As Benjamin says: 'On the breaking of this cycle maintained by mythic forms of law, on the suspension of law with all the forces on which it depends, finally therefore on the abolition of state power, a new historical epoch is founded'.[23] Divine violence cuts the Gordian knot that binds together violence and law, and, in doing so, embodies the radical dissolution and transcendence of state power. Divine violence is a transformative rupture of social relations – one that destroys the legal order, not with the intention of setting a new one up in its place, but in a more radical sense of freeing us from the hold that law has over us. For Benjamin:

> This very task of destruction poses again, in the last resort, the question of a pure, immediate violence that might be able to call a halt to mythical violence. Just as in all spheres, God opposes myth, mythical violence is confronted by the divine. And the latter constitutes its antithesis in all respects. If mythical violence is lawmaking, divine violence

> is law destroying; if the former sets boundaries, the latter boundlessly destroys them; if mythical violence brings at once guilt and retribution, divine violence only expiates, if the former threatens, the latter strikes; if the former is bloody, the latter is lethal without spilling blood.[24]

One way to understand this enigmatic idea of 'divine violence' – which strikes with the force of *justice* against legal authority, and which is 'lethal without spilling blood' – is through Georges Sorel's notion of the proletarian general strike, to which Benjamin makes explicit reference.

Sorel, inspired by the syndicalist movements and organisations in France in the nineteenth century,[25] proposed a form of autonomous workers' action as a solution to the deadlock of socialist politics. In his *Reflections on Violence* (*Réflexions sur la violence*, 1908) he considers the prospects for class struggle and worker's revolution at the turn of the twentieth century. The chief obstacle to the revolution, he argues, is the moral degeneration of the proletariat, its loss of class identity and its subsumption within the bourgeois moral universe. Proletarian moral and political energy had been dissipated through the internalisation of bourgeois values, as well as through the obfuscating role of socialist politicians whose function was to incorporate the working class into representative structures of the capitalist state and the 'social peace' – a kind of corporatist consensus between labour and capital which merely shrouded capitalism in humanitarian and social democratic ideology. Violence, Sorel argues, has an important role to play in restoring the political and moral vitality of the working class by sharpening class distinctions which had become blurred. Violence is what allows the proletariat to overcome its position of 'decadence', to spurn the hypocritical humanitarian overtures of the capitalists and socialist politicians, and to rediscover its 'egoism'.[26] In other words, violence allows the proletariat to affirm its autonomous class identity and values in opposition to that great agent of 'decadence' and 'incapacity', the modern state.

But what kind of violence is Sorel talking about here? We must pay close attention to his idea of the proletarian general strike and to his understanding of the function of myth. The proletarian general strike is a form of revolutionary direct action engaged in by workers themselves, without the mediation of the state and political parties. It is at the same time a kind of *myth*, a myth of war – specifically class war, whose centrality to Marxist theory Sorel wanted to restore. The general strike embodies the symbolism of a battlefield; it enacts the drama of a decisive battle between the proletariat and the bourgeoisie. The drama of war has the effect of galvanising the energy and passions of the working class. Sorel described the myth as 'a body of images capable of evoking instinctively all the sentiments which correspond to the different manifestations of the war undertaken by Socialism against modern society'.[27] The myth of the general strike might therefore be understood as a sort of *mise en scène*, in which all the emotional energy of previous strikes and workers' actions are concentrated to a point maximum intensity, something that produces militant and heroic affects in workers, imbuing them with warrior-like virtues of courage and self-discipline, as well as a newfound vitality: 'appealing to their painful memories of particular conflicts, it colours with an intense life all the details of the composition presented to consciousness'.[28]

This idea of myth[29] allows us to consider revolutionary politics in new ways, not so much as a form of strategic action formed around the achievement of concrete goals – although these are important too – but as a politics of *pure means*. The proletarian general strike proposed by Sorel conveys the idea of direct action in the immediacy of the present, in the here and now. Action is understood not as a means to an end but an end in itself. This is close to how Benjamin understands the notion of divine violence: it is only through the liberation of violence from the achievement of certain ends, such as the setting up of a new legal order, that violence becomes essentially non-violent, that it is 'lethal without spilling blood'. In both accounts there is an understanding of violence not in pursuit of any particular end or program, but as *pure means:* Benjamin refers to 'pure immediate violence'.[30] Such an understanding of action might be considered *ontologically anarchic* because it resists foundations, particularly legal foundations. Indeed, Benjamin's notion of divine violence – while it strikes from a sphere external to the human world – might be seen as the attempt to restore life to itself, to rescue it from the abstraction and alienation of the law, and to return it to the realm of ordinary human experience. The myth of the proletarian general strike and the notion of divine violence might both be seen in terms of the anarchist idea of prefiguration as discussed in a previous chapter – a form of ethical action that, in prefiguring the future in the present, refuses to sacrifice means to ends.

Benjamin's critical attitude towards violence of course is much more complex and refined than the vitalist celebration of violence we find in Sorel's work. We should not forget that Sorel's celebration of violence led him first to embrace Leninism, and later the politics of the far-right figure Charles Maurras and the Action Francaise, eventually coming to celebrate Mussolini's fascist activism. There is no celebration of violence whatsoever in Benjamin's work. Violence is deeply related to the movement of history and the production of culture. Cultural goods, so it is argued by Benjamin, are imbued with the suffering of the oppressed who had to manufacture these goods. Thus history and law can be redeemed, and violence expunged from them, only if we take account of the suffering of the past and the destruction of real lives in the name of progress.

This is further elucidated by Benjamin in a long essay on Kafka. Kafka's work, says Benjamin, is 'the world of offices and registries, of musty, shabby, dark rooms'.[31] This is law's 'heart of darkness'. To emancipate this world from its intrinsically looming violence the only solution is a suspension of legality, a state of exception that is however not a precipitation of Schmittian decisionism, not a sheer Wille zur Macht, a brute will to power. It is rather a taking distance from law, a disactivated law, a ruling without enforcement; or, better put, a rule pronounced but not sanctioned. Law is in this way transformed from the tumultuous and aggressive contingency of command to the non-violence of quiet reading and studying: 'The law which is studied and not practiced any longer is the gate to justice'.[32] 'Divine violence', then, is not so much 'direct action', in the form of Sorel's myth of violent collective practice, but rather a pause from violent activism, and attention to what is said and written in the rules that consequently cannot be converted into forms of coercion.

Law, from a prescriptive experience, should become a practice of mutual understanding, communication, and mediation.

Violence against violence

Notwithstanding some of these differences between Benjamin's and Sorel's conceptions of violence, Sorel's notion of the violence of the proletarian general strike nevertheless has important consequences for an anarchist politics. For Sorel, the effect of the general strike is to construct new forms of subjectivity, to create an autonomous working class 'identity' where none existed before. The worker, as an autonomous subject, does not pre-exist the general strike but is retroactively created by it. The aim of the myth of the general strike is to create a new moral and aesthetic universe, a new form of ethics, a new set of virtues. Just as the Christian martyrs distinguished themselves through their fortitude, self-discipline and commitment to moral struggle, so the proletariat must learn to discipline itself and acquire its own morality and nobility; it must develop, as Sorel puts it, '*habits of liberty* with which the bourgeoisie are no longer acquainted'.[33] Where we see Sorel's notion of ethical prefiguration as important, is in the way that it proposes the cultivation of new modes of subjectivity and the possibility of alternative social relationships and institutions based on the idea of autonomy. Freedom, we would suggest, is not something that arises spontaneously, but only comes about through practices of self-disciplining such that one's dependencies on power and familiar patterns and habits of obedience and consumption are broken. Indeed, Sorel's insistence on morality, and even a certain kind of 'purity', was in order to wean the proletariat off its dependence not only on the state and its agents of representation, but particularly on the moral culture of the bourgeoisie and the capitalist system. Perhaps, in the same way, a certain kind of 'asceticism' would be necessary to enable us to detach ourselves from the culture of consumerism and the capitalist circuits of desire in which we are so thoroughly immersed. To the extent that neoliberal capitalism governs us through our 'freedom' – our *freedom* to consume, to work and to obey – we can only break with this system and develop alternative and more genuine practices of freedom through a certain kind of self-discipline. As Sorel suggests, liberty is a new habit that we are yet to learn.

The proletarian general strike is the event that endows the proletariat with the capacity for freedom. This is largely because it is a form of autonomous direct action without any agent of mediation or direction: the workers in this scenario emancipate themselves from capitalism and the state by directly seizing control of the means of production. In this sense, the kind of revolutionary action Sorel has in mind is much closer to anarchism than socialism: 'It is impossible that there should be the slightest misunderstanding between the Syndicalists and official Socialists on this question: the latter, of course, speak of breaking up everything, but they attack men in power rather than power itself'.[34] Whereas the syndicalists destroy power, the socialists seek to possess and command it.

Sorel therefore proposes an important distinction between the *political general strike* and the *proletarian general strike*, a distinction that broadly maps onto Benjamin's distinction between mythic violence and divine violence. For Sorel, whereas the *political general strike* is orchestrated by socialist politicians and official trade unions, and is intended to exercise political control over the state and to extort concessions from the capitalist class, the proletarian general strike embodies the radical dissolution of state power through the affirmation of workers' autonomy and direct action. The two forms of action are completely different. In the case of the proletarian general strike, the dissolution of the state is not the strategic aim as such but is, rather, embodied and symbolised in the very action itself. Both forms of action involve violence, but violence of a very different kind.

For Sorel, precisely because the proletarian general strike avoids the trap of power – because it seeks autonomy from the state rather than wanting to control it – the violence it evokes ends up as a radical non-violence. The battlefield on which proletarian violence is enacted is a *symbolic* one, and militaristic action is to be understood metaphorically. The violence here is symbolic and ethical, a kind of stylised, gestural confrontation with the enemy which imbues the worker with a warrior-like nobility and virtue, yet which does not involve real physical violence:

> they are purely and simply acts of war; they have the value of military demonstrations, and serve to mark the separation of classes. Everything in war is carried on without hatred and without the spirit of revenge; in war the vanquished are not killed; non-combatants are not made to bear the consequences of the disappointments which the armies may have experienced on the fields of battle; force is then displayed according to its own nature, without ever professing to borrow anything from the judicial proceedings which society sets up against criminals.[35]

This last point is a reference to the political and legal violence of the state, a form of violence which is infinitely bloodier than proletarian violence. Here Sorel has in mind the Jacobin Terror in France in the early 1790s – the violent proscriptions and persecutions of the enemies of the revolution at the hands of the new revolutionary leadership. His point, therefore, is that forms of revolutionary action which aim to seize control of state power are much more likely to result in real violence; whereas it is precisely because proletarian autonomy wants no truck with the state at all that it manages to avoid bloodshed and sublimate its violence into a symbolic war. Indeed, Sorel refers to legal violence as bourgeois force, and reserves the term violence for the chivalrous and heroic form of proletarian warfare described above: 'the term *violence* should be employed only for acts of revolt; we should say, therefore that the object of force is to impose a certain social order in which the minority governs, while violence tends to the destruction of that order'.[36]

We can conclude from this that what makes violence *violent* in the real sense – what turns violence into *force*, as Sorel puts it – is its *state-ification;* in other words, force entails real bloodshed because it uses the mechanisms of state power to impose a social order from above. It is not merely to say that the state is an instrument of violence – and will always be the most violent of instruments due to its capacity to be so – but more that the *logic* of statism, the logic by which a certain order is imposed coercively and hierarchically upon the world, is what produces untold violence. Therein lies the danger for all revolutionary projects, bourgeois or socialist, which seek to control the reins of state power; the history of this kind of revolutionary path is soaked in blood. By contrast, the violence of autonomous revolution – or as we might call it, following Stirner, *insurrection* – because it distances itself from the state and seeks to dissolve its power, transforms itself into a kind a symbolic and ethical violence. The insurrection might be said to be a violence against an existing set of social relations, rather than violence against persons.

Anarchism and (non)violence

How does the notion of 'violence against violence' – which we have reconstructed in different ways through Sorel and Benjamin – allow us to better grapple with anarchism's own relationship with violence? As we noted at the start of the chapter, anarchism has always had a rather ambivalent relationship with violence.[37] While anarchism in the past has been no stranger to violence – from the violent 'propaganda of the deed' during the nineteenth century, to full-scale military campaigns during the Russian and Spanish Civil Wars in the twentieth century – there is at the same time the ethical problematisation of violence as a coercive and authoritarian relationship which centrally contradicts anarchist principles. Anarchism has been characterised by both violent and non-violent resistance to power, and is known as much for peaceful civil disobedience as it is for political assassinations. While there is an ethical reservation about the use of violence against persons, anarchism nevertheless maintains a close proximity to the notion of *war*. This might be understood in two senses. Firstly, there is the claim that centralised political power, whether democratic or autocratic, stands in a relationship of war with society: state power, it is argued, is not based on consent, but is a violently imposed form of domination which intervenes in social relations in irrational and destructive ways. The state is a form of organised violence, whose domination is established through the conquest of territory and the destruction of pre-existing social relationships. Secondly, if the state is a war machine, it can only be confronted with another war machine, that of the social revolution. As Bakunin declared: 'Revolution means war, and that implies the destruction of men and things'.[38] However, while this might seem like an endorsement or acceptance of wholesale violence, the anarchist social revolution would liberate people from politically instituted forms of violence: 'The Social Revolution must put an end to the old system of organization based upon violence, giving full liberty to the masses, groups, communes, and associations, and likewise to individuals themselves, and destroying once and for all the historic cause of all violence …'[39]

So, in this sense, the anarchist social revolution might be understood as a form of counter-violence, a *violence against violence*. The violence of the state – a violence that is much more excessive in any case than any form of violence opposed to it – can only be met with a counter-violence. In order to unmask the violence that the state rests upon, the state can only be confronted with another kind of violence. So, it is not a question of whether or not a revolution against state power will be violent – against such overwhelming violence and power, it cannot be anything other than violent. Rather it is a question of whether it is possible to have a form of violence that, in seeking the abolition of power, at the same time seeks the abolition of violence itself. It is not clear, then, how exactly the violence of the social revolution should be understood. While it may indeed involve real instances of violence, at the same time it is a mass action aimed against violence.

It is too simplistic to identify anarchism entirely with non-violence, notwithstanding the important pacifist traditions within anarchism, associated with the likes of Thoreau, Tolstoy and Gandhi, or with certain radical strands of Christianity[40] and Judaism.[41] Many forms of protest, dissent and civil disobedience would be meaningless without some dimension of violence, whether this involves property destruction, vandalism, sabotage and even physical confrontations with the police. Violence is ethically justifiable in several circumstances[42] – most obviously in self-defence, as well in the destruction of physical property as part of protests and direct action. Moreover, we should not assume that non-violence is always a more successful tactic in political struggles. The violent forms of protest that anarchists at times engage in are often condemned by other protestors as being self-defeating, as giving the cause a 'bad name' and living up to media stereotypes, or provoking a violent response by the police. However, as Peter Gelderloos and others have pointed out, there is little evidence to suggest that non-violence is the more effective tactic; indeed, the ideology of non-violence and peaceful civil disobedience often acts to support the system it claims to challenge.[43] Given that 'violence' is such an ambiguous term, and given the everyday 'background' violence of the structures of political and economic oppression that anarchists confront, the very debate over violence vs. non-violence as tactics of political struggles often becomes meaningless. It must be possible, then, for those engaged in political struggles to determine their own criteria for violence and to ethically transform it – in the way that both Benjamin and Sorel sought in different ways to do. Gelderloos refers to a 'diversity of tactics' in anarchist struggles and suggests the deployment of a different terminology to talk about violence – such as 'illegal', 'combative', 'conflictive' or 'forceful' actions.[44]

While coming from the opposite position to Gelderloos in affirming a politics and ethics of nonviolence,[45] Judith Butler nevertheless associates this with a kind of 'force', making it very different from pacifism. She says:

> Nonviolence does not imply the absence of force or of aggression. It is, as it were, an ethical stylization of embodiment, replete with gestures and modes of non-action, ways of becoming an obstacle, of using the solidity of the body and its proprioceptive object field to block or derail a further exercise of violence.[46]

The notion of nonviolence as 'an ethical stylization of embodiment' might be close to Sorel's notion of the mythical proletarian general strike which, as we have seen, takes place on a metaphorical 'battlefield' and has the value of 'military *demonstrations*' that are at the same time 'nonviolent' in the sense of not involving actual killing. In other words, symbolic actions – which can include physical obstruction, destroying and vandalising property, occupying spaces and so on – can have their own violence, expressing the same aggression and conveying the same *force*, as acts of real violence. Butler continues:

> When, for instance, bodies form a human barrier, we can ask whether they are blocking force or engaging in force. Here, again, we are obligated to think carefully about the

> direction of force, and to seek to make operative a distinction between bodily force and violence. Sometimes, it may seem that obstruction *is* violence – we do, after all, speak about violent obstruction – so one question that will be important to consider is whether bodily acts of resistance involve a mindfulness of the tipping point, the site where the force of resistance can become the violent act or practice that commits a fresh injustice. The possibility for this kind of ambiguity should not dissuade us of the value of this kind of practice.[47]

While not necessarily taking an explicitly anarchist position, Butler, like Gelderloos, refuses to leave it up to the law to determine the appropriate parameters of violence. The idea that the law is the only legitimate way of resolving conflicts and putting a stop to violence ignores the fact that the law has its own violence.[48] She therefore draws on Benjamin's critique of legal violence to arrive at an alternative and more ethical form of violence as nonviolence.

Moreover, as we have suggested, the real transformative *force* of radical politics lies more in the way it fosters different relationships between individuals and new modes subjectivity, new practices and forms of community. Butler associates the 'force' of nonviolence with the cultivation of new ethical sensibilities, new ways of being in the world and relating to others. We also saw that, for Sorel, the proletarian general strike – despite its romanticised vision of violence – was really a way of transforming social relations through the promotion of workers' autonomy, engendering different ways of being, living, working, relating to one another, and in encouraging new ethical sensibilities.

Here it is important to refer to Andrea Caffi's intelligent critique of violence. Caffi is one of the most cultivated and heterodox anti-authoritarian thinkers of the twentieth century. According to Caffi, we can distinguish three spheres in the present political order: first 'people', a multitude of individuals without intersubjective bonds beyond contingent, fleeting encounters; second, 'government', a structure of domination whose main tool is violence; third, 'society, a sphere where individuals meet freely and develop bonds of friendship. Now, this friendship is an alternative to violence, and it is only within this sphere of 'civility' that we can hope to make of the critique of violence a lived practice: '"Society" in principle excludes every kind of constraint and especially all forms of violence'.[49]

Caffi's approach is close to Benjamin's idea of sociality, considered a special space of understanding and mediation: 'There is a sphere of human agreement that is non-violent to the extent that it is wholly inaccessible to violence, the proper sphere of 'understanding', language'.[50] This idea is later reformulated and re-elaborated by Hannah Arendt. In her essay *On Violence*, she distinguishes three main forms of power: force, power, and violence. Now, power in the proper sense is *acting in concert* – *action* as opposed to *work* and *labour*[51] – a non-instrumental and non-strategic cooperation among subjects based on communication and understanding. Violence, on the contrary, is non-communicative. When violence is used, understanding and language no longer hold.[52] Arendt, we should add, was in some senses sharing an anarchist view of what free political institutions should be: she gives examples of 'workers' councils' or direct democracy,[53] while labelling present representative democracies as mostly 'oligarchic' regimes.

An essential part of the ethics of nonviolence is the realisation of our interdependency and shared vulnerability, and therefore the recognition of our ethical obligation towards others – both human and non-human. It is this sensibility that allows us to create a new vision of global solidarity and equality.[54] This is again exactly what Caffi stresses as the role of 'civility' and 'sociality'. Our point, then, is that rethinking violence along the lines we have suggested allows the possibility of creating new and more autonomous ways of relating to others, new forms of subjectivity and community – in other words, it allows a reconstruction of the social bond in a way that is not strictly determined by legal and state authority.

Destroy yourself: violence and the mystical experience

Central to the anarchist social project, as we have emphasised throughout, is the reconstitution of the self. How does the question of violence come into this? While we do not take an absolute moral position on violence, regarding it as legitimate in *certain* circumstances, the risk is always that violent actions not only harm other individuals but also lead to a certain corruption of one's own subjectivity. This at least was the view of the anarchist activist Gustav Landauer, who took part in the German Revolution of 1918–1919 and who was murdered by right-wing paramilitary forces after the crushing of the Bavarian Republic (*Raterepublik*). Indeed, it was precisely this context of spiralling revolutionary violence and counter-violence in postwar Germany that prompted Benjamin to write his 'Critique'. Yet, Landauer himself rejected the anarchist use of violence. The assassination by an anarchist of US President McKinley in 1901 led Landauer to criticise the use of violence by anarchists as a tool of revolution. He argued that this sort of 'propaganda by deed' was not only self-defeating – and moreover, indicative of a certain vanity and desire for recognition on the part of some anarchists – but went against the very ethical orientation of anarchism itself. It was impossible, according to Landauer, to build an anarchist society on the basis of violence: 'All violence is either despotism or authority. What the anarchists must realize is that a goal can only be reached if it is already reflected in its means. Non-violence cannot be attained by violence.'[55] Such a refusal of violence might lead some to dismiss Landauer's anarchism as anti-political but, on a different reading, it can lead to a more intense experience of the political. The 'political' anarchists who counselled violence as a means to the end of revolution were, for Landauer, 'not anarchic enough'.[56]

Indeed, for Landauer, anarchism should not be seen as an end at all, as a certain type of society that one seeks to establish, as this would inevitably involve imposing a particular vision of society upon others: 'Those who want "to bring freedom to the world" – which will always be *their* idea of freedom – are tyrants, not anarchists'.[57] Rather than seeing anarchism as a future goal to be attained, it should be something of the present; it is about how one lives in the here and now. Anarchy cannot be a society only for anarchists. Anarchism is a certain kind of disposition, a way of being and relating to oneself and to others. There is a role for violence here, but it is violence against (existing) social relationships rather than against individuals. This is why

Landauer believed that, insofar as the state itself is merely a social relationship that we reproduce through our daily interaction with other individuals, it 'can be destroyed by creating new social relationships'.[58] Here revolutionary destruction is transformed into a creative project, aimed at the reconstruction of the social bond in new ways. Revolution is not so much a direct and violent assault on political power, but rather a 'micro-political', even 'spiritual', modification of individual behaviours and relationships.

Yet this spiritual transformation also involves a kind of metaphorical *self-immolation* that is closely bound up with the mystical experience. For Landauer, anarchism is the spiritual redemption and rebirth of humanity, but one that first passes through the turmoil of the individual's soul. The possibility of anarchism is sometimes obscure and only accessible to a mystical experience, rather than something that can be articulated as a rational vision of social relations: 'Only when anarchy becomes, for us, a dark, deep dream, not a vision attainable through concepts, can our ethics and our actions become one'.[59] The mystical experience is described in terms of a metaphorical self-destruction, a kind of 'violence' that is directed *inward* – at once detaching and separating oneself from one's existing subject position and place within the world, yet at the same time creating, in this act of spiritual self-obliteration, a new relationship with the world. As Landauer puts it: 'I do this to feel one with the world in which my I has dissolved. Just like someone who jumps into the water to kill himself, I jump into the world – but instead of death, I find life. The I kills itself so that the World-I can live'.[60]

This 'violence' directed inwards is at the same time the creation of a new self, more profoundly connected with life and the world. What is interesting, from our point of view, is the way that violence is transformed through this act of spiritual oblivion; rather than being directed towards others, it is directed towards oneself, albeit in an entirely metaphorical sense. And rather than being purely destructive, it is also redemptive and creative. Violence becomes the act of *clearing the ground*; it is a form of radical self-reflexivity, accepting one's own fragility and lack of a permanent fundament, a deconstruction and reconstruction of pre-existing selves that remained attached to existing conditions and social relations, having as an end that new ones could emerge in their place, though never forgetting their intrinsic fragility.

This is no doubt a strange and paradoxical way of thinking about anarchist politics and ethics, especially in a tradition that is generally associated with the idea of the sovereignty of the individual. Yet, Landauer's point is that individual autonomy is not something that can be simply assumed to exist, as if in some natural state, but is, rather, something to be created, an ethical project to be worked on – and part of this involves a destruction of old modes of subjectivity and the invention of something new.

A coda on law and violence

An interesting debate recently emerged within the tradition of German Frankfurt School critical theory. This tradition, with some important exceptions, often ignored the question of law and legality, following the Marxist tendency to downplay the importance of 'superstructure' as opposed to the 'base' mode of economic production. A formidable exception, as we have seen, was Benjamin's *Zur Kritik der Gewalt*, but we might also remember the work by Franz Neumann, whose book *Behemoth* is still one of the best reflections on Nazi law.

The second generation of this school – namely Jürgen Habermas and Axel Honneth – was more interested in dealing with law as a significant element of a functioning of a society. Habermas devoted one of his weightiest tomes, *Between Facts and Norms*, to legal theory. The book is full of important insights and proposals about a democratic and anti-authoritarian form of legality. While, prior to this book, he believed that law was a functional 'medium' of society, in the same manner as markets and the economy, he now reshapes legal practice as a moment that can be transparent to discourse and normative arguments. Law, in this way, is redeemed and reconsidered as a sphere of conversation between citizens. But Habermas is somehow too conciliatory towards the phenomenon of legal practice and gives it a centrality in the construction of the social order that is possibly at variance with the radical, anti-authoritarian approach of the Frankfurt School.

Habermas' criticism of law, if there is one, is relatively mild, and, although at a certain point he claims that his discourse theory is somehow rooted in an anarchist utopia where human relations are ruled only by arguments and not by coercion,[61] nonetheless he does not allow room for contestation and dissent by those not willing to accept the law as it is proposed to them. Law's assumed discourse rationality seems to fully displace human life and its contingency.[62] Moreover, Habermas is only implicitly critical of the repressive reality of the rule of law. He does not question the legitimacy of punishment for instance. Violence in the law seems to be reduced only by democratising the sources of law itself. Legal rules have to pass a test of deliberative acceptability, but once this test is passed, there is no further justification needed for the application of the rule, provided at least its appropriateness to the concrete case is guaranteed.[63] Once again, as is the case in Ronald Dworkin's 'integrity' theory, justification redeems the necessity of coercion.

However, a third generation of Frankfurt School thinkers have taken up a strong critical stance towards the law, making it the central concern of their social theory. This is especially the case with Christoph Menke. In a recent short book *Recht und Gewalt*, later translated as *Law and Violence*, Menke, a philosopher rather than a lawyer, has, following the gesture of Benjamin, proposed a criticism of law as being essentially connected with violence.

Menke's criticism is carried out along four main theses. (i) That law, whose function should be to limit and counteract violence, can only do so through the use of violence. Law was born as an alternative to vengeance, which is the retribution of violence by violence in a series of actions without end. Law claims to be able to put a stop to this perpetual chain of violent acts and to pacify intersubjective relations. But it can only do it through an act of violence. This means, in this perspective, that violence is an essential element of the nature of law. (ii) That the violent character of law means that there is no possible reasoning or argument available that can effectively bridge the gap between what is law and what is not law. While the law operates through a binary code – legal–illegal – what is illegal is due to a discretionary determination of the law itself without any possible justification.

(iii) That law imposes on the parties involved in a legal contest and procedure a sort of 'curse'. They are asked to judge and convict themselves, if found legally responsible and 'guilty'. The party on trial cannot but acknowledge the legality and the rightness of the procedural outcome. In this way, she is bound to condemn herself and give up her autonomous judgment. She is coerced to abide by the trial's sentence: 'The curselike violence of legal judging is due to the fact that its legitimacy, by which it overcomes revenge, demands the convict's self-sentencing: the violence of law is the curse of self-sentencing'.[64]

(iv) Finally, that law is only possible and valid within an established polity. Law is operative and equally effective only for citizens. The 'other', the foreigner, or whoever is excluded from the polity, is banned from the precinct of law. From this criticism, one might expect an attitude of radical refusal of law and legality – but this is not Menke's proposal. For instance, it might be possible to envisage an alternative way of resolving disputes and pacifying conflict, whereby law itself could be transcended. But Menke does not believe such transcendence to be possible. Rather, he pleads for a law of the 'unwilling', an *Entsetzung* of law, using Benjamin's notion; a 'relief' or 'retreat' of law, meaning by this that a law which can be self-reflective on its own violence, might be inclined to operate through as little violence as possible. Only by reflecting on its own character as necessarily violent could law become less violent. Law's relief will be the outcome of a legality followed unwillingly, *ex fastidio*, with a guilty conscience that would induce the agents of the law to minimise the violence of their actions. 'Legal legislation is defined here by its restriction: it is defined by what it does not do.'[65]

This view of the law has been critiqued by two legal theorists, both working within the Frankfurt critical theory, Andreas Fischer-Lescano and Daniel Loick. They converge in finding Menke's thesis of the 'relief of law' too weak to meet the anti-authoritarian standards and the utopian promises of a possible law without violence and authority.

Fischer-Lescano's first objection is that we need not root law in a specific polity nor equate legal subjectivity with citizenship, as Menke claims, especially if we consider how globalised the legal world is: 'Law in a world society operates independently of the polity'.[66] Constitutionalism under globalised world conditions is more societal than strictly political.[67] This means that law can operate without producing exclusion, contrary to what Menke argues. A second objection is that the self-reflexivity of law should take an intersubjective and communicative form, one provided by a 'procedural conjunction of decision and discussion as a democratization of the legal form'.[68] Self-reflexivity, for Menke, is a way out from the violence of law, but this movement is interpreted as an individual retreat from the cruelty and definitive character of law. By self-reflexivity Menke refers to a specific virtue of the lawyer applying the law, not to a reform of the content and form of the law itself. It is a change of mood, a new feeling of detachment and suspicion towards the tool that one is asked to use, by being aware of its cutting edge, of the violence this tool is capable of. But this is consigned to the virtue of the single legal operator. There is no guarantee here that an individual sentiment could be universalised; there is no platform to do that. No institution of law is concerned with this change of mood. Once again, in this way, law remains entrenched in a monological attitude that is not invested in or subverted by a conversation with a 'third person'. A final objection, then, is that de-potentiating law – the alternative recommended by Menke – is not sufficient to redeem law from its intrinsically violent nature. We should not be satisfied with this idea of a self-reflective law, according to Fischer-Lescano. Rather we should be seeking to transcend law altogether in the name of justice. We need justice – referring to a dimension beyond law – not so much moderation and self-denial. For Fischer-Lescano, 'The utopian justice to come can be conceived only in transcending the law'.[69]

Fischer-Lescano in this way takes some distance from Menke's strategy of a 'relief' of law, which entails merely a reform of the ethics of legal agents. Rather, law has to be applied in as small a dose as possible. Here a minimalist legal doctrine would be the outcome of the self-reflexivity of a law that is acutely aware of its own terrible potentialities. Legal reasoning should, consequently, be driven more by compassion and empathy than by formal logical arguments. The genuine rationality of law would be dictated by a feeling of generosity and even piety. This is the suggestion we find in the conclusion of an essay by Fischer-Lescano, in which he develops a discussion of *Rechtskraft*, the 'force of law'.[70] True, he pleads for a more inclusive practice of democracy and normative communication where dissent and even resentment are allowed to be expressed and heard. Deliberation should accept dissent and conflict. On other hand, non-citizens, those outside the constitution, should also be asked to give their views. Outsiders must be allowed to have a voice. However, this is possible only if certain feelings can be mobilised in the legal sphere too. Only if formal law becomes mixed with human gentleness, good disposition, a love of peace and trust, do we have any hope of emancipation from hierarchy and domination. However, as we can see, this conclusion is not too distant from Menke's 'relief' or the deposing of the law as a matter of lawyers' self-reflexivity.

Loick's objections are stronger. First of all, he outlines how Menke's concept of law is basically no different from liberal legal doctrine. Menke reproposes an idea of law to which coercion is intrinsic. It is a reproposing of Kant's view: 'Right and authorization to use coercion mean one and the same thing'. But this is mostly due to a mechanical notion of what stopping or counteracting violence may imply. Coercion is inserted into the concept of law insofar as this is seen as an effective means to counteract it. But in this way a paradox is opened, since the violent, or potentially violent, means employed to bring an end to violence only ends up perpetuating it.

Experience shows, Loick contends, that 'legal coercion neither prevents breaches of law, nor does it compensate for them retrospectively, nor does it work as reliable medium for conflict resolution at all'.[71] On the other hand, Kant's concept of law is not congruent with Kant's idea of normativity and morality. Morality is only driven by a categorical imperative of justice; effective results and consequences are excluded from moral reasoning and legitimacy. Thus, a law defined through its instrumental capacity to be followed (due to the use of violence) would be illegitimate from the perspective of Kantian moral theory. Here we find a contradiction in the very system of Kant's philosophy and, especially, we could add, from the perspective of a strong concept of normativity such as the one defended by anarchism. Violence is neither effective nor legitimate, if the goal is one of justice.

Furthermore, for Loick, there are positive forms of law that are not based on coercion. He especially refers to two historical experiences: international law, and Jewish legal practice. These both operate effectively without being supported by a monopoly of violence. There is no sovereign state underpinning international law and traditional Jewish law. The former operates through free agreements, and the latter is possible through a community of interpretations and practices, not through imperative prescriptions. These two cases might be sufficient to show that the connection between law and violence is not a conceptual one, as is Menke's claim.

We have seen that Menke raises another point to qualify the law as violent – that its application cannot be based on reasoning or insight; it is, rather, always a matter of sheer decision. Menke defends a form of radical legal realism here. There is no possible rationality in the practice of law beyond a sort of will to power. On the other hand, Menke believes that rule-following cannot but be based on the fear of punishment.[72] Threat is connatural to a rule. But, to justify such a view, two assumptions must be made, both of which are debatable, rooted as they are in a specific political anthropology, namely a Hobbesian one. One should assume, according to this perspective, that human beings are *homines hominibus lupi*, in a perpetual state of war with one another.

Menke, we have seen, takes up Benjamin's idea of the 'deposing' (*Entsetzung*) of law, but he gives it a more individualist and psychological turn. The 'relief' of law which is recommended here is more a 'retreat' from the law, than the abolition or transcendence of it. In particular, once law is made consubstantial with violence, there is no way to not use violence whenever applying law. For Menke – as Loick objects – 'the task of legal criticism is not to discriminate law and violence', since such discrimination is ontologically impossible, but to discriminate different 'modes of execution' of the law, by choosing the one that might be considered less violent in the eyes of the legal operator on the basis of his virtue and empathy.[73] Law is in any case condemned to be a vehicle of violence and oppression.

This is an unsatisfactory outcome, especially from an anarchist point of view. But this is inevitable if violence is seen a part of the 'essence' of law, a position also maintained by

Kenneth Himma, an analytical jurisprudent who intends to convince us, first, that law is a concept to be defined in terms of necessary and sufficient conditions from an a priori perspective, and then tries to identify coercion as one of these essential conditions for the 'nature' of law.[74] In opposition to such a perspective one might argue that law is an interpretive concept, since what law is is essentially contested, and, at the end of the day, law is what people think and practice as law. This is what makes this discussion especially relevant. If we think that law is essentially violent, we shall have a violent practice of law. If we believe that law is not necessarily related to violence, we could have a form of law without violence or at least make some progress towards achieving it. Loick resumes this dilemma in a clear way, and we may share his conclusion: 'Once coercion and law are no longer a priori bound to each other, normative criteria are needed in order to distinguish legitimate from illegitimate hindrances of freedom: the legitimacy of coercion can no longer simply be deduced from the law itself'.[75]

Notes

1. Kelsen, *Pure Theory of Law*, p. 33.
2. Locke, *Second Treatise*, p. 268.
3. It was against the over-inflation of the term, that Hannah Arendt introduced her famous conceptual distinction between violence and power. Violence referred to a top-down relationship of coercion and domination and had a purely instrumental quality, whereas power referred to a bottom-up form of collective self-organisation ('the power of the people'). This was not to say, of course, that power could never employ violence as a means; nor did it mean that violence could never, in turn, destroy power. But violence could never *become* power, or generate it. (See Arendt, *On Violence*.)
4. See, for instance, the collection of essays that address this relationship in Austin Sarat and Thomas R. Kearns, eds., *Law's Violence: The Amherst Series in Law, Jurisprudence and Social Thought*, Ann Arbor: University of Michigan Press, 1995.
5. Cover, Robert M., 'Violence and the Word' (1986). *Faculty Scholarship Series*. Paper 2708, 1601–1629, p. 1601. http://digitalcommons.law.yale.edu/fss_papers/2708.

6. Ibid., p. 1628.
7. Walter Benjamin, 'Critique of Violence', *Reflections: Essays, Aphorisms, Autobiographical Writings*, ed. by P. Demetz, trans. by E. Jephcott. New York: Schocken Books, 1986, 277–300, p. 281.
8. There are some exceptions of course: for instance, the 'illegalist' tradition of individualist anarchism – exemplified by the Bonnot Gang in France in the early twentieth century – advocated criminality as a lifestyle and as a legitimate form of social rebellion. See Mitchell Abidor ed., *Down with the Law: Anarchist Individualist Writings form Early Twentieth-Century France*, Chicago and Edinburgh: AK Press, 2019.
9. Derrida, *Rogues*.
10. This point is elaborated by Loizdou in her book *Anarchism as an Art of Living without Law*.
11. This is also reflected in his short fragment 'The Right to Use Force' [published in the *Journal of Religious Socialism* in 1920] which is often read as a companion piece to 'Critique of Violence'. Here Benjamin defends a certain 'anarchist' position that calls into question the state's sole right to use force to the exclusion of individuals. See Walter Benjamin, *Selected Writings: 1913–1926*, ed., Marcus Bullock and Michael W. Jennings, Cambridge, MA: Harvard University Press, 1996, 231–234.
12. See also Jacques Derrida, *The Death Penalty. Volume One, The Seminars of Jacques Derrida*, ed., G. Bennington, trans., P. Kamuf, Chicago: Chicago University Press, 2014.
13. Benjamin, 'Critique', p. 286.
14. Ibid., p. 286.
15. In April 2022, the High Court ruled that the London Metropolitan police breached the rights of the organisers of the vigil in their heavy-handed response.
16. Benjamin, 'Critique', 287.
17. Ibid., 287.
18. Ibid., 295.
19. Here Geoffroy de Lagasnerie raises an interesting question of individual criminal responsibility, and why the law is geared towards producing guilty subjects rather than holding society at large to account, given that many crimes are the result of broader social and economic circumstances beyond the individual's direct control: 'Questioning the criminal justice system requires unearthing the reasons why, when confronted by an event or act, we feel the need to identify, singularize, and judge rather than understand, generalize,

and politicize: what purpose is served by an individualizing perception of events and the attribution of responsibility to singular subjects? Why create guilty subjects?' (*Judge and Punish*, p. 89).

20. Benjamin, 'Critique', 297.
21. Benjamin's example here is God's violent judgment on the company of Korah from the Old Testament (see 'Critique', 297).
22. Benjamin at the same time distances himself from what he calls a 'childish anarchism' that refuses constraints on individual behaviour of any kind and espouses the maxim 'What pleases is permitted' (Ibid., 284). However, by this he is referring more to a naïve libertarianism or even libertinism that fetishises absolute individual freedom, something far removed from anarchism as an ethical and political theory.
23. Ibid., 300.
24. Ibid., 297.
25. Particularly by the French anarcho-syndicalist, Fernand Pelloutier and the Bourses de Travaille, an autonomous trade union organisation and working-class movement that included education and mutual aid practices.
26. See Georges Sorel, *Reflections on Violence*, trans., T. E. Hulme and J. Roth, New York: Collier Books, 1961, 90–91.
27. Ibid., 127.
28. Ibid., 127.
29. We should note here that the *myth* of the general strike is at the same time very different – indeed the opposite – of what Benjamin means by mythic violence.
30. Benjamin, 'Critique', 300.
31. Walter Benjamin, 'Franz Kafka: On the Tenth Anniversary of his Death', trans., Harry Zohn in Howard Eiland and Michael W. Jennings, ed., Selected Writings: Volume 2: 1927–1934 (Cambridge, MA: Belknap Press 1999).
32. Ibid., p. 815.
33. Sorel, *Reflections*, 88.
34. Ibid., 17.
35. Ibid., 115.
36. Ibid., 172.
37. See also Elizabeth Frazer and Kimberley Hutchings, 'Anarchist Ambivalence: politics and violence in the thought of Bakunin, Tolstoy and Kropotkin', *European Journal of Political Theory*, 18(2) 2019: 259–280.
38. Bakunin, *Political Philosophy*, p. 372.

39. Ibid., 373.
40. See Jacques Ellul, *Anarchy and Christianity*, trans. by G. Bromiley, Grand Rapids, MI: Eerdmans Publishing, 1991.
41. See Martin Buber, *Paths in Utopia*, trans., R. F. C. Hull, Boston: Beacon Press, 1958.
42. This is also affirmed in Benjamin's understanding of the judgement against violence – 'Thou shalt not kill' – not as an absolute commandment, but rather as an ethical guideline 'for the actions of persons and communities who have to wrestle with it in solitude and, in exceptional cases, to take on themselves the responsibility of ignoring it' (see Benjamin, 'Critique', 298). This does not simply open the possibility of justifying real violence in certain circumstances – for self-defence for instance – but, more importantly, proposes a notion of autonomous ethical judgement as distinct from moral commandment.
43. See Peter Gelderloos, *How Non-Violence Protects the State*, Cambridge, MA: South End Press, 2007. See also G. Anders, *Gewalt Ja oder nein: Eine notwendige Diskussion*, ed. by M. Bissinger, Knaur, Munchen 1987, especially pp. 24–25.
44. Peter Gelderloos, *The Failure of Non-Violence*, Left Bank Books, 2017.
45. We should note that Gelderloos, in critiquing nonviolence, is not thereby advocating violence, but simply questioning the moralistic assumptions behind the ideology of nonviolence.
46. Judith Butler, *The Force of Nonviolence: an Ethico-Political Bind*, London: Verso, 2020, p. 19.
47. Ibid., 19.
48. Ibid., 88.
49. A. Caffi, 'A Critique of Violence', in Id., *A Critique of Violence. Writings*, transl. by R. Rosenthal, Bobbs-Merrill, New York 1970, p. 40. For a similar approach to the question of violence which is opposed to sociality and 'civility', cf. E. Balibar, *Violence and Civility: On the Limits of Political Philosophy*, Columbia University Press, New York 2015.
50. Benjamin, 'Critique of Violence', p. 245. Butler also refers to this as a different way of understanding Benjamin's notion of 'divine violence', pointing to Benjamin's claim that 'non-violent conflict resolution' See Butler, *Force*, 90).
51. See H. Arendt, *The Human Condition*, The University of Chicago Press, Chicago 1958.
52. See Arendt, *On Violence.*
53. See Arendt, *On Revolution.*
54. Butler, *Force*, 38–43.

55. Landauer, 'Thoughts on Anarchy', *Revolution and Other Writings.*
56. Ibid., p. 85.
57. Ibid., p. 87.
58. Gustav Landauer, 'Weak Statesmen, Weaker People!', *Revolution*, pp. 213–214.
59. Landauer, 'Thoughts on Anarchy', p. 88.
60. Landauer, 'Mysticism: From Separation to Community', *Revolution*, 94–108, p. 97.
61. See J. Habermas, *Between Facts and Norms: Contributions to a Discourse Theory of Law and Democracy*, William Rehg, Cambridge, MA: MIT Press, 1998.
62. Cf. A. Fischer-Lescano, *Rechtskraft*, August Verlag, Berlin 2013, pp. 70–71.
63. Cf. K. Günther, *Der Sinn für Angemessenheit. Anwendungsdiskurse in Moral und Recht*, Suhrkamp Verlag, Frankfurt am Main 1988.
64. Ch. Menke, 'Law and Violence', *Law & Literature*, Vol. 22, 2010, p. 9.
65. Ibid., p. 14.
66. Ibid., p. 185.
67. Cf. G. Teubner, 'Societal Constitutionalism: Alternatives to State-Centred Constitutional Theory?', in Christian Joerges, Inga-Johanne Sand and Gunther Teubner eds., *Constitutionalism and Transnational Governance*, Oxford: Oxford University Press, 2004, 3–28.
68. A. Fischer-Lescano, 'Postmodern Legal Theory as Critical Theory', in Menke, *Law and Violence*, p. 170.
69. Ibid.
70. A. Fischer-Lescano, *Rechtskraft*, p. 118.
71. D. Loick, 'Law Without Violence', *Law and Violence*, p. 98.
72. See Menke, 'Law and Violence', p. 21.
73. Loick, 'Law Without Violence', p. 108.
74. See Himma, *Coercion and the Nature of Law.*
75. Loick, 'Law Without Violence', p. 99.

Eight
Disobedience

The previous chapter explored the ethics of violence and considered whether violence could legitimately be deployed in resistance to the legal violence of the state. We argued that while violence is in many cases morally justifiable, it also comes with many risks, including the replication of authoritarian and coercive relationships. We therefore proposed ways that the meaning of violence could be transformed through symbolic action so that it 'does not spill blood' but at the same time retains its ethical and political *force*. Indeed, anarchism might be seen as the project of modifying our relationship to violence in such a way that political struggles become creative rather than purely destructive; so that they allow for the invention of new forms of subjectivity and more autonomous relations between individuals.

Ethical considerations of violence and nonviolence in political struggles open onto the question of civil disobedience. Once again, anarchism has an ambiguous relationship to civil disobedience, by which is meant *principled* law-breaking. Clearly, disobedience to legal authority is at the very core of anarchism; anarchism, in its fundamental rejection of sovereignty and political obligation, is the most disobedient of all radical political traditions. It is a philosophy and politics of defiance. Anarchism starts with a resounding 'No' to the claim of political obligation. It reserves the right of the individual to make his or her own rational and moral judgement about the legitimacy of the law and to autonomously decide his own course of action. The anarchist might choose, upon reflection, to comply with a particular law because it seems like the right thing to do, but this is never the same as *obeying* the law – compliance with specific laws for prudential reasons is not a recognition of legal authority. On the other hand, the anarchist might choose to not comply with the law and to resist it – whether in an individual capacity or in active collaboration with others, choosing the means appropriate to this resistance. The act of disobedience, of refusal, of non-compliance is already a form of violence if understood in the sense of Benjamin's 'divine violence'. It is something that strikes at the very heart of law's authority, invoking an alternative idea of justice beyond the law.

Yet, there are important differences between anarchism and the tradition of civil disobedience. Civil disobedience usually entails strictly *nonviolent* resistance, and, while there is certainly an anarchist tradition of 'pacifist' civil disobedience associated with the thought of Tolstoy and Thoreau, anarchism as a whole is not limited to this. Secondly, civil disobedience involves non-compliance with *specific* laws but does not necessarily call into question the whole concept of legal authority; it defies this or that law, but not the legal system in its entirety. Indeed, it often claims to be doing so out of loyalty to higher legal principles or to the constitutional order, which a particular law or government measure is said to be inconsistent with. Those who engage in civil disobedience often say that in defying a particular law, they are actually respecting the *rule of law* – something an anarchist would not usually go along with. Of course, there are different ways of thinking about civil disobedience, from liberal to more radical versions. However, civil disobedience does not, generally speaking, question the principle of legal and political authority in the radical sense that anarchism does.

Still, any anarchist legal theory must take the notion of civil disobedience seriously. Even in its milder forms, civil disobedience opens up an important space of politicisation and of autonomous ethical action, in which the boundaries of legal authority are contested. Even if proponents of civil disobedience say they are upholding the rule of law by taking direct action, they are also, at least potentially, calling into question the legal order that demands that *all* laws, insofar as they are laws, be obeyed. They are also disagreeing with the idea that the only way laws can be challenged or amended is through proper legislative processes or at the ballot box. Moreover, there is a certain value in exposing the gap between constitutional principles and particular laws.

Revealing an inconsistency between the application of the law and the principles it is supposed to enshrine is at the same time to open up cracks and fissures within the legal order and to chip away at its foundations. Above all, it is important to acknowledge the courage of individuals who engage in civil disobedience, who are prepared to risk police violence, arrest and imprisonment to defy the law, and who sometimes stake their very lives on a point of moral principle. Such dissenting actions have a certain ethical dignity and moral force that anarchists ought to recognise and respect. So, while there are important differences between anarchism and most traditions of civil disobedience – certainly the liberal 'constitutional' tradition – anarchism can be thought of as a radical form of civil disobedience. Perhaps we can speak of anarchism as 'uncivil' disobedience – as a philosophy and politics that takes disobedience beyond the limits of 'civility', that is, beyond the limits of what are considered acceptable forms of communication and action. Or perhaps we might be inclined to drop the term 'civil' altogether and see anarchism simply as 'disobedience'.[1]

However, as we shall be arguing in this chapter, to understand disobedience we need to start with the problem of *obedience*. Legal authority presupposes obedience. Legal systems assume that we will obey their directives and commands; indeed, they could not operate on any other basis. Kelsen defined legal validity in terms of its 'binding force' on the behaviour of the individual. The key question for us is to understand the nature of this 'binding force'. Is it something that is purely coercive, as Kelsen seems to suggest, or does it also rely on our *freely* consenting to be bound by it? In other words, why do we obey laws even in the absence of direct coercion, and when obedience sometimes goes against our own interests or clashes with our moral sensibilities? It is here that we encounter the fundamental enigma of political authority – what Etienne de la Boétie a long time ago termed 'voluntary servitude' (*servitude volontaire*); in other words, the mystery of our free and uncoerced consent to our own domination. The free abandonment of our own freedom, and our *desire* for our own servitude – a phenomenon that has been borne out time and time again with such disastrous consequences – is a major obstacle to radical politics and is something that any critical theory of the law, especially anarchism, must come to terms with. However, in this chapter we propose an alternative and more emancipatory interpretation of the idea of 'voluntary servitude'. We show that this ethical and political problematic of free obedience at the same time reveals the instability of power relationships and the ontological primacy of freedom over authority. The flip-side of voluntary servitude – the truth that it conceals and at the same time presupposes – is 'voluntary inservitude', in other words, *wilful disobedience.*

Anarchism and civil disobedience

In Arendt's famous essay, 'Civil Disobedience', written amidst the political upheavals and tumult of the 1960s in the US – particularly student protests against the Vietnam War – she argues that civil disobedience serves as an important check on abuses of power and as a corrective to the failing institutions of government, something that is entirely consistent with the spirit of the US Constitution. In fact, she sees civil disobedience – which she at the same time distinguishes from the more individualist and theological notion of conscientious objection – in terms of a kind of voluntary association that hearkens back to the revolutionary foundations of the republic. People come together in groups in order to resist unjust laws and government policies, and even to challenge the will of the majority, which always has the potential to become tyrannical.

Reading this essay, it is hard not to be struck by the resonances with our own time. Arendt sees civil disobedience as symptomatic of a certain crisis of legitimacy in governing political and legal institutions, a general breakdown of their authority. Indeed, she refers to a kind of 'state of emergency' in the political order, to which civil disobedience can be seen as a response.[2]

This situation of emergency is characteristic of our own time today. In the wake of ongoing and mounting crises, governing political and legal institutions seem to be in a similar state of decomposition. Pandemics, ecological catastrophes, economic instability, fuel and energy crises, all have the effect of revealing structural inequalities and institutional weaknesses, exposing the liberal democratic order to new challenges to its authority. This comes in many forms, from right-wing populism to new forms of extra-parliamentary mobilisation and dissent. Recently, for instance, we have seen movements and spontaneous mobilisations around the world against police violence, racial injustice and environmental devastation. Activists have engaged in 'illegal' tactics such as unauthorised protests and gatherings, often in violation of COVID-19 restrictions, as well as forms of direct action such as blockading motorways, pulling down statues, attaching themselves to aircraft, and shutting down city centres. Their demands – such as ending police violence against racial minorities or declaring a climate emergency – are apparently simple yet go to the heart of the political and economic order. Governments have responded to these actions with increasingly repressive legislation.[3] Yet, these disobedients are prepared to defy the law and risk serious criminal sanction on behalf of a higher moral principle; indeed, some even actively seek arrest as part of their protest tactics.[4]

While these actions and movements emerge in a more spontaneous and 'viral' way in the contemporary globalised era, they can nevertheless be seen as part of the long-established tradition of civil disobedience – one that includes mobilisations over the past two decades against economic inequality, neoliberal austerity policies and the institutions of global financial capitalism, or against political authoritarianism in different parts of the world. They are also reminiscent in some ways of the earlier Civil Rights and anti-war movements in the US in the 1960s, or of Gandhi's campaign of nonviolent resistance to British colonial rule in India. Indeed, the idea of civil disobedience and the withdrawal of consent from authority has a long genealogy going back to Renaissance humanism and early modern thought – something we shall explore in this chapter. Yet, how should such actions and campaigns be understood from the perspective of anarchist theory? Clearly, anarchism is an important part of this dissenting tradition. As we have already noted, anarchism rejects the principle of political obligation and asserts, in Godwin's words, the 'right to private judgement' over legal authority. Notwithstanding the reservations of some philosophical anarchists,[5] this exercise of 'private judgement' is also a *political* act; it is not confined to the individual's solipsistic withdrawal into his own conscience, but can also involve a collective withdrawal of consent from the political order.[6] Anarchism is an *activist* philosophy, and has long been associated with the struggles of workers, women, the poor, indigenous people, the colonised, cultural, racial and sexual minorities, and even struggles on behalf of non-human species and the natural environment. Moreover, anarchism, more so than other radical philosophies, is based on the principle of direct action rather than the pursuit of political objectives through parties or revolutionary vanguards.

The anarchist principle of disobedience, of non-compliance with the law, is perhaps best summed up by Henry David Thoreau in his famous essay 'Civil Disobedience' [1849]: 'It is for no particular item in the tax bill that I refuse to pay it. I simply wish to refuse allegiance to the state, to withdraw and stand aloof from it effectually'.[7] Thoreau's seemingly inconsequential act of non-compliance – refusing to pay taxes in protest against slavery and the US war against Mexico, which led him to spending a night in jail – is at the same time a declaration of war against the state. The simple act of disobedience becomes a withdrawal of allegiance from the state, a refusal to comply with its directives and commands. If the state is a machine, the disobedient individual jams himself in its cogs and mechanisms to stop their working. As Thoreau says: 'If the injustice has a spring, or a pulley, or a rope, or a crank, exclusively for itself, then perhaps you may consider if the remedy will not be worse than the evil; but if it is of such a nature that it requires you to be the agent of injustice to another, then I say, break the law. Let your life be a counter-friction to stop the machine'.[8] In other words, if the law forces you to act against your conscience, then you should refuse to comply; even simple acts of resistance can wear down the machine. The key element here is the withdrawal of consent. This is not so much a constituting action, in the sense of the revolutionary seizure of power. Rather, following the distinction we drew in a previous chapter, it is much closer to Stirner's idea of the insurrection: 'a working forth of me out of the established'.[9]

In the act of withdrawing consent from the political and legal order, civil disobedience is clearly in accordance with the anti-authoritarian ethos of anarchism. There are, however, some important differences, at least with regard to more liberal interpretations of civil disobedience, which tend to see principled lawbreaking as a form of constitutional fidelity. From this perspective, in engaging in civil disobedience, the individual is said to be acting out of loyalty to the liberal political order as a whole, defying a particular law or policy because it is inconsistent with higher legal or constitutional principles. This is precisely how John Rawls understands civil disobedience, which he allows in liberal societies only under limited circumstances. Rawls defines civil disobedience in the following terms:

> a public, nonviolent, conscientious yet political act contrary to the law usually done with the aim of bringing about a change in the law or policies of the government. By acting in this way one addresses the sense of justice of the majority of the community and declares that in one's considered opinion the principles of social cooperation among free and equal men are not being respected.[10]

Civil disobedience is considered problematic for 'more or less just' democratic societies in which citizens recognise and respect the legitimacy of the constitution. The problem arises, according to Rawls, because of a conflict of obligations: on the one hand of citizens to the laws imposed by a legislative majority, following the correct procedures of a liberal democracy, and on the other, of the individual to his or her own conscience and sense of justice. In other words, if one accepts the democratic rules of the game – the idea that laws are determined by majority rule – then how can one justify even principled lawbreaking by minorities? This is why Rawls imposes so many conditions and limitations on civil disobedience – limitations that anarchists would regard as intolerable.

Firstly, as we have seen, civil disobedience must be *public*. Rawls says:

> Not only is it addressed to public principles, it is done in public. It is engaged in openly with fair notice; it is not covert or secretive. One may compare it to a public speech,

and being a form of address, an expression of profound and conscientious political conviction, it takes place in the public forum.[11]

Yet this would seem to rule out whistleblowing – leaking information about government lying or corporate coverups and malfeasance – which, given the risks involved, is usually done by individuals in secret. The kinds of public, visible actions Rawls has in mind, such as protests and sit-ins, seriously limit the scope of civil disobedience, imposing conditions that simply do not apply today in the age of internet communication technologies which have transformed the notion of the 'public' space and have enabled new kinds of resistance, including electronic whistleblowing and hacktivism.[12] Indeed, the actions of Julian Assange, Chelsea Manning and Edward Snowden – all of whom have paid a heavy price for their exposure of US government lies, cover-ups and abuses of power – as emblematic of a new kind of civil disobedience that completely overturns the accepted categories of the public space, citizenship and democracy.[13] Assange, Manning and Snowden are exemplars of a new type of political subject who defies the regime of visibility, representation and inclusion within the political order. Their actions do not take place in the public space – in the way that Rawls stipulates – but, on the contrary, in the anonymous space of the Internet. Rather than seeking to appear in the political-legal order, to stand up and be counted, in the Arendtian sense, they operate in a clandestine space, engaging in a withdrawal, a 'line of flight' from the state order. However, this does not make their action any less political. Indeed, anonymity, the concealing of identity, the refusal of visibility and representation becomes a new kind of political action and constitutes an alternative space for freedom and autonomy. As Geoffroy de Lagasnerie says: 'The practice of anonymity enables one to act politically without constituting oneself as an identifiable subject. Anonymous subjects are not subjects who appear. On the contrary they dissolve as public subjects and organize their own invisibility.'[14]

Therefore, the gesture of invisibility and anonymity – which we also see in the wearing of masks in protests – becomes the means and symbol for a different and more anarchistic politics of disobedience, one that challenges the traditional idea of the democratic space that Rawls saw as central. Anonymity also allows for the constitution of a new kind of political subject: rather than the legally recognised citizen, whose rights and duties are prescribed by the state, we are seeing the emergence of disobedient subjectivities who determine their own autonomous identity and modes of action and communication. In today's societies of surveillance and hypervisibility, in which everyone must present themselves for identification and conform to legally prescribed categories of subjectivity, perhaps the most radical gesture is the refusal of identification and the withdrawal from the order of visibility. This is a politics of *dis-identification*, something that is close, once again, to Stirner's insurrection. As Foucault put it, in questioning the political valency of 'identity' and the liberal notion of the individual whose identity is always determined by the state even as he asserts his legal rights against it: 'Maybe the target nowadays is not to discover what we are but to refuse what we are. We have to imagine and to build up what we could be to get rid of this kind of political "double bind," which is the simultaneous individualization and totalization of power structures.'[15]

Secondly, Rawls says that civil disobedience must be nonviolent. Yet, as we have already discussed, the meaning of violence/nonviolence is a complex issue. Rawls' definition would certainly exclude actions that many activists would regard as legitimate, such as property damage, or confrontations with the police, or the sabotage of military installations, animal testing laboratories, government communication systems. Anarchist civil disobedience might be nonviolent, as was the case with Thoreau, or as we find in the pacifist writings of Tolstoy;[16] or it might be violent, as with the actions of the US abolitionist John Brown. As the American anarchist Voltairine de Cleyre – who reflected on Brown's violent assaults on the institutions of slavery – said: 'Direct action may be the extreme of violence, or it may be as peaceful as the waters of the Brook of Shiloa'.[17] Indeed, for de Cleyre, the main distinction was not between violence and nonviolence, but rather between direct and indirect, or 'political', action – in other words, democratic representation. The latter, she argued, was often pointless, and led to a loss of autonomy and independence.

This touches on the third condition that Rawls imposes: that civil disobedience is 'conscientious yet political'. In other words, civil disobedience is said to have a communicative function and is an appeal to the majority's sense of justice. Rawls elaborates: 'civil disobedience is a political act not only in the sense that it is addressed to the majority that holds political power, but also because it is an act guided by political principles, that is, by the principles of justice which regulate the constitution and social institutions generally'.[18] The key problem for Rawls is that in 'more or less just' societies, disobeying laws that have been democratically determined according to constitutional procedures requires special justification. The minority of dissenters must therefore appeal to the majority to change particular laws and must, in doing so, be guided by the same principles of constitutional justice and procedural fairness that everyone has agreed to. In other words, in defying specific laws and policies, civil disobedients at the same time remain bound by the constitutional principles and institutions of the society they are part of. The civil disobedient dissents from particular laws but not from the political order itself; he or she still must still recognise the legitimacy and moral authority of this order and its right to make laws. A particular law or policy may be challenged if it is clearly inconsistent with constitutional principles of liberty and equality. However, for the most part, as members of 'more or less' functional liberal societies based on the constitutional principles of liberty and equality, we have a duty to obey.[19]

Yet, from an anarchist point of view, the existence of liberal and democratic institutions and procedures does not confer legitimacy; political obligation can by no means be derived from some hypothetical notion of consent to the liberal democratic order. 'Just' institutions can – indeed often *do* – produce unjust outcomes; 'just' laws are implemented in unjust ways, even if the correct procedures are followed and checks and balances applied. The ongoing and endemic problem of excessive police violence and overly punitive systems of incarceration in some of the most rule-bound liberal democracies in the world should make this immediately obvious. They cannot be seen simply as aberrations to be corrected, or insufficiencies to be ameliorated, but rather as the violent and coercive 'underside' of sovereignty. Therefore, in contesting specific laws the anarchist is not acting out of loyalty to the constitution or respect for the majority will; rather, disobedience should be understood as a registering of dissent from the political order itself. This does not mean that there is no value in seeking legal reform, or in pointing out the inconsistency between particular laws and constitutional principles. Seeking to make laws less onerous, oppressive and unjust within the existing legal system by asserting extra-parliamentary pressure on lawmakers and public opinion is an entirely worthwhile endeavour. However, anarchism reinterprets the very meaning and significance of civil disobedience to indicate a form of action that, even if its immediate aims are limited, calls into question the very principle of state sovereignty that forms the basis of any political order, liberal democratic or otherwise.

Rawls' highly circumspect concession to civil disobedience is therefore premised on a more general claim about our duty to obey the law in constitutional liberal democracies – in other words, a general 'fidelity to the law'. However, can we turn this premise around and talk about a duty to *disobey*? This is the position that Candice Delmas takes in her critique of Rawls. She argues that if we can be said to have a moral, rather than simply legal, duty to obey the law – according to Rawls' notion of justice – then we have an equally compelling moral duty to disobey a law that is *unjust*. This is more than a *right* of resistance; it is resistance as a *moral duty*, something that flows from the very nature of political obligation. Moreover, resistance against injustice might legitimately involve violence, and might not always be public and communicative in the manner that Rawls stipulates. It may involve forms of political discourse and action which transgress the 'rules of the game' and offend the sensibilities of the majority. Here, Delmas invokes the notion of 'uncivil' as opposed to 'civil' disobedience. Uncivil disobedience is disruptive, it questions the limits of political participation and the norms of 'civility': 'Uncivil disobedience also questions the rules of public engagement, the standards and boundaries of civility and public reason: who gets to speak, as well as where, when, and how'.[20] Many contemporary forms of protest and activism might be regarded as uncivil in this sense: movements for racial justice, like Black Lives Matter, and climate justice, like Extinction Rebellion, Insulate Britain and Just Stop Oil, as well as digital hacktivism and whistle-blowing, challenge accepted liberal democratic notions of political communication and action. Certainly, the notion of uncivil disobedience invoked by Delmas is much closer to anarchism in the way it disrupts the traditional notion of the public sphere. However, Delmas distinguishes her position from that of philosophical anarchists, for whom the absence of political obligation is without any practical consequences, and whose position thus amounts, in her eyes, to a certain 'toothlessness'.[21] For Delmas, on the contrary, disobedience itself is a political obligation.

We would largely agree with Delmas' position. But where does this political obligation to resist come from? It clearly does not arise from one's loyalty to an existing political community, as this is precisely the principle that is being challenged in the act of dissent. If it arises, on the other hand, from a sense of natural justice, then it seems we are not very far away from the position of the philosophical anarchist for whom the question of obedience to the law depends on the individual's moral conscience and right of private judgement. Perhaps, alternatively, resistance can be seen as an extension or radicalisation of the democratic principle of collective self-determination. It is here that Robin Celikates proposes a radical democratic model of civil disobedience, in contrast once again to the liberal democratic model put forward by Rawls. Radical democratic civil disobedience exceeds the norms and institutions of liberal democracy and aims at a *democratisation* of democracy.[22] Civil disobedience can be seen as an insurrectionary process and an expression of the constituting power of the *demos* that aims at a renewal of democratic political life. Similarly to Delmas, Celikates questions the limitations of the liberal account of civil disobedience put forward by Rawls (as well as Dworkin). Celikates argues, in contrast, that civil disobedience might legitimately involve violent disruption and property damage, as well as going against the majority will. However, rather than adopting the term 'uncivil' disobedience, as Delmas does, he argues for a renegotiation of the term 'civil' to include understandings of citizenship and modes of action otherwise excluded in the liberal model: 'The consequence of the radical democratic critique of identifying the "civil" in civil disobedience with a strict commitment to nonviolence cannot be an embrace of violence'.[23] In other words, while not ruling out violence per se – and while remaining critical of the ideology of nonviolence – radical democratic civil disobedience at the same time recognises the ethical and political risks of violence; something that is close to the anarchist position. Moreover, the liberal constitutional model of civil disobedience, which sees it only as a last resort, neglects the way that the usual channels of democratic communication and decision-making remain inaccessible to most people or become hegemonised by oligarchic interests. Therefore, civil disobedience, on Celikates' reading, should not be seen as an outlier to democracies – only to be tolerated in exceptional circumstances – but as central to the very understanding of democracy. As he puts it:

> Rather than being viewed as the actions of individual rights-bearers, civil disobedience represents an essentially collective and political practice of contestation, in which the vertical form of state authority (or *constituted power*) is confronted with the horizontal constituting power of the association of citizens or of those who are governed.[24]

We largely agree with this radical democratic reinterpretation of civil disobedience; Celikates' model comes closest to the anarchist position. Disobedient acts of principled law breaking – where the lawmaking authority of the sovereign state is challenged – opens up an important space of political contestation and democratic renewal. However, is constituting power the most appropriate category to think about this? As we suggested in a previous chapter, the problem with the constituting power of the demos is that it remains within the conceptual logic of sovereignty and therefore within the order of *constituted* power that it contests. There is a fundamental ambiguity in the notion of constituting power, in that it derives from the idea of the people or demos as sovereign over the legal order and as having the power to change it; yet, in doing so, it presupposes the formation of a new sovereign legal order with its own coercive structure.

Celikates recognises that the radical democratic model of civil disobedience is challenged by the realities of globalisation, the emergence of transnational activism, alternative forms of digital disobedience and activism which do not take place in traditional visible political spaces, as well as indigenous struggles for self-determination against Western-centric forms of hegemony imposed by the modern nation state.[25] Yet, he does not elaborate on how this relatively traditional idea of the democratic will-making power of citizens of bounded polities can really accommodate these new, 'deterritorialised' forms of politics. Celikates' model of civil disobedience – despite its radical departure from the liberal model – is still hinged to the state and to the traditional model of citizenship.

Therefore, while there are many points of convergence between anarchism and the theory of civil disobedience – and certainly with the radically democratic and 'uncivil' theories discussed above – we can perhaps agree with James D. Ingram who, in his anarchist critique of civil disobedience, argues that: 'Civil disobedience presupposes a state, a legitimate authority that governs a territorial community through binding law'.[26] In other words, the main difference, as we see it, between the anarchist tradition and the theory of disobedience – despite some important parallels – is that anarchism does not begin from the ontological presupposition of state sovereignty. Anarchism does not assume the inevitability of the state as the only way to organise social life; rather, the state can be displaced by alternative forms of community based on voluntary and cooperative relationships between individuals and by the development of non-coercive legal frameworks. Despite the common claim that we have the right – or even duty – to dissent from the law, most theories of disobedience do not go along with the anarchist claim that alternatives to the centralised sovereign state can be found. Indeed, it is striking that they try to distance themselves, in one way or another, from the anarchist position.

The problem of obedience

We want to argue that to understand disobedience – what it means, how it can be justified, and what its limits should be – we need to start with the opposite problem of *obedience*. If disobedience is seen as an occasional disruption of the political order, or as a corrective to unjust laws, then perhaps the more important, yet troubling, question is why we obey political authority in the first place. Why should obedience be seen as the default position, the norm, and disobedience the exception? As the anarchist Howard Zinn once famously put it: 'Civil disobedience is not our problem. Our problem is civil obedience'. Our voluntary obedience to authority, our compliance with unjust laws and policies, our consent to systems of domination, inequality and organised violence, is surely one of the central enigmas of politics. While legal and political systems certainly wield coercive power, they for the most part rely upon our willing consent. So, the question we must engage with, as critical political and legal theorists, is precisely why we continue to obey authority even in the absence of coercion.

This raises deep political and ethical problems yet, surprisingly, it is a question that is not usually confronted in most of the literature on civil disobedience. While some level of obedience and compliance is necessary for the functioning of any society, it becomes an ethical and political problem when it occurs under conditions that adversely affect the interests of those who obey, or when it means engaging in actions that seriously clash with one's moral sensibilities. In other words, why do we submit to authority even when it goes against our interests? Why do we go along with commands we know to be wrong in some deep moral sense? How are repressive and totalitarian regimes able to maintain the loyalty and consent of millions of their citizens? How are states able to organise atrocities and genocides on a mass scale, relying on the complicity of ordinary people in participating at all levels in systems of persecution, violence and murder? How do capitalist enterprises ensure, without the need for coercion, not only the willingness of their employees to allow their labour to be exploited, but to actively identify with their employer's desires.[27]

Is voluntary obedience simply a question of ideological domination, or what the Marxists used to call 'false consciousness', or is something else going on here? Of course, psychoanalysis and critical theory have long engaged with this problem. Freud, in his study of the psychodynamics of groups, was perplexed by the way that individuals within group settings behaved very differently to when they were on their own, abandoning their freedom and even their own sense of self-preservation, and displaying 'an extreme passion for authority' or, in the words of the observer of group behaviour, Gustav Le Bon, 'a thirst for obedience' whereby members of groups identified absolutely with the figure of the leader, supplanting their own ego for his.[28] A similar line of enquiry was pursued in the early twentieth century by Wilhelm Reich, who studied the mass psychology of fascism in Germany, and who argued that the popular appeal of National Socialism could not be reduced to ideological obfuscation or 'false consciousness' but, rather, to an active desire for one's own domination, arising from an internalised authoritarianism and conservative beliefs and attitudes concerning sexuality. As in Freud's analysis, there was a combination of identification with the figure of the Führer and the complete and voluntary submission to his authority.[29] According to Reich, the authoritarian and repressive organisational structures of the family, church, and the state were internalised within the individual psyche, establishing fertile ground for an attraction to fascism. For Reich, and for many other thinkers, the desire for one's own domination and the desire to dominate others were but two sides of the same coin, reflecting the authoritarian organisation of the psyche. The mystery of obedience to authority has been central to many investigations into domination, violence and prejudice, whether Arendt's ethical and political concern with the 'banality of evil' in understanding the moral complicity in atrocities of Nazi bureaucratic functionaries like Adolf Eichmann;[30] or the idea of the 'authoritarian personality' put forward by Adorno;[31] or the various social psychology experiments conducted by Stanley Milgram in the 1960s and Philip Zimbardo in the 1970s, which emphasised the willingness of seemingly ordinary people to comply with immoral commands and to inflict pain and suffering on others simply because they were ordered to do so by figures of authority.

However, the question of voluntary servitude becomes more enigmatic, and at the same time more acute, in late modernity with the breaking down of patriarchal structures of authority, such as the family, organised religion, governing institutions and even traditional, hierarchically organised workplaces and businesses. In the era of what Lacan foreshadowed as the 'decline of the paternal function' – in other words, the death of the symbolic figure of the Father – it is perhaps hard to know who our Masters are today. And yet, the mystery of voluntary servitude is that we obey as never before. Indeed, the desire for new masters of all kinds perhaps accounts for the particular appeal of populist political leaders who, on the one hand, openly transgress the symbolic authority of institutions and offices in a parodic performance of sovereignty, and on other, seek to institutionalise new forms of power and hierarchy.

La Boétie's question

To gain a better insight into this phenomenon of voluntary servitude, we turn to the thinker who first coined the term and who enquired into its reasons and its ethical and political implications. Etienne La Boétie was a French sixteenth-century thinker and writer in the civic humanist tradition,[32] best known for his close relationship with essayist Michel de Montaigne. La Boétie's most famous work, *Discours de la Servitude Volontaire,* which Montaigne called a 'text written in honour of liberty against tyrants',[33] was most likely written around 1549 when he was a law student at the University of Orléans, and was published clandestinely in 1577. The text was written against the backdrop of a revolt against the French king Henry II in protest against the imposition of the *gabelle* or salt tax. Subsequently, it had a complex and ambiguous history, circulated by Huguenots and monarchomachs in their opposition to the French crown. It has been seen as call to resistance against unjust tyrannical rule, and it had a significant impact on the tradition of political dissent and civil disobedience,[34] being influential among anarchists, particularly Tolstoy and Benjamin Tucker.

La Boétie starts with the observation that people often consented to tyrannical authority, voluntarily sacrificing their own interests, freedom, property and even their lives, to the will of one man, when they were not coerced in any way:

> For the present, I should like to understand how it happens that so many men, so many villages, so many cities, so many nations, sometimes suffer under a single tyrant who has no other power than the power they give him; who is able to harm them only to the extent to which they have the willingness to bear with him; who could do them absolutely no injury unless they preferred to put up with him rather than contradict him.[35]

For La Boétie, people's self-subjection to the will of the tyrant constitutes a genuine mystery, because it involves the free abandonment of their freedom to one individual who, in himself, has no power over them other than that with which they endow him. He goes on to say that this voluntary subjection cannot be explained as cowardice, because the people so vastly outnumber the tyrant (and his henchmen) that they cannot possibly be acting out of fear: 'When not a hundred, not a thousand men, but a hundred provinces, a thousand cities, a million men, refuse to assail a single man from whom the kindest treatment received is the infliction of serfdom and slavery, what shall we call that?'[36] Rather, as La Boétie puts it, the people are charmed and seduced by the tyrant, even though he has none of the personal qualities that would normally inspire loyalty. For La Boétie, this enthrallment to the figure of the tyrant/leader is a genuine enigma, an inexplicable moral sickness, a kind of perversion that he struggles to name: 'What monstrous vice, then, is this which does not even deserve to be called cowardice, a vice for which no term can be found vile enough, which nature herself disavows and our tongues refuse to name?'[37]

What is unaccountable, for La Boétie, is that people would so willingly abandon their freedom. Freedom is seen as a natural condition. We are intended for freedom, and yet for some reason we choose to give it up and submit ourselves to tyrannical rule, with all the violence, oppression and insecurity this entails. We have essentially forgotten this natural predisposition, so inured have we become to domination. This idea of freedom as an uncorrupted natural state of being, as opposed to the artificiality and corruption of servitude, is reflected in La Boétie's claim that even animals resist the slightest constraint upon their freedom, unlike denatured humans who have been raised under the yoke; paradoxically, animals understand freedom much better than us, and will fight to the death to preserve what we have so easily given up.[38]

Even stranger, voluntary servitude is not a passive condition but an *active*, even frenetic abandonment of freedom; it is something we energetically devote ourselves to. La Boétie observed the ways in which we continually renew and strengthen the bonds of our own servitude every day through the repetition of submissive practices, rituals and behaviours. Just as Spinoza was perplexed by the way that men 'will fight for their servitude as if they were fighting for their own deliverance, and will not think it humiliating but supremely glorious to spill their blood and sacrifice their lives for the glorification of a single man',[39] so for La Boétie it is as if we go out of our way to increase our own domination.[40]

La Boétie offers three tentative explanations for this strange condition. Firstly, he says that behaviours of servitude become normalised and a matter of habit and custom – a 'habituation to subjection': 'This is why men born under the yoke and then nourished and reared in slavery are content, without further effort, to live in their native circumstance, unaware of any other state or right, and considering as quite natural the condition into which they were born'.[41] Second, he points to the propagandistic and ideological function of despotism. Tyrants make a spectacle of their own power, which has a stupefying effect on the masses: 'Plays, farces, spectacles, gladiators, strange beasts, medals, pictures, and other such opiates, these were for ancient peoples the bait toward slavery, the price of their liberty, the instruments of tyranny'.[42] There is a parallel here with what Guy Debord called 'societies of the spectacle', in which power in modern capitalist societies is maintained through the circulation of images, and through media, sports and entertainment spectacles and corporate events designed to project a series of brands, norms and consumerist values.[43] Third – and this is perhaps La Boétie's most compelling explanation – tyrants establish around themselves a network of dependencies based on fear and self-interest; a kind of pyramid of power, in which the tyrant's immediate circle of counsellors and henchmen themselves maintain a series of servants and dependents, creating an organisational ecosystem involving vast numbers of people, all of whom identify with the tyrant's desires. As La Boétie says: 'The consequence of all this is fatal indeed. And whoever is pleased to unwind the skein will observe that not the six thousand but a hundred thousand, and even millions, cling to the tyrant by this cord to which they are tied.'[44] It is self-interest and the hope of advancement that leads people into this entangled web of relations, and yet, for La Boétie, they pay a high price in the loss of their independence and freedom, living in fear of the capricious will of the tyrant.[45]

Ontological anarchy

How should La Boétie's enigmatic thesis of voluntary servitude be interpreted? It has at times been read in a pessimistic, even conservative way, which says that men are born to submit to authority, that they become willing slaves to the sovereign.[46] However, as we have indicated, it is also possible to derive a much more radical, even anarchistic, message from his text. The key insight from La Boétie's study of voluntary servitude is that power presupposes, and indeed is dependent upon, obedience; the power of the tyrant, which seems, on the one hand, so overwhelming and inspires such fear and veneration, is a kind of illusion created by our obedience and the abandonment of our own freedom. In other words, we project onto the tyrant the image of absolute power, thus retroactively *constituting* his power over us. The power of the tyrant does not pre-exist obedience and compel it by force, but is, rather, only *our* power in an inverted form, created through the abandonment of our own freedom. Put simply, power is a thing made by its subjects, rather than being forcibly imposed upon them. As La Boétie says:

> He who thus domineers over you has only two eyes, only two hands, only one body, no more than is possessed by the least man among the infinite numbers dwelling in your cities; he has indeed nothing more than the power that you confer upon him to destroy you. Where has he acquired

> enough eyes to spy upon you, if you do not provide them yourselves? How can he have so many arms to beat you with, if he does not borrow them from you? The feet that trample down your cities, where does he get them if they are not your own? How does he have any power over you except through you?[47]

The image here is reminiscent of the Hobbesian Leviathan, only in reverse. Individuals who have freely abrogated their freedom constitute the body of the sovereign; the weapons he uses against us – his eyes, arms and feet – are really our capacities and powers that we have relinquished to him. However, the implications of this are completely different in La Boétie's account. The tyrant's body politic is shown to be a specular illusion – the powers of the sovereign are in reality nothing; when stripped of his illusion of authority, he is shown to be nothing more than a 'little man' with only two eyes, two hands and one body. In fact, as La Boétie says, the tyrant is really the 'least man' among you. Moreover, unlike in the Hobbesian image, where individuals are captured and enthralled by the specular image of the One – gazing up at their sovereign with eyes of reverence and awe – La Boétie counsels people to simply turn their backs on the sovereign, to no longer recognise his authority, at which point his power collapses like a statue whose foundations have been removed:

> From all these indignities, such as the very beasts of the field would not endure, you can deliver yourselves if you try, not by taking action, but merely by willing to be free. Resolve to serve no more, and you are at once freed. I do not ask that you place hands upon the tyrant to topple him over, but simply that you support him no longer; then you will behold him, like a great Colossus whose pedestal has been pulled away, fall of his own weight and break into pieces?[48]

In other words, if all power comes from the people and is constructed through their willing consent, then this at the same time exposes the *powerlessness of power*, the fragility and instability of all systems of domination, which all depend at some level on consent and complicity. What La Boétie's analysis reveals, then, is the *ontologically anarchic* structure of authority, the fact that, as a relationship, authority is inherently unstable and, in a sense, lacking and ungrounded. Paradoxically, what La Boétie shows us is the ontological freedom as the other side of power; the great secret of power is freedom. Power and authority are constituted through the free abdication of our own freedom; but this freedom can reclaimed through a simple act of free will, through wilful indocility or what Foucault once called 'voluntary inservitude'.[49] One whole century before the shadow of Leviathan loomed up over our horizon, La Boétie had already disturbed its foundations by revealing the freedom that lay behind it, the freedom which Hobbes tried to make us forget.

The ontological primacy of freedom is also a point emphasised by the anarchist anthropologist, Pierre Clastres, who argued that state-dominated societies were unnatural and resulted from a historical misfortune, whereby we suddenly switched from a condition of primitive freedom and equality to one of alienation, servitude and division between oppressors and oppressed. By contrast, he argued, 'Primitive societies refuse power relations by preventing the *desire for submission from coming into being*'.[50] Clastres' contention is that when La Boétie formed his ideas about the naturalness of liberty and the unnatural condition of servitude, he was writing against the backdrop of the intense historical encounter between the state-dominated societies of Europe and the free and stateless societies of the New World, for whom the desire for submission was entirely unknown. For Clastres, then, the radical nature of La Boétie's thinking lay in the idea that domination is not inevitable and that there is another way of living: 'The young La Boétie transcends all known history to say: something else is possible'.[51] Ontological anarchy – as revealed by Clastres and La Boétie[52] – means that *nothing is set in stone*, and that *something else is always possible.*

The anarchist republic

As we have mentioned, La Boétie's notion of the withdrawal of consent from authority has been particularly influential in the tradition of civil disobedience. Indeed, Thoreau's exhortation that we no longer comply with unjust laws and become instead the counter-friction against the machinery of the state seems to directly recall La Boétie's words on how to resist the tyrant:

> Obviously there is no need of fighting to overcome this single tyrant, for he is automatically defeated if the country refuses consent to its own enslavement: it is not necessary to deprive him of anything, but simply to give him nothing; there is no need that the country make an effort to do anything for itself provided it does nothing against itself.[53]

La Boétie does not proscribe any kind of revolutionary program. Rather, the key thing is that we refuse to participate in behaviours of servitude; it is not so much that we act against the tyrant but that we *no longer act against ourselves*. In other words, La Boétie understands resistance, first and foremost, as an act of *self*-emancipation, whereby we extricate ourselves from the illusion of his power.

Yet, although La Boétie seems to be counselling mostly 'peaceful' resistance, it is way too simplistic to confine his understanding of dissent to the liberal model of constitutional civil disobedience. As John Holloway says, La Boétie's politics of refusal should rather be seen as the starting point of every act of resistance: 'The break begins with refusal, with No. No, we shall not tend your sheep, plough your fields, make your car, do your examinations'.[54] In other words, La Boétie's great 'No' to power can be understood as the ontologically anarchic starting point for *all* forms of dissent, even radical dissent, from authority. The message we can take from La Boétie's withdrawal of consent is this: *you were always free, but you just didn't know it*. This idea of ontological freedom – the primacy of freedom over power – is very close to the anarchist notion of prefiguration we have discussed: rather than waiting for the great liberating event – organised by the revolutionary party – prefiguration is a self-enacted freedom that is realised in the present moment, and which involves the creation of autonomous spaces, relations and forms of existence in the here and now.

The radical dimension of La Boétie's politics of disobedience therefore lies in its presenting to us the possibility of an alternative ontology of free and autonomous life – not so much a different set of institutions and laws that would guard against tyranny – but, rather, the image of a different set of 'natural' ungoverned social and ethical relations between individuals. In presenting a counter-image to the totalising, unifying figure of the tyrant – the One – La Boétie shows that real freedom lies in the *plurality* of human relationships. In other words, the power of the tyrant is in the way it presents a fantasy image of wholeness and unity, an artificial totality into which people seek to incorporate themselves. Thus, the many – whose power otherwise exists in pluralistic and egalitarian relations of difference and singularity – come to identify with and submit to the figure of the One. As Miguel Abensour puts it, the *all ones* [*tous uns*] become the *All One* [*tous un*].[55] Here it is important to recall that the alternative title of La Boétie's text was *L'Contre Un* or the *Counter-One*, suggesting not only an opposition to monarchical power, but an unmasking of the plurality of human relations behind the false image of the single leader. La Boétie's point is that this ontological plurality, whose *undoing* is the basis of tyrannical power, is something that can be renewed through practices of refusal, resistance, and the construction of alternative relationships between individuals.

These alternative relations are constituted by friendship, equality and solidarity, rather than domination. Freedom is that of the natural bonds of companionship and an original condition of plurality and equality, from which domination is absent. The tyrannical relationship emerges on the basis of the destruction of these bonds and their replacement by a new and artificial set of relations. Resistance therefore involves the renewal or reinvention of the original set of relations. This explains La Boétie's interest in friendship as an antidote to tyranny. Friendship is the polar opposite of tyranny because it is a relationship of trust, respect, and equality, from which domination is absent.[56] By contrast, the tyrant has no friends, only dependents and subjects, those who serve him out of fear and self-interest: 'The fact is that the tyrant is never truly loved, nor does he love'.[57] Inequality of this kind destroys the very possibility of genuine friendship.

La Boétie's alternative image of social relations is of a certain kind of republic, but it is a republic of friends, rather than a republic of laws. La Boétie certainly employs classical republican tropes – both in his analysis of tyranny and his evoking of alternative ideal city-states of Athens, Sparta, Rome and Venice – however, the image of autonomous and freely formed relationships of equality and solidarity that he puts forward, suggests the possibility of *anarchist republic*; a republic without a state, a republic of friends.

Notes

1. See Elena Loizidou, ed., *Disobedience: Concept and Practice*, New York: Routledge, 2013.
2. Hannah Arendt, 'Civil Disobedience', *Crises of the Republic*, San Diego, New York, London: Harcourt Brace, 1972, 49–102, pp. 101–102.
3. A series of new criminal justice and public order bills introduced in the UK over 2021–2022, in response to a wave of protests by Black Lives Matter and Extinction Rebellion activists, and the toppling of the statue of the slave trader Edward Colston in Bristol in 2021, expanded the scope of protest-related offences – such as 'locking on' – and massively increase police powers to crack down on 'disruptive' protests, including on the grounds of exceeding noise limits, as well as bringing in harsher penalties for damaging public monuments. (See the Public Order Bill 2022; and the Police, Crime, Sentencing, and Courts Bill 2021.)
4. The climate justice movement Extinction Rebellion sees mass arrest as a key element in their protest strategy.
5. See, for instance, A. John Simmons, who distinguishes between philosophical and political anarchism. Christopher Heath Wellman and A. John Simmons, *Is there a Duty to Obey the Law?*
6. William E. Scheuerman distinguishes between philosophical anarchism, which simply questions the principle of political obligation, and political anarchism which implies active resistance to state authority. See *Civil Disobedience*, Cambridge: Polity Press, 2018, p. 191.
7. Henry David Thoreau, 'Civil Disobedience' [1849] Mozam Book, 2002, p. 24.
8. Ibid., 15.
9. Stirner, *The Ego and its Own*, 32.
10. John Rawls, *A Theory of Justice. Revised Edition*, Cambridge, MA: Harvard University Press, 1999, p. 320.
11. Ibid., 321.

12. See Bernard E. Harcourt, *Exposed: Desire and Disobedience in the Digital Age*, Cambridge MA: Harvard University Press, 2015.
13. See de Lagasnerie, *The Art of Revolt.*
14. Ibid., 51.
15. Michel Foucault, 'The Subject and Power', *Critical Inquiry*, Vol. 8, No. 4 (Summer, 1982), 777–795, p. 785.
16. For Tolstoy, violence was 'the indispensable condition of power', and was incompatible not only with Christianity but with anarchist principles. See 'The Kingdom of God is Within You, Or Christianity not as a mystical teaching but as a new concept of life' [1894] The Anarchist Library https://theanarchistlibrary.org/library/leo-tolstoy-the-kingdom-of-god-is-within-you.
17. Voltairine de Cleyre, 'Direct Action' [1912] The Anarchist Library https://theanarchistlibrary.org/library/voltairine-de-cleyre-direct-action.
18. Rawls, *A Theory of Justice*, p. 321.
19. However, as Peter Singer objects, 'if disobedience is an appeal to the community, why can it only be an appeal which the community already accepts? Why could one not be justified in disobeying in order to ask the majority to alter or extend the shared conception of justice?' Peter Singer, *Democracy and Disobedience*, Clarendon, Oxford 1973, p. 88.
20. Candice Delmas, *A Duty to Resist: When Disobedience should be Uncivil*, Oxford: Oxford University Press, 2018, 64.
21. Ibid., 10–11.
22. Robin Celikates, 'Radical Democratic Disobedience', in William E. Scheuerman, ed., *The Cambridge Companion to Civil Disobedience*, Cambridge: Cambridge University Press, 2021, 128–152.
23. Ibid., 136.
24. Ibid., 141–142.
25. Ibid., 144–146.
26. James D. Ingram, 'Anarchism: Provincializing Civil Disobedience', in Scheuerman, 178–200, p. 178.
27. See Frederic Lordon, *Willing Slaves of Capital: Spinoza and Marx on Desire*, trans., G. Ash, London: Verso, 2014.
28. S. Freud, *Group Psychology and the Analysis of the Ego*, trans., J. Strachey, London: Hogarth Press, 1949.
29. W. Reich *The Mass Psychology of Fascism*, New York: Orgone Institute Press, 1946.
30. H. Arendt, *Eichmann in Jerusalem: A Report on the Banality of Evil*, New York: Penguin, 2006.

31. T. W. Adorno, F. Brunswik, D. J. Levinson, R. N. Sanford, *The Authoritarian Personality*, London: W. W. Norton & Co., 1993.
32. Keohane, N. O. (1977) The radical humanism of Etienne de la Boétie. *Journal of the History of Ideas* 31(1): 119–130.
33. Montaigne, M. de (1877) 'Of Friendship'. In: *Essays of Michel de Montaigne*, trans., C. Cotton, ed., W. Carew Hazlitt, Project Gutenberg.
34. See, for instance, Roland Bleiker, *Popular Dissent, Human Agency and Global Politics*. Cambridge: Cambridge University Press, 2000.
35. E. de La Boétie, *The Politics of Obedience: The Discourse of Voluntary Servitude*. Kurz, Harry (trans.) and Rothbard, Murray (ed.). Auburn, Alabama: The Mises Institute, 1975, 43–44. Available at: https://cdn.mises.org/Politics%20of%20Obedience.pdf.
36. Ibid., 44.
37. Ibid., 44.
38. Ibid., 52.
39. B. de Spinoza, B. de, *Theologico-Political Treatise*, ed., J. Israel. Cambridge: Cambridge University Press, 2007, 16.
40. Frédéric Gros refers to this as 'surplus obedience': 'Each person always obeys more than is genuinely required by the situation of submission. And it is this excess that gives political power its hold'. See *Disobey! A Guide to Ethical Resistance, trans.*, David Fernbach, London: Verso, 2020, 42.
41. La Boétie, *The Politics of Obedience*, 55.
42. Ibid., 65.
43. G. Debord, Society of the spectacle. *Marxists Internet Archive*, 1967. Available at: www.marxists.org/reference/archive/debord/society.htm.
44. La Boétie, *The Politics of Obedience*, 72.
45. Ibid., 79.
46. On the different historical interpretations of La La Boétie's thesis, see Miguel Abensour (2011) 'Is there a proper way to use the voluntary servitude hypothesis?' *Journal of Political Ideologies* 16(3): 329–348.
47. La Boétie, *The Politics of Obedience*, 48.
48. Ibid., 48–49.
49. M. Foucault, What is Critique? In: *What is Enlightenment? Eighteenth Century Answers and Twentieth Century Questions*, ed. James Schmidt. Berkeley: University of California Press, 1996, 382–398, p. 386.

50. P. Clastres, *Archaeology of Violence,* trans., J. Herman. New York: Semiotext[e], 99, 1994.
51. Clastres, *Archaeology,* 94. In his comment on La Boétie's *Discours,* Clastres stresses three points. The French humanist proceeds from the fact of subjection to authority being a cause of suffering for human beings. Obeying a power and being coerced is unnatural. La Boétie is one of the first to speak of 'natural rights' of freedom for human beings. The second point Clastres stresses is the contingency of domination. Authority and hierarchical division between commander and commanded is not intrinsic to society. From these two points a fundamental conclusion is drawn: a different order of society is in principle possible, one without subjection and hierarchy. See P. Clastres, 'Liberté, Malencontre, Innombrable', in É. de la Boétie, *Le discours de la servitude volontaire,* ed. by P. Léonard, Payoy, Paris 2002, pp. 27 ff.
52. See the discussion on Clastres and La Boétie in Stathis Gourgouris, *The Perils of the One,* New York: Columbia University Press, 2019.
53. La Boétie, *The Politics of Obedience,* 46.
54. J. Holloway, *Crack Capitalism,* London: Pluto Press, 2010, 17.
55. Abensour, 'Is there a proper way to use the voluntary servitude hypothesis?', 34–35.
56. La Boétie, *The Politics of Obedience* 77.
57. Ibid.

Nine
Human Rights

The previous chapter considered the question of civil disobedience and the right to resist unjust laws. The right to resist presupposes some notion of natural justice or right that is beyond the positive order of the law. From a legal positivist perspective, there can be no notion of justice or rights outside the socially constituted order of legal norms; all rights come from law and only exist as legal facts. Natural rights – or the rights of Man – were, as Jeremy Bentham put it, 'nonsense upon stilts', and 'anarchical fallacies'. From the alternative natural law tradition – going back to Aquinas and the medieval scholastics and later forming the basis of classical liberal notions of individual rights – there is a moral order that exceeds man-made laws, whether divinely constituted or endowed in man's natural humanity and reason. In opposition to legal positivist theory and economic utilitarianism, Ronald Dworkin argues that individuals have rights which they can claim against the state, and which somehow exist prior to the rights created by law: 'Individual rights are political rights held by individuals. Individuals have rights when, for some reason, a collective goal is not a sufficient justification for denying them what they wish, as individuals, to have or to do, or not a sufficient justification for imposing a loss or injury upon them.'[1] Rights for Dworkin are 'trumps' that are instrumental in safeguarding individuals against unjustified state coercion and a disproportionate implementation of collective goods. And they are deontologically construed, so that no functionalist or teleological interpretation of them would be allowed. Rights in this sense cannot be balanced or filtered through an economic principle of efficiency or proportionality. While Dworkin's account seeks to avoid 'metaphysical assumptions' that such rights are divinely ordained or derive from nature, he nevertheless proposes an idea of justice that is not fully accounted for by law and which can, at times, 'trump' existing laws or act as a way of exerting pressure on lawmakers. It is precisely this idea of justice beyond law that forms the basis for our modern conception of human rights, and which innumerable campaigns and international legal agreements that assert the rights of individuals against abuse, oppression and state violence rely upon to make their claims.

However, the problem from an anarchist perspective is that even though the idea of a natural order of rights can be asserted against political and legal authority, rights are usually determined by, and thus subordinate to, the sovereign state. This is not merely to point to the weakness of individual rights in the face of state power and the principle of national sovereignty – a weakness and ineffectuality that is visible on a daily basis, despite the salutary efforts of human rights campaigners around the world – but also to the way that individual rights form the ideological foundations of the modern liberal state. The great revolutionary declarations of the eighteenth century, which formed the basis of the American and French Revolutions, enshrined the idea of natural individual rights and even the right of resistance to tyrannical authority. Yet, as the radical political tradition from Marx to the anarchists showed, these 'sacred' rights merely integrated the individual into the order of the state and the circulation of the market. The rights of man thus functioned as the ideological framework and support for the modern liberal state and the capitalist economy. As Marx observed in his famous essay 'On the Jewish Question', the rights of man simply enshrined the principle of security as 'the supreme concept of civil society'; that is the security and preservation of the bourgeois individual and his rights to property.[2] For Marx, the discourse of rights, in its individualising or 'atomising' effect, so far from freeing the individual, merely inscribed him within a double order of subjection to the state and to the market, whose formal division into different spheres of life became the basis for a new regime of domination. The political emancipation afforded by the rights of man and by the principle of legal equality in effect did not succeed in offering a truly human emancipation.[3] Similarly, Bakunin, while at times invoking the notion of 'human rights' as a means to emancipation, was perfectly aware of the way the modern state hegemonised the notion of rights, distorting their meaning and their revolutionary legacy. The state, protects its own citizens only; it recognizes human rights, humanity, civilization within its own confines alone. Since it recognises no rights outside itself, it logically arrogates to itself the right to exercise the most ferocious inhumanity toward all foreign populations, which it can plunder, exterminate, or enslave at will.[4]

The universal rights of man have therefore too often become the rights of the state. Rather than being applicable to everyone, equally and everywhere, they are narrowed to the confines of national citizenship. Bakunin thus identifies the central contradiction between the idea of universal human rights and the principle of state sovereignty upon which they inevitably founder: the problem is that if human rights are left up to nation states to determine, then they will be circumscribed, limited, allowed to some but denied to others. The 'states of emergency' which have characterised liberal democracy from its inception – from Locke's idea of 'prerogative powers' to recent COVID-19 lockdowns – point to way that individual rights have become the plaything of power, serving as the ideology of the modern (neo)liberal state while being restricted, ignored or wholly abandoned when they no longer suit the exigencies of government or the priorities of the market.

Therefore, from the anarchist point of view, there is always a tension between rights and the law. Put simply by the French anarchist Paraf-Javal,

> Either man has no rights! Or man has rights. If man has no rights, no man has the right to exercise any right. No man has the right to establish any law. If man has rights, it is not to demand of the law – (that is to say of the arbitrary wills of others) – the permission to have them. He must determine them logically and exercise them freely, if necessary *despite the law*.[5]

As a matter of fact, it is in a sense the very notion of a right that is opposed to the notion of law. A law generally consists of a prescription to be followed or to be obeyed. A law produces duties. But a right has a normative status that is opposed to a duty. It is a freedom or a power. Hobbes is explicit on this: 'For though they that speak on this subject, use to confound Jus, and *Lex*, Right and Law; yet they ought to be distinguished; because RIGHT, consisteth in liberty to do or to forbeare; Whereas LAW, determineth, and bindeth to one of them: so that Law, and Right, differe as much as Obligation, and Liberty; which in one and the same matter are inconsistent'.[6] The question is then how it might be conceivable and possible for law, as a command, that requires and imposes subjection, to give freedom or power to the addressee of the command. Thus, rights or a state legal order based on commands, is a permanent source of paradox and contradiction. Rights are indeed a threat to the state, that historically prefers to convert them into privileges, concessions or benefits bestowed on specific groups (thus denying their universal character or their inalienability), or better directly converting them into duties, or else reshaping them as virtues of a good law-abiding subject.

There is a fundamental contradiction at the heart of the liberal attempt to establish a legal order on the basis of individual rights. If we have no natural rights, then we do not have the right to establish a legal system. If, however, we *do* have natural rights, as the liberal claims, then these rights are *preeminent* over law and cannot be determined by them. That means that the individual can exercise his autonomous right to 'private judgement' over the law and to choose whether or not to obey it.

However, this line of reasoning, rather than simply demonstrating the inadequacy of human rights in the face of legal authority, suggests that rights can at times serve as a genuine foundation for resistance to the law. It is therefore too easy to regard the anarchist position on human rights as being purely a critical one. Where the anarchist position differs from the Marxist one in this respect, is that while anarchism is well aware of the limitations of human rights and their ideological functioning within the state-capitalist order, it also contends that the idea of rights can be redeemed and radicalised. Indeed, anarchists in the classical tradition saw themselves as the true inheritors of the radical legacy of the Enlightenment and the French Revolution; they were the ones who would carry the burning torch of the rights of man through to their radical conclusion. We cannot forget that the idea of human rights is first defended against the conservative criticism (for instance, the one deployed by Edmund Burke in his *Reflections on the Revolution in France*) by two writers considered forerunners of anarchist political philosophy. We here refer to Mary Wollstonecraft and William Godwin, both staunch promoters of a free polity based on human rights. According to them such rights are to be granted to every human being (including women and children) and they are not possessive or proprietary entitlements, as is the case in John Locke and in the conservative stance adopted by Burke. Property is not listed by either Godwin or Wollstonecraft as one of the fundamental rights. As Wollestoncraft writes in her terse essay *A Vindication of the Rights of Man*, 'property, I do not scruple to aver it, should be fluctuating'.[7] In other words, it should not have the absolute character that is instead granted, for instance, to free speech or individual autonomy as a political liberty. The rights of man, expanded and turned against the principle of state sovereignty and the capitalist market, and against every form of domination, of men against women for instance, could become genuinely emancipatory. As a matter of fact, rights are universalised as human and fundamental first by erasing the border between public and private sphere that is a pillar of liberalism. According to classical liberals, rights are only active in the public sphere, only within the intercourse between state and citizens, but not in the area of social and intersubjective relations, not within family or the workplace for instance. The essential difference, then, between anarchism and liberalism therefore consists in the expansion of the area of application of rights to the entire sphere of human relations and affairs. For liberalism domination can be justified by functionalist structures (as is the case of market capitalism) or by natural needs (as is the case of patriarchal family). On the contrary, for anarchism, domination is never ever justified: the normativity of autonomy applies everywhere. There is no social conduct that could be opaque to a principled anti-authoritarian attitude of equal concern and self-determination.

This chapter will therefore explore some of the ambiguities in anarchism's position on human rights. We will show how the anarchist critique of rights is developed together with a foundational justification of rights. This allows for a radical reinterpretation of their relationship to law and political authority. Thinking through the aporias of Hannah Arendt's notion of the 'right to have rights' – and taking this paradoxical formula in a distinctly anarchist direction – this chapter will argue that the idea of human rights can be transformed, extended and rethought today. At a time when, as is commonly acknowledged, international human rights are in a state of crisis – when they are openly violated around the world, abused by authoritarian regimes, disdained by right-wing populists, and ignored or traduced by the liberal democracies who claim to act in their name; when, in particular, the rights of the stateless founder against the borders of the nation state – it is necessary to rethink their meaning and significance today.

Human rights and the anarchist tradition

As we have suggested, the anarchist position on human rights is marked by a certain ambivalence. On the one hand, the classical anarchists of the nineteenth and early twentieth century saw themselves as the radical inheritors of the legacy of the French Revolution. As part of the Enlightenment tradition that embodied the rational spirit of progress and human emancipation, anarchists like Bakunin, Proudhon, Kropotkin, Rudolf Rocker, and many others, invoked the liberatory potential of human rights. The Declaration of the Rights of Man and the Citizen set humanity on a new course towards its emancipation after languishing so long under political absolutism and religious obscurantism. In the words of Bakunin:

> Since the Revolution has confronted the masses with its own gospel, a revelation not mystical but rational, not of heaven but of earth, not divine but human – the gospel of the Rights of Man; since it has proclaimed that all men are equal and equally entitled to liberty and to a humane life – ever since then, the masses of people in all Europe, in the entire civilized world, slowly awakening from the slumber in which Christianity's incantations had held them enthralled, are beginning to wonder whether they, too, are not entitled to equality, to liberty, and to their humanity.[8]

The French Revolution, notwithstanding its mostly limited, bourgeois character, embodied the principles of liberty and equality which, for anarchists, are the fundamental basis for justice and humanity. These principles, once recognised and taken seriously, would inspire revolutions everywhere.

However, the rights of man had to be taken beyond their liberal bourgeois framework and expanded to include positive *social* rights. For Bakunin, the connection between liberty and equality had to be taken seriously – one was meaningless without the other. Not only does freedom mean that *everyone* else should be *equally* free – the freedom of others is not a threat to one's freedom but an *enhancement* of it[9] – but freedom must also be accompanied by equality in a more substantial material sense. As Bakunin put it: 'We are convinced that liberty without socialism is privilege, injustice; and that socialism without liberty is slavery and brutality'.[10] For Proudhon, to simply talk about negative, political rights was insufficient and only meant the enshrinement of capitalist property rights and the expropriation of the proletariat. Political rights therefore had to be accompanied by social rights. In pointing to the gap between the French Revolution's promise of equality and the stark realities of material inequality and capitalist exploitation, Proudhon argued for political rights to be accompanied by social rights: 'Equality of political rights necessarily implies the equality of social rights'.[11] However, social rights, for anarchists, meant more than simply protections against poverty, but the rights to acquire the means of production, the right of the individual worker to benefit fully from the fruits of his or her labour. Indeed, in insisting on social rights accompanying individual political rights, and in combining the principles of economic equality and political liberty, anarchism saw itself as embodying the best traditions of liberalism and socialism.[12]

Part of this radicalisation of rights was the recognition that rights were not simply granted by governments or guaranteed by the liberal constitutional order. Rather, rights were the result of political struggles on the part of the working-class. As Rocker put it:

> Political rights do not originate in parliaments; they are rather forced upon them from without. And even their

> enactment into; law has for a long time been no guarantee of their security. They do not exist because they have been legally set down on a piece of paper, but only when they have become the ingrown habit of a people, and when any attempt to impair them will meet with the violent resistance of the populace.[13]

Even basic rights political rights like the right to vote and the extension of universal suffrage were the result of hard-fought victories over the liberal bourgeois capitalist regime that had been forced to concede them. Anarchism therefore seeks to extricate the idea of rights from the framework of liberal bourgeois ideology and return them to their revolutionary origins.

The reason why rights can be exerted against the state in this way, and continually expanded beyond their current limits, is because they spring from a 'natural' substratum outside the order of 'man made' laws and political institutions. For Bakunin, human rights emerged from natural laws, which he distinguished from political laws, that were artificial and imposed by state institutions and privileged classes in their own interests. Our defiance of these 'artificial' and 'immoral' laws was at the same time based on our 'involuntary' obedience to the laws of nature, insofar as they constituted our very humanity and created the conditions for human solidarity.[14] For Kropotkin, the awareness of human solidarity emerges from our natural biological instinct towards mutual aid, something we have inherited from animal species, and which forms the basis for the principle of justice:

> It is the unconscious recognition of the force that is borrowed by each person from the practice of mutual aid; of the close dependency of everyone's happiness upon the happiness of all; and of the sense of justice, or equity, which brings the individual to consider the rights of every other individual as equal to his own.[15]

In opposition to the liberal notion of rights, which essentially reduced rights to the 'economic rights' of the individual[16] and, in effect, denied rights to women and the working class, Kropotkin asserted the real equality of rights based on the ethical principles found in nature. While this understanding of natural rights might sound similar to the classical liberal doctrine of the rights enjoyed in the 'state of nature', the anarchist interprets these rights as being intrinsically *against* the principle of political authority which corrupts and alienates them. In other words, unlike in liberal theory, rights are not what serve to establish the political and legal order but what remain fundamentally opposed to it, disrupting its foundations and providing a moral and rational basis for an alternative system of social relations.

Furthermore, because rights are *human* in this way, embodying natural principles of justice and human solidarity, they must be genuinely universal and apply to everyone everywhere. This is perhaps the most radical aspect of the anarchist account of human rights. Rights, for anarchists, are universal; they transcend race, culture, religion, gender, age, social class, and especially borders. 'Nostra patria è il mondo intero', 'Our fatherland is the entire world', are the first words of an old Italian anarchist song. For an anarchist, human rights are cosmopolitan; they transcend the polity and imply the idea of human solidarity across borders. The emancipatory potential of human rights was constrained, first, by a reference only to a special class of human beings, paradigmatically, to bourgeois white males. It was then constrained and belittled by the principle of national sovereignty, which limited their application, granting them to citizens – if only in a restricted way – while denying them to outsiders. This contradiction is intolerable to anarchists. Anarchists are the heirs to emancipatory promise of cosmopolitanism, expressed in Diogenes' claim that he was a citizen of no polis but the *cosmos*.[17] This is why anarchism has always invoked the idea of international working class solidarity, why they have been involved, since the late nineteenth century, in various forms of transnational activism and human rights campaigns, why they have supported anti-colonial resistance movements,[18] joined international brigades to fight Fascism,[19] and defended the rights of asylum seekers and 'undocumented migrants'.[20] For anarchists, one of the worst tyrannies is that imposed at the border. The principle of national sovereignty is inherently exclusionary and unjust. In rejecting this principle, and invoking an alternative horizon of 'cosmopolitan right' and transnational solidarity, anarchism can be seen as one of the first genuinely global human rights movements,[21] one that should, at the same time, be radically distinguished from liberal and neoliberal notions of global human rights[22] or from any idea of global Empire.[23] For anarchists, human rights can never be adequately expressed in the idea of national citizenship, 'nationality', which, for Bakunin, only meant one's servitude to the state. Rather, a genuine socialist (or anarchist) republic, as opposed to simply a political republic, was a 'republic of men' rather than a 'republic of citizens'.[24]

Human rights and bare life

Yet, Bakunin's distinction between a community of men and a community of citizens, touches on one of the central ambiguities in the idea of human rights. Who exactly is the bearer of human rights? Is it man in his abstract humanity, or is it the citizen of the national polity? This ambiguity was highlighted in Max Stirner's critique of liberalism and the republican state. In granting rights to individuals, the state constructs the individual as a 'citizen', at least as far as those rights are defined and positively determined by the state authority and not by citizens themselves. In this way, the state inscribes the individual within its order of domination by imposing a certain generalised identity upon him that has no regard for his singularity and the plurality of human conditions and statuses. In other words, within the liberal state order, one has rights only insofar as one conforms to one's state-imposed identity as citizen and takes on certain duties and obligations:

> 'Equality of political rights' has, consequently, the meaning that every one may acquire every right that the state has to give away, if only he fulfils the conditions annexed thereto – conditions which are to be sought only in the nature of the particular right, not in a predilection for the person (*persona grata*).[25]

Rights are therefore not the means to liberation but the path to a new form of subjection. It is not so much that in imposing this new order of rights the modern state divides 'man' from the 'citizen' but, rather, makes 'man' the foundation of the 'citizen. In doing so, it creates a new kind of exclusion and alienation: an individual who fails to live up to his moral responsibilities as 'man' – now defined through his duties as 'citizen' – is deemed unworthy of humanity. This is a status Stirner refers to as un-man:

> But what concept is the highest to the state? Doubtless that of being a really human society, a society in which everyone who is really a man, that is, *not an un-man*, can obtain admission as a member. Let a state's tolerance go ever so far, toward an un-man and toward what is inhuman it ceases.[26]

Here Stirner highlights the paradox of human rights: once rights become formalised, they create a caesura within the idea of the human, dividing an idealised concept of man from those who fall outside this category and who become subject to exclusion and domination.

Therefore, the problem of human rights is the natural substratum from which they are said to arise, a substratum which becomes the target of the biopolitical calculations of the modern state. This is why it is perhaps too simplistic to assert, as the classical anarchists were inclined to do, the principle of human rights – based on an ontologically 'pure' idea of nature – against the artificial principle of state sovereignty. As Stirner's radical critique of rights shows, it is precisely this natural identity – Man, the human – which becomes incorporated into the state, serving as its ideological (Stirner would say *theological*) support. In other words, Man is not against the state but part of it.

Stirner's critique of human rights foreshadows that of Giorgio Agamben, who also points to the ambiguities that appear once rights become the foundation of the political order. In the French Declaration of the Rights of Man and the Citizen, in its various iterations, there is an uncertainty about whether the basis of rights lies in one's membership of a political community or in one's natural biological identity, one's 'bare life'. According to Agamben, this ambiguity between man and citizen that lies at the foundations of the modern state marks the passage by which 'bare life' (*zoe*) comes to be included in the sovereign order in the *form of its exclusion*: bare life – life in its pre-political biological essence – becomes the basis of a biopolitical rationality which endlessly produces new forms of exclusion and domination, new divisions between those deemed worthy of citizenship (and therefore of rights) and those not considered properly part of the polity on the basis of their birth, race or other markers of identity. So, while rights declarations have a radical potential, which the anarchists recognised, they also marked the inscription of the subject within the biopolitical order of the nation state, producing new zones of exception and sovereign violence.[27]

Agamben's main reference on this question is Hannah Arendt's famous critique of human rights in *The Origins of Totalitarianism* (1951), in which she pointed to the failures of human rights and international institutions in protecting refugees between the two World Wars. These conflicts led to a decomposition of the old nation state order and to the displacement of millions of people who, denied their citizenship and the protections of a political community, had nothing to fall back upon but their human rights, the rights they could claim on the basis of their 'bare' humanity. However, as Arendt famously put it:

> The Rights of Man, after all, had been defined as 'inalienable' because they were supposed to be independent of all governments; but it turned out that the moment human beings lacked their own government and had to fall back on their minimum rights, no authority was left to protect them and no institution was willing to guarantee them.[28]

When the rights of man were initially formulated, they were conflated with the rights of the citizen; however, the radical separation of 'man' from the 'citizen' made evident by the appearance of millions of stateless and displaced people, threw the idea of human rights into crisis. It was now apparent that without the protections afforded by citizenship and law – by membership of a political community and the civic rights which come with this – those abstract human rights became practically meaningless. Thus, the tragic paradox of the rights of man was that, in Arendt's words,

> If a human being loses his political status, he should, according to the implications of the inborn and inalienable rights of man, come under exactly the same situation for which the declarations of such general rights provided. Actually the opposite is the case. It seems that a man who is nothing but a man has lost the very qualities which make it possible for other people to treat him as a fellow-man.[29]

In other words, the rights of man, insofar as they are based on a general concept of humanity, did not provide any protections to people who were no longer members of a defined polity. Rather than guaranteeing that people were shown equal respect and dignity as human beings, human rights consigned people to their bare life, to their abstract humanity, leaving them vulnerable to the predations of others. It is only in their political and legal identity as members of a polis, that human beings can be properly recognised: 'Man, it turns out, can lose all his so-called Rights of Man without losing his essential quality as a man, his human dignity. Only the loss of a polity itself expels him from humanity.'[30] For Arendt, what is crucial in the condition of statelessness is the loss of legal status and protections that come from living under the rule of law. In comparing the stateless person with the lowliest criminal, she shows that the criminal is better off because at least he has a legal identity and is afforded certain protections under the law. The stateless person, on the other hand, is deprived of citizenship and is no longer regarded as a legal person; his human identity, upon which his human rights are supposedly based, only has meaning in terms of his legal identity. Once this is lost, his human identity is lost as well. Put simply, we are only recognisable as human beings insofar as we are citizens and legal persons. This is why, as Arendt shows, one of the first things that Nazis did was to strip Jews of their legal status as citizens – something that paved the way for their eventual extermination.

So, it is the absence of political community and the consequent loss of legal status that, according to Arendt, consigned millions of stateless people to their fate. As she puts it:

> The calamity of the rightless is not that they are deprived of life, liberty and the pursuit of happiness, or of

> equality before the law and freedom of opinion – formulas which were designed to solve problems *within* given communities – but that they no longer belong to any community whatsoever. Their plight is not that they are not equal before the law, but that no law exists for them; not that they are oppressed but that nobody wants even to oppress them.[31]

The condition that Arendt described applies to our own time today, in which, according to UNHCR figures, stateless people, displaced and refugees around the world number in the many tens of millions, and where their human rights claims, supposedly protected by international institutions, are met with callous indifference by the nation states to which they appeal. In their indistinct, abstract humanity – their bare life – they are treated simply as 'superfluous' people, not to be oppressed but simply ignored, shut away in camps on the peripheries of states or deported to other countries where they remain out of sight, out of mind.[32]

The 'right to have rights': ontological anarchy

Arendt's analysis has implications not only for liberal ideas of universal human rights and international human rights frameworks – whose failure in the face of state sovereignty is everywhere evident – but also for an anarchist approach to human rights discussed above. Arendt seems to be suggesting that human rights cannot simply be asserted as a moral principle against nation states, at least not in the manner proposed by the classical anarchists; indeed, human rights are essentially meaningless outside the political and legal order. The human being has no status, no significance outside his legal identity and his identity as a citizen. In other words, if one asserts human rights against the state, then upon what basis does one do so? This becomes a purely moral position, based on some abstract, empty idea of the individual, rather than a genuinely political position, which can only be derived from being part of a political community where one engages directly with others. This would seem to imply that it is only as a citizen and as a member of a polity that one can take politically valid action, and that an individual only has rights insofar as these rights are legally recognised by the political community. It is here that her famous formula of the 'right to have rights' takes on crucial significance:

> We become aware of the existence of the right to have rights (and that means to live in a framework where one is judged by one's actions and opinions) and a right to belong to some kind of organized community, only when millions of people emerged who had lost and could not regain these rights because of the new global political situation.[33]

Such a conclusion would seem to render the idea of anarchist human rights essentially invalid. Or does it? This all depends on how this ambiguous formula – the 'right to have rights' – is interpreted. Certainly on one reading, Arendt is saying that the fundamental right – the right without which all other rights are meaningless – is the right to citizenship, the right to nationhood; there are no rights outside of law, and no politics outside of the state. Such an interpretation would seem to agree with Edmund Burke's famous critique of the French Revolution – which Arendt cites approvingly – where he said that rights derive from the nation and that he recognised only the inherited 'rights of Englishmen' not the inalienable 'rights of Man'.[34] This accords with the positive law tradition that sees rights as only having meaning *within* a particular legal order.

However, such an interpretation ignores Arendt's critique of the principle of sovereignty, which she regarded as essentially anti-political. Politics, for her, was inherently pluralistic, and presupposed difference and the recognition of one's equal freedom with others – principles which are, as we have seen, *anarchistic*. Power, in its genuine political sense, was a bottom-up, rather than a top-down, relationship.[35] Moreover, we should remember that the historical models of politics from which Arendt drew her inspiration were not only the Roman Republic and the American Revolution but, more directly, the spontaneously organised and autonomous workers councils that emerged in Hungarian Revolution in 1956.[36] All this suggests a very different and much more anarchistic conception of political life and action, one that is irreconcilable, or at least in tension, with the idea of state sovereignty. Furthermore, Arendt was famously critical of all forms of nationalism. Therefore, it is simply not tenable to confine Arendt's view of politics and political existence to the idea of citizenship and the national community.

There is, then, another way to read Arendt's concept of the 'right to have rights', one that is much closer to the anarchist position. The 'right to have rights' can mean the right to a 'city', a community where people truly and effectively decide about the rules they follow. Here we could speak of a 'virtuous circle' of citizenship rights, in so far as I obey only the rules that I have myself deliberated upon, agreed and issued. This is an anarchist principle. The 'rights to have rights' can thus mean membership of different kinds of non-state political communities, communities that are self-organised and self-determined, and based on bottom-up, non-hierarchical and decentralised forms of decision-making. It seems clear that Arendt does not rule out the possibility of alternative forms of political life, belonging and legal recognition that are outside the nation state and are not governed by the principle of national sovereignty. Indeed, one example of such communities might be precisely the transnational activist networks and organisations that support and defend the rights of asylum seekers and refugees today, and which have emerged in the cracks and at the margins of states.[37] We of course acknowledge the very real desire and need of refugees and asylum seekers to have their status legally recognised by nation states. Rather, our point is that the 'crisis' of statelessness – which is just as real in our time as it was in Arendt's – is also a crisis of the idea of the nation state and of the idea of citizenship as being the only marker of political recognition and significance. In other words, there is no reason why we must confine our understanding of political community and political life to the bounded community of the nation state, and, indeed, the increasing mobility that we see today – migrants crossing borders and thereby contesting the principle of national sovereignty – will demand new conceptual models of politics and different understandings of community.

Such alternative, non-sovereign conceptions of community and politics suggest the possibility of a different approach to the question of human rights. If we take the notion of the 'right to have rights' simply as the *right to politics* – rather than the right to membership of any particular polity – then we can view this fundamental right in an *ontologically anarchic* way, as that which allows a plurality of different understandings of political life and the invention of new rights. In other words, we might view the 'right to have rights' as a kind of *groundless* ground, as a contingent space of invention from which new forms of politics and new conceptions of rights can emerge. This should be understood in terms of Arendt's claim of revolutions being *new beginnings* that coincide with the idea of freedom,[38] and her idea that natality is the fundamental condition of politics: 'the new beginning inherent in birth can makes itself felt in the world only because the newcomer possesses the capacity of beginning something anew, that is, of acting'.[39] In other words, the 'right to have rights' – as the right to political life – is both an instituting *Grund-right* (similar to Kelsen's *Grundnorm*), as well as something that, in its radical indeterminacy, unpredictability and groundlessness, unsettles all existing political and legal principles, endlessly posing the question of the limits of existing rights and political communities and allowing for the invention of new ones.[40] This is not, however, a locus of decisionist, ex nihilo commands. Rights are based on the fundamental dignity of rights holders, vulnerable beings, beings who are existentially fragile and phenomenologically 'naked', who can suffer, who ask for an identity, and therefore deserve care, protection and recognition through an act of public mutual reflexivity. This can only be offered by an anarchist polity centred on the principles of equal and mutual concern and individual self-determination.

The anarchy of rights

An ontologically anarchic view of rights – which sees rights as having no natural identity or foundation – is somewhat different from the classical anarchist position, in which rights were based on a notion of human rationality and nature derived from a certain humanist and rationalist conception of man. However, if we see this in terms of a certain 'deconstruction' of the idea of rights, we can also recognise the way that it allows for their continual reinterpretation. The history of human rights since the eighteenth century shows how their conceptual limits have been subject to ongoing political contestation, resulting in their expansion to include those traditionally excluded, such as women, the working class, children, racial minorities, indigenous people, and even the natural environment and non-human species. These are struggles which anarchists have always been part of. Anarchism itself can therefore be seen in terms of a certain 'deconstruction' of rights, one that takes the language and meaning of rights beyond their historical limits and original Enlightenment formulation. The latter example of 'animal rights'[41] is the terrain for perhaps the most radical challenge to the traditional conception of human rights today: the idea that animals can have legal rights,[42] and are therefore worthy of the same or similar degrees of respect, protection, dignity and equal treatment as human beings utterly transforms our accepted understanding of human rights, disturbing the very ontological distinction between the human and non-human. While there is of course a danger of anthropomorphising animals in attributing legal rights to them, something that runs the risk of reinforcing existing discursive hierarchies, we would nevertheless emphasise the radical potential of such endeavours. The broader idea of ecological rights once again has the potential to disturb the traditional ontological foundations of human rights and to transform them in a more radical way. The idea of the rights of nature – the claim that the natural world and non-human entities and ecosystems have rights and need to be protected from the extractive practices of capitalism[43] – is very different, even radically opposed, to the traditional idea of 'natural rights', which is entirely anthropocentric. We think here of Locke's idea of the natural right to 'subdue the earth'. An ontologically anarchic reading of the 'right to have rights', by contrast, can produce new 'inhuman'[44] or even 'posthuman'[45] conceptions of rights, emancipation and community.

Our point, then, is that an anarchist approach – while traditionally rooted in Enlightenment rationalism and humanism – at the same time allows an ongoing transformation of the conceptual limits of human rights, opening them to new forms of contestation and to new political subjects.

Michel Foucault, in his lecture series on war in 1976, referred enigmatically to the possibility of a 'new right' in opposition to the old rights of sovereignty; a right that would be 'both anti-disciplinary and emancipated from the principle of sovereignty'.[46] While he does not elaborate on what this 'new right' could mean, it is clear that he contrasts this with the legal authority of the sovereign and the disciplinary mechanisms of the state, the two forms of constraint between which the modern subject is caught. In other words, to simply assert one's legal rights as an individual against the power of the state is insufficient. As Foucault argues, the figure of the liberal individual, with his so-called rights and freedoms, is at the same time part of the state order he imagines he opposes. Rather, 'We have to promote new forms of subjectivity through the refusal of this kind of individuality which has been imposed on us for several centuries'.[47]

Therefore, this 'new right' that Foucault speaks of should be interpreted as the right to invent new modes of subjectivity, new ways of living, new ways of relating to others and to ourselves that are no longer tied to the liberal idea of the individual. This notion of right reflects Foucault's later concerns with the 'care of the self' – the ethical practices of self-constitution and *askesis* found in the cultures of Greek and Roman antiquity. Here individuals, albeit in highly circumscribed cultural settings, elaborated their own ways of relating to themselves and to others outside of the institutional constraints that apply to the modern individual. Such ethical practices and forms of self-disciplining were, according to Foucault, practices of freedom in the sense that they were designed to limit the desire for domination and to enhance one's own sense of autonomy and self-mastery.[48] Foucault was primarily interested in the *self-constitution* of the subject as a form of resistance to the subjectifying and biopolitical power of the modern state, and the way that a certain understanding of rights could facilitate such practices of self-formation.[49] Rights were tools that could be used in what Reiner Schürmann refers to as the project of 'constituting oneself as an anarchistic subject'.[50]

How, then, should anarchists approach the question of human rights? Let us say that rights offer a convenient language in which to make certain claims – for freedom, equal concern, empowerment – and in this sense they are extremely important discursive tools in political struggles. However, they should be treated simply *as* tools, and we should not invest too much in them. They are at best an imperfect language, in themselves insufficient for expressing the new forms of human autonomy and community that anarchism aims to foster. Neither anarchist morality nor its possible and prospective legality are grounded on rights. Rather, they are based on a more fundamental and intimate form of common, intersubjective good.

Notes

1. Ronald Dworkin, *Taking Rights Seriously*, Cambridge, MA: Harvard University Press, 1978.
2. Karl Marx, 'On the Jewish Question', *The Marx-Engels Reader: Second Edition*, ed., Robert C. Tucker, New York and London: W. W. Norton & Co., 1978, 26–52, p. 43.
3. It is on the basis of this critique of the limitations of bourgeois rights – or rather the reduction of rights to bourgeois law – that Christophe Menke invokes the idea of a 'new right' which he sees as a kind of revolt against the unjust conditions out of which bourgeois justice is formulated. See *Critique of Rights*, Cambridge: Polity Press, 2020.
4. Mikhail Bakunin, 'Federalism, Socialism, Anti-Theologism' (1876) Marxists.org (Bakunin archive): www.marxists.org/reference/archive/bakunin/works/various/reasons-of-state.htm.
5. Paraf-Javal, 'The Rights of Man and the Law' (1902) The Libertarian Labyrinth: www.libertarian-labyrinth.org/working-translations/paraf-javal-the-rights-of-man-and-the-law-1902/.
6. Thomas Hobbes. *Leviathan*, ed. by C. B. Macpherson, Penguin, Harmondsworth 1982, p. 189.
7. M. Wollstonecraft, *A Vindication of the Rights of Man*, OUP, Oxford 2008, p. 23.
8. Bakunin, 'Federalism, Socialism, Anti-Theologism'.
9. Bakunin, 'God and the State'.
10. Bakunin, Political Philosophy, p. 269.
11. Proudhon, 'Manifesto of Sixty Workers from the Seine Department' (1864) in Guérin, *No Gods, No Masters*, pp. 103–110.

12. See Rudolf Rocker, 'Anarchism and Anarcho-Syndicalism', Rudolf Rocker Reference Archive, www.marxists.org/reference/archive/rocker-rudolf/misc/anarchism-anarcho-syndicalism.htm.
13. Rocker, 'Anarchism and Anarcho-Syndicalism'.
14. Bakunin, *Political Philosophy*, p. 168.
15. Kropotkin, *Mutual Aid*, pp. 4–5.
16. See Kropotkin, *Ethics: Origin and Development*, The Anarchist Library, 1922, p. 25.
17. See Carl Levy, 'Anarchism and Cosmopolitanism', *Journal of Political Ideologies*, 16:3, 265–278.
18. See Benedict Anderson, *Under Three Flags: Anarchism and the Anticolonial Imagination*, London: Version, 2005. See also Maia Ramnath, *Decolonizing Anarchism: An Anti-authoritarian History of India's Liberation Struggle*, Oakland CA: AK Press, 2011.
19. Morris Brodie, 'Volunteers for Anarchy: The International Group of the Durruti Column in the Spanish Civil War', *Journal of Contemporary History*, 56(1): 2021, 28–54.
20. Natasha King, *No Borders: The Politics of Immigration Control and Resistance*, London: Zed Books, 2016.
21. See Mark Bray, 'Beyond and Against the State: Anarchist Contributions to Human Rights History and Theory', *Humanity: An International Journal of Human Rights, Humanitarianism, and Development*, Volume 10, Number 3, Winter 2019, pp. 323–338.
22. See Samuel Moyn on the ambiguous relationship between neoliberal globalisation and human rights. *Not Enough: Human Rights in an Unequal World*, Cambridge, MA: Belknap Press, 2018.
23. See Costas Douzinas on the difference between a radical cosmopolitan understanding of human rights and the notion of liberal globalisation. *Human Rights and Empire: The Political Philosophy of Cosmopolitanism, Abingdon*: Routledge-Cavendish, 2007.
24. Mikhail Bakunin, *Bakunin on Anarchy*, ed., and trans., S. Dolgoff. New York: Vintage Books, 1971, pp. 118–119.
25. Stirner, *The Ego and Its Own*, 93.
26. Ibid., 158–159.
27. Giorgio Agamben, *Homo Sacer: Sovereign Power and Bare Life*, trans., Daniel Heller-Roazen, Stanford CA: Stanford University Press, 1998, pp. 128–129.
28. Hannah Arendt, *The Origins of Totalitarianism*, Orlando Austin New York San Diego London: Harcourt, 1968, pp. 291–292.

29. Ibid., p. 300.
30. Ibid., p. 297.
31. Ibid., pp. 295–296.
32. The latest asylum-seeker policy introduced by the UK government in 2022, which will see asylum seekers and 'illegal' border crossers deported to Rwanda, is a perfect example of this approach.
33. Arendt, *The Origins of Totalitarianism*, pp. 296–297.
34. Ibid., p. 299.
35. See Arendt, *On Violence*.
36. See Arendt, *On Revolution*, pp. 266–267.
37. See Leslie Gauditz on the Noborder network as a new type of political community. 'The Noborder Movement: Interpersonal Struggle with Political Ideals', *Social Inclusion*, 2017, Volume 5, Issue 3, pp. 49–57.
38. See Arendt, *On Revolution*, p. 29.
39. Hannah Arendt, *The Human Condition*. Second Edition, Chicago and London: University of Chicago Press, 1958, p. 9.
40. This is an interpretion that is supported by Étienne Balibar: 'while legitimizing the notions of power and authority, she [Arendt] finds a means of lodging a paradoxical principle of *anarchy – of* "nonpower" or the contingency of authority – at the very heart of *arché*, or the authority of the political. We are thus led to reinterpret the absence of foundation or groundlessness of rights not only as a logical thesis, but as a practical thesis that is itself political, even if in an essentially antinomic mode.' See *Equaliberty: Political Essays*, trans., James D. Ingram, Durham, CA: Duke University Press, 2014, 168–169.
41. For an anarchist perspective on animal rights, see Bob Torres, who links the industrialised mass slaughter of animals with the domination of the broader capitalist economy. *Making a Killing: The Political Economy of Animal Rights*, Oakland, CA: AK Press, 2007.
42. See Costas Douzinas, *The Radical Philosophy of Rights*, Abingdon, Oxon: Routledge, 2019; and Cass R. Sunstein and Martha Nussbaum, eds., *Animal Rights: Current Debates and New Directions*, Oxford: Oxford University Press, 2004.
43. See, for instance, Cormac Cullinan, 'The Legal Case for the Universal Declaration of Mother Earth' 2010; and the 'Universal Declaration of the Rights of Mother Earth' drawn up at the World People's Conference on Climate Change and the Rights of Mother Earth in Cocochamba Bolivia in 2010. www.garn.org/universal-declaration/.

44. See Stephanie deGooyer, Alistair Hunt, Linda Maxwell and Samuel Moyn, *The Right to Have Rights*, London: Verso, 2018.
45. See Erica Cudworth and Stephen Hobden, *The Emancipatory Project of Posthumanism*, London: Routledge, 2018.
46. Foucault, *Society must be Defended*, p. 40.
47. Foucault, 'The Subject and Power', p. 785.
48. See Michel Foucault, 'The Ethics of the Concern for Self as a Practice of Freedom' (Interview 1984) in *Ethics*: Subjectivity and Truth, Volume 1. ed., Paul Rabinow, trans., Robert Hurley, London: Penguin, 2000, pp. 281–301.
49. See Ben Golder, *Foucault and the Politics of Human Rights*, Stanford CA: Stanford University Press, 2015.
50. Reiner Schürmann, 'On Constituting Oneself as an Anarchistic Subject', in *Tomorrow the Manifold: Essays on Foucault, Anarchy and the Singularization to Come*, ed., Malte Fabian Rauch and Nicolas Schneider, Zurich: Diaphanes, 2019, 7–30.

Conclusion

Law without Coercion: On the Possibilities of an Anarchist Legal System

A Dutch legal scholar Thom Holterman, once posed the question, 'how can an anarchist be interested in law and legal science?', the corollary to which was, 'how can a lawyer be interested in anarchism?' He says:

> Speaking for myself, I see anarchism as a fountain of inspiration, a paradigm which allows me to think in quite a different way within the scope of legal sciences than traditionally is done. On the one hand, this paradigm contains the perspective to make suggestions for a new and different societal organization. On the other hand it gives the possibility to criticize the (existing) legal reality. Accordingly it is not at all strange that the notions developed by some anarchists and some legal scholars converge quite dramatically.[1]

This book has sought to explore this, perhaps not altogether surprising, convergence between anarchism and law, and to construct some sort of paradigm for an anarchist legal philosophy. We have, on the one hand, used anarchist theory as a litmus test for law, taking full account of anarchism's radical critique of legal authority and political obligation. Every legal theory must be able to answer the fundamental question posed by the anarchist: 'why must I obey the law?' If law cannot provide a persuasive answer to this question, without violating its own claims to justice and legitimacy – and very often it cannot – then we have the right to disobey. On the other hand, we have argued that it is too simplistic to see anarchism as an outright rejection of the law. Anarchism, we have sought to show, has a much more nuanced approach to the question of law, and there is room within anarchist theory for an alternative conception of law: *law without coercion*. Anarchists do not reject law as such, only statist law, that is, law that is unilaterally and hierarchically imposed by a sovereign. Instead, they favour a form of law that is multilateral, interactive and, as Holterman suggests, derives from a social reality that produces social norms, particularly that of mutualism, which operates as a regulative principle for coordinating behaviour.[2] There is the recognition that some form of law would be needed in anarchist societies, simply as a way of organising basic functions, duties and responsibilities. However, as Holterman puts it: 'The old idea about coordination is that the coordinating force comes from above and intervenes from outside. The anarchist approach is: coordination is felt necessary by the smaller organizations and local communities, which then build 'coordinating knots'.[3]

Over the course of our investigations into questions of political obligation, sovereignty, legal foundations, violence, civil disobedience, and human rights, we have chartered an uncertain terrain between the demands of the law and the principles of anarchism. There is no one clear way of approaching an anarchist legal philosophy. Indeed, to lay down a definitive model of an anarchist legal system would go against the very grain of anarchism, which not only embodies a diversity of theoretical perspectives but also a plurality of practices and an ongoing experimentation in fostering new forms of freedom and autonomy. However, we have argued that anarchism should be seen as an *instituting*, rather than simply a destituting, practice. Bakunin's famous 'urge to destroy' was also a 'creative urge': the desire to create in the place of the old institutions of domination and violence, alternative, non-authoritarian institutions. Although anarchism is often associated in the popular imagination with the wild spontaneity of life that reacts against the rigidifying effect of institutions – and indeed Bakunin defined anarchy as 'the mutiny of all local passions and the awakening of spontaneous life at all points'[4] – it is equally concerned with the way that alternative kinds of institutions can foster new and freer modes of existence. We should therefore not see life and institutions as opposed. As Roberto Esposito puts it: 'What else is life, after all, if not a continuous institution, a capacity for self-regeneration along new and unexplored paths?'[5] Indeed, anarchism has long been associated with countless experiments in alternative and more autonomous forms of social organisation, from anarchist federations and republics – as we saw in the historical experience of the Spanish Civil War – to the 'everyday anarchism'[6] of activist networks, mutual aid organisations, social centres and cooperatives. All these communities and social movements, even the most horizontally organised, can be considered 'institutions' in the sense that they seek to engender certain regular norms and codes of conduct among their participants and to open up new scope for human action.[7] However, the key point here is that these 'rules' do not operate as fixed and rigid constraints, but rather as ethical guidelines that are, moreover, decided collectively and are open to ongoing challenge and contestation. They would be mostly *constitutive*, increasing people's capacity of action, rather than regulative, in the sense of limiting such capacity.[8] If such rules can be considered laws, they are very different from those of most legal systems: they are not coercive, do not involve violent sanctions and punishments, and are not arranged according to the hierarchical sovereign principle of command and obedience. Their aim is the coordination of behaviours in order to promote and enhance the freedom and autonomy of the community's members. This aim reflects the basic anarchist principle that individual freedom can only be realised in association with the freedom of others. As Bakunin put it, 'I am free only when all human beings surrounding me – men and women alike – are equally free'.[9] If this is the case, then the exercise of one's freedom requires a certain coordination with the freedom of others. Anarchist law might be understood as a non-coercive, non-authoritarian and open-ended ethical framework in which to achieve this.

Hermann Amborn's ethnographic study of legal systems in traditional tribal communities in the Horn of Africa gives us some clues as to how anarchist law might operate. Building on the anarchist anthropologist Pierre Clastres' idea that indigenous Amazonian tribes were 'societies against the state', in which power was decentralised and there was no alienation between 'rulers' and 'ruled' – the tribal chief only had informal power – Amborn points to the polycephalic structure of the tribal communities he studies. Here power does not flow from the top downwards, and there is no formal hierarchy or centralised authority. Rather, they are rhizomatically organised and non-hegemonic – that is, anarchist. In such societies, law functions as a series of non-coercive, fluid norms which encourage rather than compel behaviour, and which arise from the interactions that condition community life rather than being imposed from the above in an alienating fashion. Law operates more as a system of social communication, rather than a form of command. The focus is on peaceful and consensual conflict resolution, rather than inflicting of punishments and sanctions. Law, moreover, is pluralistic, flexible, adaptable to different situations, and works through a complex interplay with customs and traditions. Legal institutions, as Amborn puts it, must be

> filled with life, redeveloped and reframed, to stave off the danger that they will ossify, and their intended results be translated into their opposite. To preserve the vitality of institutions, a vigilant confrontation with contemporary questions is necessary, and along with it, measures and rules negotiated hand in hand with assemblies. These rules are not inflexible laws but instead rules of play, as it were, for the political. They activate the freedom to employ power on the part of the many and curb its misuse.[10]

Here we are reminded of Miguel Abensour's ontologically anarchic understanding of law and legal institution (discussed in Chapter 5) as creating a kind of conflictual space in which existing rules can be contested and in which the tendency of power to become centralised and ossified is resisted; anarchist law creates a contingent space for political experimentation, an 'incessant "new disorder" that reinvents the political realm beyond the state, and even against it'.[11]

Yet, even though anarchist law operates as a flexible series of rules and as an open space for the invention of new political practices and behaviours, this does not mean that it is devoid of ethical coordinates or principles of justice. Legal anarchist Gary Chartier argues that law is necessary to structure stateless societies and, similarly to Amborn and others, he envisages a polycentric legal order of overlapping legal regimes based on consent and voluntary agreement rather than on coercion. In his extensive elaboration of an anarchist legal order, he proposes that it reflect certain normative principles of justice, such as the recognition of pre-existing rights, principles of equal respect and fairness and, above all, what he calls the non-aggression maxim (NAM) – in other words, the principle that coercion against other individuals is an illegitimate violation of their autonomy. It is not up to the law to determine or impose any one vision of justice or the good life – something that would go against the anarchist idea of a plurality of moral visions and perspectives – but simply to protect individuals in their freedom to choose how to live. As he puts it:

> Though different actual legal regimes in a stateless society would doubtless adopt different rules, the maxim of non-aggression and the prohibitions on violating people's bodies and on interference with their possessory claims that underlie it provide a clear and intelligible framework for the legal rules it would be reasonable for just institutions in a stateless society to implement ... Such rules would leave no room for attempts to foster virtue using the force of law or to employ the law to prevent or end non-aggressive injuries – often important, but appropriately addressed by non-forcible means.[12]

Perhaps the best way to think about the relationship between law and justice is to follow Walter Benjamin's enigmatic claim that 'The law which is studied and not practiced any longer is the gate to justice'.[13] This at least is the approach taken by critical theorist Daniel Loick who, in line with this anarchist trajectory of thought we have been tracing, argues for a form of law without sovereignty and thus, without coercion. What would law without enforcement – a law that is 'studied but not practiced' – look like? Here Loick draws on Jewish thinkers like Benjamin, Franz Rosenzweig and Hermann Cohen to think about how law might be binding without at the same time involving coercive sanctions. For the neo-Kantian Cohen, for instance, 'obedience' does not come through fear of punishment so much as through a sense of being morally obligated to law. Coercion is actually superfluous because moral law aligns with our inclinations, with our moral and rational imperatives. Although, as Loick points out, Cohen is no anarchist and, indeed, views the state as the realisation of the highest moral good, he nevertheless sees the state as comprising a series of legal norms which take the place of coercion and whose function is to promote human autonomy; law would not be enforced by the state as such, only acknowledged and freely assumed by individuals.[14] In the case of Rosenzweig, by contrast, the universality of the law is replaced with the singularity of the ethical command, which comes from God but which nevertheless creates non-coercive social bonds and, indeed, a community based on shared ethical practices rather than the positive laws of the state. This is a sort of messianic community in which the law retreats, revealing in its wake human relations based on neighbourly love, care and ethical responsibility for the other – a community of ethical practices that is *indifferent* to state sovereignty.[15] We could call this an anarchist community. While these three thinkers discussed by Loick approach the question of law in very different ways, they all share a certain vision of life without sovereignty – without *arché* or the principle of authority.

But why is law still important to an anarchist community? Loick makes a distinction between the *abolition* of the law – which he regards as utopian – and its *deposition*, where it continues to be present and to regulate human conduct, but in a non-coercive and unobtrusive way. Indeed, the presence of the law has the virtue of relieving the individual of the burden of having to constantly make decisions and moral judgements about every aspect of their lives and the life of the community:

> The codification of rules can guard against a condition of constant anxiety about responsibility, in which state sovereignty may have been overcome, but in its place, quasi-sovereign abilities are demanded of the people themselves. The establishment of law also frees them from the responsibility to constantly make moral judgements in their everyday lives, so they can limit themselves to considering questions of personal prudence.

> They are allowed to pursue their purely personal interests in the framework of the permitted, and also to completely withdraw themselves mentally from the law.[16]

We need to consider the way that law not only opens up a space of collective deliberation and political decision-making, but also – in an opposite sense – frees us from the burden of having always to be making decisions, from the endless meetings, discussions and debates with fellow community members, from the tedious procedures and requirements of consensus-building, so that we can simply get on with our own lives. As Oscar Wilde once quipped, 'the trouble with socialism is that it takes up too many evenings'. Perhaps the same might be said about anarchism. If an anarchist society intends to promote human flourishing, then one of the virtues of having a legal system as a regular pattern of rules and norms would be to free up our time for our individual pursuit of the good life. Anarchists would want a legal system that allows them to be involved in shaping and reshaping it when required, but which otherwise leaves them alone and interferes with their daily lives as little as possible.[17]

Let us think of law, then, as a practice of freedom. Law can never supplant life, nor should it seek to do so. Law cannot do everything, and we should not look to law to resolve every single problem or conflict, something that Kropotkin warned us about. Indeed, in an anarchist society there should be greater scope for ad hoc agreements between individuals based on trust and mutual reciprocity. However, if designed in the right way, laws as institutions can provide a useful framework for resolving disputes and for coordinating human behaviour towards greater cooperation and sociability. The key element of anarchist law is that it promotes human autonomy and freedom, and it can only do this if it operates in a non-coercive way and if it remains flexible and open to adaptation according to changing circumstances. Law should reflect, or at least not obstruct, the mutability of life and the plural paths of freedom that one may follow.

Notes

1. Thom Holterman, 'Anarchism and Legal Science', *ARSP: Archiv für Rechts- und Sozialphilosophie / Archives for Philosophy of Law and Social Philosophy*, 1993, Vol. 79, No. 3 (1993), 349–359, p. 350.
2. Ibid., p. 351. Holterman refers to such rules as 'traffic schemes' – schemes which produce a certain regular pattern or order of behaviour, but which are mutually decided.
3. Ibid., p. 354.
4. Mikhail Bakunin, *Selected Writings*, ed., Arthur Lehning, London: Jonathan Cape, 1973, pp. 179–180.
5. Esposito, *Institution*, p. 1.
6. We borrow this idea of anarchism as a series of everyday practices from the British anarchist Colin Ward. See *Anarchy in Action*, San Francisco: PM Press, 2017.
7. See M. La Torre, *Law as Institution*, Springer, Berloin 2010.
8. See ibid.
9. Bakunin, *Political Philosophy*, p. 267.
10. Amborn, *Law as Refuge of Anarchy*, p. 176.
11. Abensour, *Democracy against the State*, p. 123.
12. Chartier, *Anarchy and Legal Order*, p. 3.
13. Benjamin cited in Daniel Loick, *A Critique of Sovereignty*, trans., Amanda DeMarco, London and New York: Rowman & Littlefield, 2019, p. 194.
14. Ibid., p. 200.
15. Ibid., p. 209.
16. Ibid., p. 211.
17. Here a certain radical articulation of J. S. Mill's 'harm principle' – as the principle according to which legal interference is confined to the prevention of real harm to others – might operate as some kind of model for anarchist law.

Bibliography

Abensour, M. 'Is there a proper way to use the voluntary servitude hypothesis?' *Journal of Political Ideologies* 16(3) 2011: 329–348.

Abensour, M. *Democracy against the State. Marx and the Machiavellian Moment*. Trans. M. Blechman and M. Breaugh. Cambridge: Polity. 2011.

Abidor, M. ed., *Down with the Law: Anarchist Individualist Writings from Early Twentieth-Century France*. Chicago and Edinburgh: AK Press. 2019.

Adorno, T. W., Brunswik, F., Levinson, D. J., Sanford, R. N. *The Authoritarian Personality*. London: W. W. Norton & Co., 1993.

Agamben, G. *State of Exception*. Trans. Kevin Attell. Chicago and London: University of Chicago Press. 2005.

Agamben, G. *The Kingdom and the Glory: For a Theological Genealogy of Economy and Government* (Homo Sacer *II*, 2). Trans. by L. Chiesa. Stanford, CA: Stanford University Press. 2011.

Agamben, G. 'What is a destituent power (or potentiality)?' trans., Stephanie Wakefield. *Environment and Planning D: Society and Space* 2014, volume 32, 65–74.

Agamben, G. *Where are We Now? The Epidemic as Politics*. London: Eris. 2021.

Agamben, G., Benvenuto, S., and Esposito, R. 'Coronavirus and Philosophers' in *European Journal of Psychoanalysis*, February to May 2020.

Alexy, R. *Law's Ideal Dimension*. Oxford: Oxford University Press. 2021.

Amborn, H. *Law as Refuge of Anarchy: Societies without Hegemony or State*. Trans., Adrian Nathan West. Cambridge, MA: MIT Press. 2019.

Anders, G. *Gewalt Ja oder nein: Eine notwendige Diskussion*, ed. by M. Bissinger, Munchen: Knaur. 1987.

Anderson, B. *Under Three Flags: Anarchism and the Anticolonial Imagination*, London: Verso. 2005.

Arendt, H. *The Human Condition*. Chicago: University of Chicago Press. 1958.

Arendt, H. *The Origins of Totalitarianism*, Orlando Austin New York San Diego London: Harcourt. 1968.

Arendt, H. *On Violence*. New York: Harvest. 1970.

Arendt, H. *Crises of the Republic*, San Diego, New York, London: Harcourt Brace. 1972.

Arendt, H. *On Revolution*, London: Penguin. 1990.

Arendt, H. *Eichmann in Jerusalem: A Report on the Banality of Evil*. New York: Penguin. 2006.

Austin, J. *The Province of Jurisprudence Determined*. Cambridge: Cambridge University Press. 1995.

Bakunin, M. 'The Political Theology of Mazzini and the International' [1871]. The Anarchist Library. https://theanarchistlibrary.org/library/mikhail-bakunin-the-political-theology-of-mazzini-and-the-international (accessed 22/03/2023).

Bakunin, M. 'Federalism, Socialism, Anti-Theologism' (1876) Marxists.org (Bakunin archive): www.marxists.org/reference/archive/bakunin/works/various/reasons-of-state.htm (accessed 23/03/2023).

Bakunin, M. 'God and the State' [1882]. The Anarchist Library. https://theanarchistlibrary.org/library/michail-bakunin-god-and-the-state (accessed 22/03/2023).

Bakunin, M. *Marxism, Freedom and the State*, trans. K. J. Kenafick. London: Freedom Press. 1950.

Bakunin, M. *The Political Philosophy of Bakunin*. Ed., G. P. Maximoff. London: The Free Press of Glencoe. 1953.

Bakunin, M. *Bakunin on Anarchy*, ed., and trans., S. Dolgoff. New York: Vintage Books, 1971.

Bakunin, M. *Selected Writings*, ed., Arthur Lehning, London: Jonathan Cape. 1973.

Balibar, É. *Spinoza et le politique*. Paris: Presses universitaires de France. 2011.

Balibar, É. *Equaliberty: Political Essays*, trans., James D. Ingram, Durham, CA: Duke University Press. 2014.

Balibar, É. *Violence and Civility: On the Limits of Political Philosophy*. New York: Columbia University Press. 2015.
Balibar, É. *Spinoza politique. Le transindividuel*, Presses universitaires de France, Paris 2018.
Benjamin, W. 'Critique of Violence', *Reflections: Essays, Aphorisms, Autobiographical Writings*, ed. by P. Demetz, trans. by E. Jephcott. New York: Schocken Books. 1986, 277–300, p. 281.
Benjamin, W. 'Zur Kritik der Gewalt', in Id., *Sprache und Geschichte: Philosophische Essays*, ed. by R. Tiedemann. Stuttgart: Reclam. 1992.
Benjamin, W. 'The Right to Use Force'. *Selected Writings: 1913–1926*, ed., Marcus Bullock and Michael W. Jennings. Cambridge, MA: Harvard University Press. 1996. 231–234.
Benjamin, W. 'Franz Kafka: On the Tenth Anniversary of his Death', trans., Harry Zohn in Howard Eiland and Michael W. Jennings, ed., Selected Writings: Volume 2: 1927–1934. Cambridge, MA: Belknap Press. 1999.
Benjamin, W. 'On the Concept of History', Selected Writings, Vol. 4: 1938–1940, ed. by H. Eiland and M. W. Jennings, trans. by E. Jephcott. Cambridge, MA: Harvard University Press, 2003. 389–400.
Benson, B. *The Enterprise of Law: Justice without the State*, Oakland, CA: The Independent Institute. 2011.
Berlin, I. 'Equality', In Id., *Concepts and Categories*, ed. by T. Hardy, 2nd ed., Princeton, NJ: Princeton University Press. 2013.
Berti, G. N. *Il pensiero anarchico dal Settecento al Novecento*, Lacaita, Manduria. 1998.
Bleiker, R. *Popular Dissent, Human Agency and Global Politics*. Cambridge: Cambridge University Press. 2000.
Bloch, E. *The Principle of Hope*, Cambridge MA: MIT Press. 1986.
Bookchin, M. *The Ecology of Freedom*. Oakland CA: AK Press. 1982.
Bottici, C. *Anarchafeminism*. London: Bloomsbury. 2021.
Bourdieu, P. *Sur l'État. Cours au Collège de France 1989–1992*. Paris: Raisons d'agir/Seuil. 2012.
Bray, M. 'Beyond and Against the State: Anarchist Contributions to Human Rights History and Theory', *Humanity:*

An International Journal of Human Rights, Humanitarianism, and Development. 10, 3 (Winter 2019): 323–338.

Brodie, M. 'Volunteers for Anarchy: The International Group of the Durruti Column in the Spanish Civil War'. *Journal of Contemporary History*, 56(1): 2021, 28–54.

Buber, M. *Paths in Utopia*, trans., R. F. C. Hull. Boston: Beacon Press. 1958.

Butler, J. *Notes Towards a Performative Theory of Assembly*. Cambridge Massachusetts and London: Harvard University Press. 2015.

Butler, J. *The Force of Nonviolence: An Ethico-Political Bind*, London: Verso. 2020.

Cacciari, M. *The Withholding Power: An Essay on Political Theology*, trans., Edi Pucci, London: Bloomsbury. 2018. 14.

Caffi, A. 'A Critique of Violence', in Id., *A Critique of Violence. Writings*, transl. by R. Rosenthal. New York: Bobbs-Merrill. 1970.

Campbell, T. *The Legal Theory of Ethical Positivism*. London: Routledge. 1996.

Castoriadis, C. *L'institution imaginaire de la société*, Paris: Seuil. 1975.

Castoriadis, C. 'La découverte de l'imagination'. *Libre*, Vol. 3. 1978.

Castoriadis, C. 'La 'polis' grecque et la création de la démocratie', in Id., *Domaines de l'homme*. Paris: Seuil. 1999.

Castoriadis, C. *Pouvoir, politique, autonomie, in Id., Le monde morcelé*. Paris: Seuil. 2000.

Cesare, D. di. *The Political Vocation of Philosophy*. Trans., David Broder. Cambridge: Polity Press. 2021.

Cesare, D. di. *The Time of Revolt*. Cambridge: Polity Press. 2021.

Chartier, G. *Anarchy and Legal Order: Law and Politics for a Stateless Society*. Cambridge: Cambridge University Press. 2013.

Clastres, P. *Archaeology of Violence*, trans., J. Herman. New York: Semiotext[e] 99. 1994.

Clastres, P. 'Liberté, Malencontre, Innombrable', in É. de la Boétie, *Le discours de la servitude volontaire*, ed. by P. Léonard. Paris: Payoy. 2002.

Cleyre, V. de. 'Direct Action' [1912] The Anarchist Library: https://theanarchistlibrary.org/library/voltairine-de-cleyre-direct-action (accessed 22/03/2023).

Colson, D. 'Anarchist Readings of Spinoza'. *Journal of French Philosophy*, Vol. 17. 2007.

Cooper, M. 'The Alt-Right: Neoliberalism, Libertarianism and the Fascist Temptation'. *Theory, Culture & Society* (Special Issue: *Post-Neoliberalism*), 38: 6 (2021), 28–50.

Cover, R. M., 'Violence and the Word' (1986). *Faculty Scholarship Series*. Paper 2708, 1601–1629, p. 1601. http://digitalcommons.law.yale.edu/fss_papers/2708.

Cudworth, E. and Hobden, S. *The Emancipatory Project of Posthumanism*. London: Routledge. 2018.

Cullinan, C. 'The Legal Case for the Universal Declaration of Mother Earth' 2010; 'Universal Declaration of the Rights of Mother Earth'. World People's Conference on Climate Change and the Rights of Mother Earth (Cocochamba Bolivia 2010) Global Alliance for the Rights of Nature www.garn.org/universal-declaration/ (accessed 23/03/20230).

Debord, G. *Society of the Spectacle*. Marxists Internet Archive, 1967. Available at: www.marxists.org/reference/archive/debord/society.htm (accessed 20/03/2023).

deGooyer, S., Hunt, A., Maxwell, L., and Moyn, S. *The Right to Have Rights*, London: Verso. 2018.

Deleuze, G. *Introduction*, in *Instincts & institutions*, ed. by G. Deleuze. Paris: Hachette. 1953.

Deleuze, G. *Spinoza – philosophie pratique*. Paris: Éditions de Minuit. 1981.

Delmas, C. *A Duty to Resist: When Disobedience should be Uncivil*. Oxford: Oxford University Press. 2018.

Derrida, J. 'Force of Law: The "Mystical Foundation of Authority"', in Drucilla Cornell et al. eds. *Deconstruction and the Possibility of Justice*. New York: Routledge. 1992. 3–67.

Derrida, J. *Negotiations. Interventions and Interviews, 1971–2001*, ed., and trans., E. Rottenberg. Stanford CA: Stanford University Press. 2002.

Derrida, J. *Rogues. Two Essays on Reason*. Stanford: Stanford University Press. 2005.

Derrida, J. *The Death Penalty. Vòlume One, The Seminars of Jacques Derrida*, ed., G. Bennington, trans., P. Kamuf. Chicago: Chicago University Press. 2014.

Douzinas, C. *Human Rights and Empire: The Political Philosophy of Cosmopolitanism*. Abingdon: Routledge-Cavendish. 2007.

Douzinas, C. *The Radical Philosophy of Rights*. Abingdon, Oxon: Routledge. 2019.

Douzinas, C. *The End of Human Rights*. Oxford: Hart Publishing. 2000.

Dworkin, R. *Taking Rights Seriously*. Cambridge, MA: Harvard University Press. 1978.

Dworkin, R. *Law's Empire*. Oxford: Hart. 1998.

Dworkin, R. *Justice for Hedgehogs*. Cambridge, MA: The Belknap Press. 2011.

Dyzenhaus, D. ed., *Law as Politics: Schmitt's Critique of Liberalism*. Durham NC: Duke University Press. 1998.

Dyzenhaus, D. *Legality and Legitimacy: Carl Schmitt, Hans Kelsen and Herman Heller in Weimar*. Oxford: Oxford University Press. 2000.

Egoumenides, Magda. *Philosophical Anarchism and Political Obligation*. London: Bloomsbury. 2014.

Ellul, J. *Anarchy and Christianity*, trans. by G. Bromiley. Grand Rapids, MI: Eerdmans Publishing. 1991.

Esposito, R. *Immunitas: The Protection and Negation of Life*. Cambridge: Polity Press, 2011.

Esposito, R. *Instituting Thought: Three Paradigms of Political Ontology*. Trans., Mark William Epstein. Cambridge: Polity Press. 2021.

Esposito, R. *Institution*, trans. Z. Hanafi. Cambridge: Polity Press. 2022.

Eulau, H. F. 'The Depersonalization of the Concept of Sovereignty', *The Journal of Politics*, Vol. 4, No. 1 (Feb., 1942): 3–19.

Ferreira da Silva, D., and Harris, M., eds. *Postcolonialism and the Law*. London: Routledge. 2017.

Ferrell, J. 'Against the Law: Anarchist Criminology', *Recent Developments in Criminology: Towards Disciplinary Diversity and Theoretical Integration*. Ed., Stuart Henry. London: Routledge. 2016.

Feyerabend, P. *Against Method: Outline of an Anarchist Theory of Knowledge*. London: Verso. 1993.

Finnis, J. *Natural Law and Natural Rights*. Oxford: Clarendon. 1980.

Firth, R. *Disaster Anarchy: Mutual Aid and Radical Action*, London: Pluto Press, 2022.

Fischer-Lescano, A. *Rechtskraft*. Berlin: August Verlag. 2013.

Foucault, M. 'Revolutionary Action: "Until Now"' in *Language, Counter-Memory, Practice*, ed., Donald Bouchard. Oxford: Basil Blackwell. 1977. 218–233.

Foucault, M. 'The Subject and Power', *Critical Inquiry*, Vol. 8, No. 4 (Summer, 1982): 777–795.

Foucault, M. 'What is Critique?' In: *What is Enlightenment? Eighteenth Century Answers and Twentieth Century Questions*, ed. James Schmidt. Berkeley: University of California Press. 1996, 382–398.

Foucault, M. 'The Ethics of the Concern for Self as a Practice of Freedom' (Interview 1984) in *Ethics: Subjectivity and Truth*, Volume 1. ed., Paul Rabinow, trans., Robert Hurley, London: Penguin. 2000. 281–301.

Foucault, M. *Society must be Defended: Lectures at the College de France*, 1975–76, ed., Mauro Bertani and Alessandro Fontana, trans., David Macey. New York: Picador. 2004.

Foucault, M. *The Birth of Biopolitics: Lectures at the College de France, 1978–79*, ed., Michel Senellart. Basingstoke, Hampshire: Palgrave Macmillan. 2008.

Frazer, E. and Hutchings, K. 'Anarchist Ambivalence: politics and violence in the thought of Bakunin, Tolstoy and Kropotkin'. *European Journal of Political Theory*, 18(2) 2019: 259–280.

Freud, S. *Group Psychology and the Analysis of the Ego*, trans., J. Strachey. London: Hogarth Press. 1949.

Gallie, W. B. 'Essentially Contested Concepts'. *Proceedings of the Aristotelian Society*, Vol. 56 (1956), 167–198.

Gans, C. *Philosophical Anarchism and Political Disobedience*. Cambridge: Cambridge University Press. 2012.

Gauditz, L. 'The Noborder Movement: Interpersonal Struggle with Political Ideals', *Social Inclusion*. 5, 3 (2017): 49–57.

Gehlen, A. *Urmensch und Spätkultur: Philosophische Ergebnisse und Aussagen*, 6th ed., ed. by K. S. Rehberg, Vittorio Klostermann. Frankfurt am Main. 2004.

Gelderloos, P. *How Non-Violence Protects the State*, Cambridge, MA: South End Press. 2007.

Gelderloos, P. *The Failure of Non-Violence*. Seattle: Left Bank Books. 2017.

Godwin, W. *Enquiry Concerning Justice* (1793). Ontario: Batoche Books. 2001.

Godwin, W. *Enquiry Concerning Justice and Its Influence on Modern Morals and Happiness* (3rd ed., 1798), ed. I. Kramnick. Harmondsworth: Penguin. 1985.

Golder, B. *Foucault and the Politics of Human Rights*, Stanford CA: Stanford University Press. 2015.

Gourgouris, S. *The Perils of the One*. New York: Columbia University Press. 2019.

Graeber, D. *Debt. The First 5000 Years*. Brooklyn, New York: Melville House. 2011.

Graeber, D. *The Democracy Project: A History, a Crisis, a Movement*. London: Penguin. 2014.

Graeber, D. *The Utopia of Rules: On Technology, Stupidity and the Secret Joys of Bureaucracy*. Brooklyn, N. Y.: Melville House. 2015.

Graeber, D. and Wengrow, D. *The Dawn of Everything: A New History of Humanity*. London: Allen Lane. 2021.

Green, L. *The Authority of the State*. Oxford: Clarendon Press. 1988.

Gros, F. *Disobey! A Guide to Ethical Resistance*, trans., David Fernbach. London and New York: Verso. 2020.

Günther, K. *Der Sinn für Angemessenheit. Anwendungsdiskurse in Moral und Recht*, Frankfurt am Main: Suhrkamp Verlag. 1988.

Gurvitch, G. *L'idée du droit social: notion et système du droit social*. Paris: Sirey. 1932.

Habermas, J. *Between Facts and Norms: Contributions to a Discourse Theory of Law and Democracy*, trans., William Rehg. Cambridge, MA: MIT Press. 1998.

Hacker, P. M. S. 'Sanction Theories of Duty'. *Oxford Essays on Jurisprudence*, ed. by A. W. B. Simpson. Oxford: Clarendon. 1973.

Harcourt, B. E. *Exposed: Desire and Disobedience in the Digital Age*. Cambridge MA: Harvard University Press. 2015.

Hart, H. L. A. *The Concept of Law*. Clarendon: Oxford. 1961.

Hart, H. L. A. 'Problems of the Philosophy of Law', in Id., *Essays in Jurisprudence and Philosophy*. Oxford: Clarendon. 1983.

Hauriou, M. *Aux sources du droit. Le pouvoir, l'ordre et la liberté*. Paris: Cahiers de la Nouvelle Journée. 1933.

Hegel, G. W. F. *Grundlinien der Philosophie des Rechts*. Frankfurt am Main: Suhrkamp Verlag. 1986.

Himma, K. E. *Coercion and the Nature of Law*. Oxford: Oxford University Press. 2020.

Hobbes, T. *Leviathan* [1651] Chapter XVII www.gutenberg.org/files/3207/3207-h/3207-h.htm.

Hobbes, T. *Leviathan*, ed. by C. B. Macpherson. Harmondsworth: Penguin, Harmondsworth. 1982.

Holloway, J. *Crack Capitalism*, London: Pluto Press. 2010.

Holterman, T. 'Anarchism and Legal Science', *ARSP: Archiv für Rechts- und Sozialphilosophie / Archives for Philosophy of Law and Social Philosophy*, 79, 3 (1993): 349–359.

Hostis. 'Destituent Power: An Incomplete Timeline', The Anarchist Library (1 November 2020): https://theanarchistlibrary.org/library/hostis-destituent-power-an-incomplete-timeline (accessed 23/03/2023).

Jellinek, G. *System der subjektiven öffentlichen Rechte*, Tübingen: Mohr. 1905.

Jellinek, G. *Allgemeine Staatslehre*, III ed., Darmstadt: Wissenschaftliche Buchgesellschaft. 1960.

Kant, Immanuel. 'Das Ende aller Dinge', in Id., *Ausgewählte Kleine Schriften*, Hamburg: Felix Meiner. 1965.

Kant, I. *Metaphysik der Sitten*, ed. by H. Ebeling. Stuttgart: Reclam. 1990.

Kantorowicz, H. 'The Concept of the State', *Economica*, No. 35, February 1932, pp. 5–6.

Kelsen, H. 'Gleichheit vor dem Gesetz', *Veroffentlichung der Deutschen Staatsrechtslehrer*, Vol. 3. Berlin: Walther de Gruyter. 1927.

Kelsen, H. *Der soziologische und juristische Staatsbegriff*, II ed., Tübingen: Mohr, Tubingen. 1929.

Kelsen, H. *Reine Rechtslehre*, I ed., Wien: Deuticke. 1934.

Kelsen, H. *Pure Theory of Law*, trans., Max Knight. Berkely and Los Angeles: University of California Press. 1967.

Kennedy, D. 'The Role of Law in Economic Thought: Essays on the Fetishism of Commodities'. *American University Law Review* 34, 939. 1985.

Keohane, N. O. 'The Radical Humanism of Etienne de la Boétie. *Journal of the History of Ideas* 31(1) 1977: 119–130.

King, N. *No Borders: The Politics of Immigration Control and Resistance*. London: Zed Books. 2016.

Kinna, R. and Prichard, A. 'Anarchism and Non-Domination', *Journal of Political Ideologies*, 24(3) 2019: 221–240.

Kramer, M. *Critical Legal Theory and the Challenge of Feminism*. Lanham, MA: Rowman & Littlefield. 1995.

Kropotkin, P. *Mutual Aid: A Factor in Evolution*. McCure, Phillips & Co. 1902.

Kropotkin, P. *Ethics: Origin and Development* [1922] *The Anarchist Library*: https://theanarchistlibrary.org/library/petr-kropotkin-ethics-origin-and-development (accessed 23/03/2023).

Kropotkin, P. *The State: Its Historic Role*. London: Freedom Press. 1943.

Kropotkin, P. 'Law and Authority: An Anarchist Essay'. Anarchy Archives: http://dwardmac.pitzer.edu/Anarchist_Archives/kropotkin/lawauthority.html (accessed 23/03/2023).

La Boétie, É de. *The Politics of Obedience: The Discourse of Voluntary Servitude*. Kurz, Harry (trans.) and Rothbard, Murray (ed.). Auburn, Alabama: The Mises Institute, 1975, 43–44. Available at: https://cdn.mises.org/Politics%20of%20Obedience.pdf.

La Torre, M. 'On Two Distinct and Opposed Version of Natural Law: Inclusive versus Exclusive'. *Ratio Juris*, Vol. 19. 2006.

La Torre, M. *Law as Institution*, Berlin: Springer. 2010.

La Torre, M. 'The Hierarchical Model and H. L. A. Hart's Concept of Law', *Revus – Journal for Constitutional Theory and Philosophy of Law*, 21 (2013): 141–162.

La Torre, M. *Nostra legge è la libertà: Anarchismo dei Moderni*. Roma: Derive Approdi. 2017.

La Torre, M. *Nostra legge è la libertà: Anarchismo dei Moderni*. Roma: DeriveApprodi. 2017.

La Torre, M. *La justicia de la tortura. Sobre Derecho y fuerza*. Madrid: Trotta. 2022.

Lagasnerie, G. de. *The Art of Revolt: Snowden, Assange, Manning*. Stanford CA: Stanford University Press. 2017.

Lagasnerie, G. de. *Judge and Punish: The Penal State on Trial*. Trans., L. Vergnaud. Stanford, CA: Stanford University Press. 2018.

Landauer, Gustav. *Revolution and Other Writings: A Political Reader*. Edited and Translated by Gabriel Kuhn. Oakland, CA: PM Press. 2010.

Laudani, R. *Disobedience in Western Political Thought: A Genealogy*. Cambridge: Cambridge University Press. 2013.

Lesage, J de La Haye. *The Abolition of Prison*, trans., Scott Branson, Oakland CA: AK Press. 2021.

Levy, C. 'Anarchism and Cosmopolitanism'. *Journal of Political Ideologies*, 16:3 (2022): 265–278.

Locke, J. *Two Treatises of Government*, ed. P. Laslett. Cambridge: Cambridge University Press. 1988.

Loick, D. *Anarchismus zur Einfuehrung*. Hamburg: Junius Verlag. 2017.

Loick, D. *A Critique of Sovereignty*, trans., Amanda DeMarco, London and New York: Rowman & Littlefield. 2019.

Loizidou, E. ed., *Disobedience: Concept and Practice*. New York: Routledge. 2013.

Loizidou, E. *Anarchism: An Art of Living without Law*. Abingdon, Oxon: Routledge. 2023.

Lordon, F. *Willing Slaves of Capital: Spinoza and Marx on Desire*, trans., G. Ash. London: Verso. 2014.

Luhmann, N. *Rechtssoziologie*, II ed., Opladen: Westdeutscher Verlag. 1983.

Luhmann, N. *Das Recht der Gesellschaft*. Frankfurt am Main Suhrkamp.1990.

MacCormick, N. *H. L. A Hart*, London: Arnold. 1980.

MacCormick, N. and Weinberger, O. *An Institutional Theory of Law*. Berlin: Springer. 1986.

McCormick, J. *Carl Schmitt's Critique of Liberalism: Against Politics as Technology*. Cambridge: Cambridge University Press. 1997.

McLaughlin, P. *Anarchism and Authority: A Philosophical Introduction to Classical Anarchism*. Aldershot, Hampshire: Ashgate. 2007.

Marneros, C. '"It is a Nomos Very Different from the Law": On Anarchy and the Law'. *Acta Universitatis Lodziensis: Folia Juridica* 92 (2021): 125–139.

Marx, K. 'On the Jewish Question'. *The Marx-Engels Reader: Second Edition*, ed., Robert C. Tucker. New York and London: WW Norton & Co. 1978. 26–52.

Meier, H. *Carl Schmitt and Leo Strauss: The Hidden Dialogue*, trans. by J. Harvey Lomax. Chicago, IL: University of Chicago Press. 1995.

Meier, H. *The Lesson of Carl Schmitt: Four Chapters on the Distinction between Political Theology and Political Philosophy*, trans., Marcus Brainard. Chicago & London: University of Chicago Press. 1998.

Menke, C. 'Law and Violence', *Law & Literature*, Vol. 22, 2010, 9.

Menke, C. *Law and Violence: Christophe Menke in Dialogue*. Manchester: Manchester University Press. 2018.

Menke, C. *Critique of Rights*. Cambridge: Polity Press. 2020.

Menkel-Meadow, C. 'Feminist Legal Theory, Critical Legal Studies, and Legal Education, or "The Fem-Crits Go to Law School"'. *Journal of Legal Education*, 38: 1/2 (March–June 1988). 61–85.

Messer-Kruse, T. *The Trial of the Haymarket Anarchists*. London: Palgrave Macmillan. 2011.

Montaigne, M. de. 'Of Friendship'. In: *Essays of Michel de Montaigne*, [1877] trans., C. Cotton, ed., W. Carew Hazlitt. Project Gutenberg: www.gutenberg.org/files/3600/3600-h/3600-h.htm (accessed 23/03/2023).

Montaigne, M. de. *Essais*, book 3, Ch. 13. www.gutenberg.org/files/3600/3600-h/3600-h.htm.

Moyn, S. *Not Enough: Human Rights in an Unequal World*. Cambridge, MA: Belknap Press. 2018.

Negri, A. *Insurgencies: Constituent Power and the Modern State*, trans. M. Boscagli. Minneapolis, MN: University of Minnesota Press. 1999.

Neumann, F. *Behemoth: The Structure and Practice of National Socialism 1933–1944*, Chicago: Ivan R. Dee. 2009.

Oakeshott, M. *On Human Conduct*. Oxford: Oxford University Press. 1991.

Olivecrona, K. *Law as Fact*, I ed., Copenhagen: Musgrave. 1939.

Paraf-Javal, 'The Rights of Man and the Law' (1902) The Libertarian Labyrinth: www.libertarian-labyrinth.org/working-translations/paraf-javal-the-rights-of-man-and-the-law-1902/.

Pascal, B. *Pensées*, ed. by M. Le Guern. Paris: Gallimard. Paris. 1977.

Peterson, E. *Theological Tractates*, ed. and trans. by M. J. Hollerich, Stanford, CA: Stanford University Press. 2011.

Guérin, D. *No Gods, No Masters: An Anthology of Anarchism*. Oakland, CA: AK Press, 2005.

Proudhon, P-J. *Système des contradictions économiques, ou philosophie de la misère*, 2 vols., Paris: Marcel Rivière. 1923.

Proudhon, P-J. *De la création de l'ordre dans l'Humanité, ou Principe d'organisation politique*, ed. by C. Bouglé and H. Moysset. Paris: Marcel Rivière. 1929.

Proudhon, P-J. *Du principe fédératif et oeuvres diverses sur les problems politiques européens*. Ed. C. Bouglé and H. Moysset, Marcel Rivière. Paris. 1959.

Proudhon, P-J. *De la Justice dans la Révolution et dans l'Église*, Vol. 2. Paris: Fayard. 1988.

Proudhon, P-J. *What is Property?*, ed. by Donald R. Kelley and Bonnie G. Smith, Cambridge: Cambridge University Press. 1994.

Proudhon, P-J. *Property is Theft!: A Pierre-Joseph Proudhon Anthology*, ed. by Iain McKay, Oakland, California: AK Press. 2011.

Radbruch, G. *Rechtsphilosphie*, ed. by R. R. Dreier and S. L. Paulson. Heidelberg 1999.

Ramnath, M. *Decolonizing Anarchism: An Anti-authoritarian History of India's Liberation Struggle*. Oakland CA: AK Press. 2011.

Rawls, J. 'Constitutional Liberty and the Concept of Justice', in *Rights*, ed. by D. Lyons. Belmont, Cal.: Wadsworth. 1979.

Rawls, J. *A Theory of Justice*. Revised Edition. Cambridge, MA: Harvard University Press. 1999.

Raz, J. *The Morality of Freedom*. Oxford: Oxford University Press. 1986.

Raz, J. *Ethics in the Public Domain*. Oxford: Oxford University Press. 1995.

Raz, J. *The Authority of Law*, 2nd ed. Oxford: Oxford University Press. 2009.

Reich, W. *The Mass Psychology of Fascism*. New York: Orgone Institute Press. 1946.

Rocker, R. 'Anarchism and Anarcho-Syndicalism', *Rudolf Rocker Reference Archive* www.marxists.org/reference/archive/rocker-rudolf/misc/anarchism-anarcho-syndicalism.htm (accessed 22/03/2023).

Rocker, R. 'Nationalism and Culture' [1933] The Anarchist Library https://theanarchistlibrary.org/library/

rudolf-rocker-nationalism-and-culture (accessed 20/07/2022).

Romano, S. *The Legal Order*. London: Routledge. 2017.

Ross, A. *On Law and Justice*. Los Angeles: University of California Press. 1958.

Rubinelli, L. *Constituent Power: A History*. Cambridge: Cambridge University Press. 2020.

Sarat, A. and Kearns, T. R., eds., *Law's Violence: The Amherst Series in Law, Jurisprudence and Social Thought*. Ann Arbor: University of Michigan Press. 1995.

Scarpelli, U. *Cos'è il positivismo giuridico*. Milano: Comunità. 1965.

Scarpelli, U. *Le 'proposizioni giuridiche' come precetti reiterati*, in 'Rivista internazionale di filosofia del diritto', Vol. 44., 1967, pp. 465–482.

Scheuerman, W. E. *Civil Disobedience*. Cambridge: Polity Press. 2018.

Scheuermann, W. E. *The End of Law: Carl Schmitt in the Twenty-First Century*, Second Edition. London: Rowman and Littlefield International. 2020.

Scheuerman, W. E. ed., *The Cambridge Companion to Civil Disobedience*. Cambridge: Cambridge University Press. 2021.

Schmitt, C. 'Der Führer schützt das Recht: Zur Reichstagsrede Adolf Hitlers vom. 13. Juli 1934', *Deutsche Juristen-Zeitung*, 20 July 1934.

Schmitt, C. *Roman Catholicism and Political Form*, trans. by G. L. Ulmen. Westport, CT: Greenwood Press. 1996.

Schmitt, C. *The Leviathan in the State Theory of Thomas Hobbes: The Meaning and Failure of a Political Symbol*, trans. by G. Schwab and E. Hilfstein. Westport, CT: Greenwood Press. 1996.

Schmitt, C. *The Crisis of Parliamentary Democracy*, trans. by E. Kennedy. Cambridge, MA: MIT Press. 2000.

Schmitt, C. *Political Theology: Four Chapters on the Concept of Sovereignty*. Trans., George Schwab. Chicago: University of Chicago Press. 2005.

Schmitt, C. 'The Age of Neutralizations and Depoliticizations', trans., Matthias Konzen and John P. McCormick, in *The Concept of the Political*, trans. by G. Schwab. Chicago, IL: University of Chicago Press. 2007, 80–96.

Schmitt, C. *The Concept of the Political*, trans. by G. Schwab. Chicago, IL: University of Chicago Press. 2007.

Schmitt, C. *Constitutional Theory*, trans. by J. Seitzer. Durham, NC: Duke University Press. 2008.

Schmitt, C. *Dictatorship: from the Origin of the Modern Concept of Sovereignty to the Proletarian Class Struggle*. Cambridge: Polity 2013.

Schmitt, C. *Ex Captivitate Salus*, ed., Andreas Kalyvas and Federico Finchelstein, trans., Matthew Hannah. Cambridge: Polity Press. 2017.

Schürmann, R. *Heidegger on Being and Acting: From Principles to Anarchy*. Trans., C-M Gros. Bloomington: Indiana University Press. 1987.

Schürmann, R. *Tomorrow the Manifold: Essays on Foucault, Anarchy and the Singularization to Come*, ed., Malte Fabian Rauch and Nicolas Schneider, Zurich: Diaphanes. 2019.

Searle, J. *Speech Acts: An Essay in the Philosophy of Language*, New ed., Cambridge: Cambridge University Press. 1970.

Sieyès, A. *What is the Third Estate?* [1789], p. 13. "Sieyès, "What Is the Third Estate?" [1789]. *Liberty, Equality, Fraternity: Exploring The French Revoution*. https://revolution.chnm.org/d/280 (accessed 22 March 2023).

Simmons, A. John. 'The Anarchist Position: A Reply to Klosko and Senor' Philosophy and Public Affairs, Vol. 16. 1979.

Simmons, A. John. *Moral Principles and Political Obligations*. Princeton: Princeton University Press. 1979.

Singer, P. *Democracy and Disobedience*. Oxford: Clarendon. 1973.

Sorel, G. *Reflections on Violence*, trans., T. E. Hulme and J. Roth. New York: Collier Books. 1961.

Spinoza, B. de, *Theologico-Political Treatise*, ed., J. Israel. Cambridge: Cambridge University Press. 2007.

Steinberg, J. 'Spinoza and Political Absolutism', eds. Yitzhak Melamed and Hasana Sharp, *Spinoza's Political Treatise: A Critical Guide*. Cambridge: Cambridge University Press. 2008. 175–189.

Stirner, M. *Der Einzige und sein Eigentum*, ed. by A. Meyer. Stuttgart: Reclam. 1981.

Stirner, M. *The Ego and Its Own*. Trans., Steven Byington, ed., David Leopold. Cambridge: Cambridge University Press. 1995.

Stone, M., Wall, I. R., and Douzinas, C., eds., *New Critical Legal Thinking: Law and the Political*. Abingdon, Oxon: Routledge. 2012.

Strauss, L. *Spinoza's Critique of Religion*. Chicago: University of Chicago Press. 1997.

Stringham, Edward, ed. *Anarchy and the Law: The Political Economy of Choice*. Oakland CA: The Independent Institute. 2006.

Sunstein, C. R. and Nussbaum, M., eds. *Animal Rights: Current Debates and New Directions*, Oxford: Oxford University Press. 2004.

Swain, D., Urban, P., Malabou, C., and Kouba, P., eds. *Unchaining Solidarity: Mutual Aid and Anarchism with Catherine Malabou*. Lanham, Maryland: Rowman and Littlefield. 2022.

Tarello, G. *Storia della cultura giuridica moderna. Assolutismo e codificazione del diritto*, and G. Fassò, *Storia della filosofia del diritto*, Vol. 2, Il Bologna: Mulino. 1970.

Taubes, J. *The Political Theology of Paul*. Stanford, CA: Stanford University Press. 2003.

Taubes, J. 'Carl Schmitt: Apocalyptic Prophet of the Counterrevolution', in Taubes, *To Carl Schmitt: Letters and Reflections*, trans., Keith Tribe. New York: Columbia University Press. 2013. 1–18.

Teubner, G. 'Societal Constitutionalism: Alternatives to State-Centred Constitutional Theory?', in Christian Joerges, Inga-Johanne Sand and Gunther Teubner eds., *Constitutionalism and Transnational Governance*, Oxford: Oxford University Press, 2004, 3–28.

Thoreau, H. D. 'Civil Disobedience' [1849] Mozam Book. 2002.

Tifft, L. and Sullivan, D. *The Struggle to be Human: Crime, Criminology and Anarchism*. Cienfuegos Press. 1980.

Tolstoy, L. 'The Kingdom of God is Within You, Or Christianity not as a mystical teaching but as a new concept of life' [1894] The Anarchist Library https://theanarchistlibrary.org/library/leo-tolstoy-the-kingdom-of-god-is-within-you (accessed 22/03/2023).

Torres, B. *Making a Killing: The Political Economy of Animal Rights*, Oakland, CA: AK Press. 2007.

Tushnet, M. 'Marxism as Metaphor' (1983) 68 *Cornell Law Review* 281.

Unger, R. M. *The Critical Legal Studies Movement*. Cambridge, MA: Harvard University Press. 1986.

Vahinger, O. *Die Philosophie des Als Ob*. Hamburg: Felix Meiner. 1920.

Vinx, L. *The Guardian of the Constitution: Hans Kelsen and Carl Schmitt on the Limits of Constitutional Law*. Cambridge: Cambridge University Press. 2015.

Ward, C. *Anarchy in Action*, San Francisco: PM Press. 2017.

Weber, M. *Gesammelte Politische Schriften*, ed. by J. Winckelmann. Tubingen: Mohr. 1980.

Wellman, Christopher Heath and Simmons, A. John. *Is there a Duty to Obey the Law?* Cambridge: Cambridge University Press. 2005.

Wilson, M. *Rules without Rulers: The Possibilities and Limits of Anarchism*. Winchester UK: Zero Books. 2014.

Winch, P. *The Idea of Social Science and Its Relation to Philosophy*. London: Routledge & Kegan Paul. 1985.

Wittgenstein, L. *Philosophische Untersuchungen*, Frankfurt am Main: Suhrkamp. 1977.

Wolff, R. P. *In Defense of Anarchism*. University of California Press: Los Angeles. 1970.

Wollstonecraft, M. *A Vindication of the Rights of Man*. Oxford: Oxford University Press. 2008.

Index

EU representative:
Easy Access System Europe
Mustamäe tee 50, 10621 Tallinn, Estonia
Gpsr.requests@easproject.com

www.ingramcontent.com/pod-product-compliance
Lightning Source LLC
Chambersburg PA
CBHW071016280326
41935CB00011B/1375

* 9 7 8 1 3 9 9 5 1 3 1 9 7 *